Contents

KU-036-838

v

901 PER

Marxism and

This book is due for return on or before the last date shown below.

Theory and History
Series Editor: Donald MacRaild

Published

Marxism and History   *Matt Perry*

Forthcoming titles include

Cultural History   *Anna Green*
Social Theory and Social History   *Donald MacRaild*
Postmodernism and History   *Willie Thompson*

Marxism and History

Matt Perry

palgrave

First published 2002 by
PALGRAVE
Houndmills, Basingstoke, Hampshire RG21 6XS and
175 Fifth Avenue, New York, N.Y. 10010
Companies and representatives throughout the world

PALGRAVE is the new global academic imprint of
St. Martin's Press LLC Scholarly and Reference Division and
Palgrave Publishers Ltd (formerly Macmillan Press Ltd).

ISBN 0–333–92244–1

This book is printed on paper suitable for recycling and
made from fully managed and sustained forest sources.

A catalogue record for this book is available
from the British Library.

Library of Congress Cataloging-in-Publication Data
Perry, Matt, 1967–
    Marxism and history / Matt Perry.
      p. cm. – (Theory and history)
    Includes bibliographical references and index.
    ISBN 0–333–92244–1 (pbk.)
    1. Philosophy, Marxist. 2. Marxian historiography. I. Title. II. Series.

B809.8 .P37 2002
901—dc21

                                                    2001053161

10   9   8   7   6   5   4   3   2   1
11   10   09   08   07   08   05   04   03   02

Typeset in Great Britain by
Aarontype Ltd, Easton, Bristol

Printed in Malaysia

7 Marxism and Postmodernism in History

Conclusion

Acknowledgements

This book has gestated over a long period of time and benefited from formal and informal education. One of the central claims made by Marxist historians is that involvement in current events and political struggles allows insight into the historical process. My own experience confirms this proposition. I owe a debt of gratitude to the outstanding individuals who have taught me about history and politics: the women from Trentham pit camp; the striking ambulance drivers, signal workers and Timex workers; those in the Heathtown Anti-Poll Tax Union, in the campaigns against the Nazis in Bloxwich and Cannock, in the anti-war protests and the comrades in Wolverhampton and Newcastle Socialist Workers' Party. Part of Marxist history's enduring legacy is to attempt to register the efforts of such people. I would like to acknowledge the scholarly assistance I have received as well. Don MacRaild has been a tireless series editor who has diligently read my manuscripts and engaged me in stimulating discussion. I would like to express my appreciation of David Martin, Mike Haynes, Terka Acton and John Charlton for their support and for their patience with the draft version of this book. Also, thank you, Christine.

MATT PERRY

Introduction

'For Marx was before all else a revolutionist ... And, consequently, Marx was the best-hated and most calumniated man of his time ... Bourgeois, whether conservative or ultra-democratic, vied with one another in heaping slanders upon him. All this he brushed aside as though it were a cobweb, ignoring it, answering only when extreme necessity compelled him ... His name will endure through the ages, and so will his work!'

F. Engels's graveside speech (1883)[1]

'Who', asked a BBC poll, 'is the greatest thinker of the millennium?' Karl Marx topped the list.[2] Another survey, this time of the USA's Library of Congress – the world's largest library – found that, with nearly 4000 works, Karl Marx was the sixth most written about individual ever (Jesus Christ came first and Lenin third).[3] For all his celebrity, Karl Marx remains an enigma; in the words of Engels's eulogy, the 'best hated' man of his times, and one difficult to overlook: for some a genius, for others a monster. His legacy is an elusive riddle, either an Orwellian nightmare or a world rid of exploitation and oppression; his ideas are either bankrupt or immanently relevant.

Whatever their view of Marx, few would dispute the statement that some of the greatest historians of the past few decades have described themselves as Marxists and that this philosophy has exerted a profound impression upon history and social science. Marx has endured. As George Iggers noted, the contribution of Marx to history cannot simply be measured by the work of Marxist historians alone. Much of it came second-hand through modern social theorists who, like Weber, defined themselves in opposition to Marx.[4] Eric Hobsbawm, one of the world's most renowned historians (and himself a Marxist), even asserted that Marx was 'the main force in "modernizing" the writing of history'.[5] At the same time Marx has undoubtedly remained academic history's 'best hated' thinker.

At the moment there are few works that specifically address Marxist historiography. The university library shelves strain under the weight of basic introductions to Marx, or discussions of Marxist theories of society, alienation, economics, class and so on. But there is little written specifically about Marxist historical writing. Stephen Rigby's *Marxism and History* examined Marx's theory of history whilst paying less attention to his historical writing. Likewise, Alex Callinicos in *Making History* elaborated Marx's philosophy of history but was less concerned with Marx's historical writing. Harvey Kaye's well-known primer concentrates on the British Marxist historians. None of these books examines the historical writing of key early Marxists along with academic Marxist historians of the past few decades. An important lacuna therefore exists in the study of Marxism and history.

If Marxism is taken to mean all those who have described themselves as such, then this book would be an unmanageable project. Instead this is an attempt to discuss Marxist history from some of its best examples in a critical but constructive synthesis. Marxist history encompasses such a broad genus of writers that it would be impossible to give a comprehensive account. Selection is therefore necessary but is not simply concerned with the management of the material; it is also required to rescue the spirit of Marxism from those who falsely bear its name.

This book seeks to provide an introduction to both the Marxist view of history and Marxist historical writing. It is aimed primarily at history students who would find this kind of text more useful than sociological and philosophical renditions of Marxism. It is my intention to avoid the dual snare of either 'dumbing down' or lapsing into jargon and technical shorthand. When specialist terminology is used, it is shown in bold for the first reference in each chapter, and these words and phrases are explained in the Glossary.

My purpose is to acquaint the reader with the key themes and issues of the school of Marxist historical writing. As this is not the kind of terrain where neutrals are easily found, I do not feign objectivity. As a Marxist, a historian, and an educator, my own position locates me as a very minor participant in this school. The strength of this sympathetic vantage point is that the themes of this book are ones that I routinely grapple with myself. The weakness is that I am open to the criticism of soft-soaping Marxism. Anticipating this charge, I would simply make two points. First, Marx's method, if faithfully applied, is a critical and sceptical one that subjects its premises to the scrutiny of doubt and the test of practice. Second, there is no virtue, from a Marxist point of view, in presenting an idealised unrealistic version of Marxism that would not stand up in a basically hostile intellectual environment. My goal therefore is to explain Marxism, within the constraints of the textbook format, in a critical and rigorous manner, taking on board the challenges of, for instance, **Stalinism** and **postmodernism**.

With initial introductions to Marx, first impressions count. Too often, students are stranded in a dark and sinister labyrinth. In the shadows lurk unfamiliar terminology, ugly translations and silhouetted figures whose exotic and menacing names are whispered without explanation. Whilst Marxism can be made very complex and technical, the basics are relatively straightforward and, it might be argued, connect with our own experiences of life. Whereas Chapter 2 deals with this in greater depth, here is a short elaboration of Marx's views on society.

▶ **The basics of Marxism**

Marx's most rudimentary observation was that labour set humans apart from the animal kingdom. Adult life for most people on the planet has always consisted of a daily routine of toil. The French slang rhyme '*métro, boulot, dodo*' (metro, work, sleep) captures this in contemporary form. Who we are and how we are perceived are wrapped up to a considerable extent with the labour we perform. For instance, the question 'What do you do?' invites an answer that explains what you do *at* work ('I'm a teacher'), or why you do not work ('I'm a student' or 'I'm a pensioner'). Although the forms of work vary enormously both today and in the past, labour is like the DNA of human history: ever-present, imperceptibly shaping and reshaping society.

For much of human history, labour has consisted of gathering, scavenging and hunting in small egalitarian bands. Past a certain point in history, that all changed. As labour became more productive with such innovations as settled agriculture and the domestication of plants and animals, communities were able to produce a surplus above and beyond the bare necessities of food, shelter and clothing. From this moment, it was no longer necessary for all to work because some individuals or groups could live by the work of others. After this profound transition, human societies divided into rulers and ruled, exploiters and exploited: that is, class-based societies emerged.

Class society is so much part of our experience that we do not usually give it a second thought or, if we do, we accept it as part of human nature; the boss at work, the stark contrasts between rich and poor, the social 'pecking order', even the authority of the university principal or the school head: these are all expressions of a society divided by class. As regards **exploitation**, the humdrum of workaday life masks the way in which others benefit from our toil through profits, dividends and executive bonuses. Even the term 'exploitation' is reserved in common parlance for exceptionally low wages rather than the norm. For Marx, exploitation was literally daylight (and legal) robbery conducted not by a masked highwayman but by every employer, every lord of the manor and every slave master. But crucially the process of exploitation does not go on unchallenged. Because of it, classes have opposing interests. Whilst ruling classes in history may want lower wages or greater tribute or harder work on the plantation, the exploited want the reverse. Class conflict is therefore inherent in class society, and hence the famous opening line of *The Communist Manifesto*: 'The history of all hitherto existing societies is the history of **class struggle**'.

This is not to say that things have always been the same; far from it. Contemporary global capitalism is very different from Ancient Rome or medieval France. As human technology, knowledge and skills have advanced, society has become more complex, more civilised. To understand these great epochal shifts, Marx again turned to the character of labour, exploitation and production. In Ancient Rome, the exploitation of slave labour predominated; in medieval France, feudal lords exploited serfs (peasants of a servile status); in modern **capitalism**, large capitalist employers exploit people who are personally free but work for a wage. Different class divisions, forms of conflict, levels of productivity and historical possibilities belong to these different stages of social and economic development. History can be divided accordingly into **modes of production**: the ancient or slave mode, the feudal mode and the capitalist mode (and so on). After a long human odyssey, taking many different paths, passing through different phases of development, we have ultimately reached modern capitalist society. Because of the abundance created by capitalist society, Marx and Engels maintained that this mode of production opened the new possibility of a classless society: socialism. They devoted their life's work to the achievement of this goal.

▶ Three generations of Marxist history

Entering active politics in the 1840s, Marx and Engels might be considered the first of three broad 'generations' of Marxists, roughly equivalent to the human life span. There is a historical and intellectual logic to treating the Marxist tradition in three epochs. Different ages are shaped by different great events. They have their illusions and their own spirit of the times. Marx and Engels witnessed the spectacular growth of smoke-stack and railway capitalism in a world dominated by European empires. In politics, socialism eclipsed liberalism as the most significant revolutionary ideology and mass trade unions and socialist parties grew across Europe. The middle generation of Lukács, Trotsky and Gramsci had to grapple with quite different problems in an age of extremes. They witnessed two world wars, the Russian revolution (as well as its degeneration) and the depression of the 1930s. In contrast, the third generation had to make Marxism relevant to a world dominated by Cold War divisions, a long economic boom, radicalisation in the 1960s and reaction in the 1980s. The close of the third generation was marked by the **fall of communism** and the triumphalist claims of neo-liberal exponents of global capitalism. The twilight of the third phase leaves us wondering about the dawn of a new fourth generation of Marxist historians, under what conditions it might develop and prosper, and what signs exist at present.

The book is thus organised to deal with the manner in which Marxism as a system of thought has altered with the changing tempo and character of world history over the last 150 years. Despite this evolution, Marxism embodies strong elements of intellectual continuity and there is an intergenerational coherence to its historical methods and analyses. Chapter 1 plots the landscape of Marxist history, identifying some of the peaks of achievement as well as the sheer range of its study and the great contrasts of subject matter, style and method. Like this text in general it selects the best examples and is intended as a gateway to a wider body of scholarship. It would be impossible to do justice to the analytical disputes over these works and also provide a guide to such a spectrum of writing. Whilst the ensuing chapters concentrate in the main on particular texts, this chapter is intended to indicate the dimensions of the Marxist school as a whole. These dimensions are significant because they reveal the value and flexibility of Marxism as a tool of historical research. Some Marxists have excelled at traditional forms of historical research; others have innovated. Marxist historians have examined history from above, the history of great men, as well as turning traditional history on its head and giving a voice to the common people. Marxist historians have scrutinised both long- and short-run historical developments in addition to history at the macro- and the micro-level. They have contributed to the theoretical and conceptual development of history as a discipline, just as they have conducted pioneering empirical research. This diversity is more than the result of random selection of research projects but stems from the very character of Marxism, which stresses the importance and connections of contending elements of human history. The recent malaise of Marxist history cannot therefore be ascribed primarily to the unsatisfactory results of its research. It has much more to do with the changing intellectual climate, institutional context and (most importantly) the fallout from Stalinism and the collapse of the Eastern Bloc. These issues are raised, especially the relationship between Stalinism and Marxist history, and they are returned to in the following chapters.

After the opening survey of Chapter 1, more detailed chapters begin with the work of Marx and Engels. It would be wrong to underestimate the pertinence of history to Marxism. Marx and Engels did not consider history to be a distinct subdivision of their thought; their view of the world was historical in essence. That is, they attempted to conceptualise and explain the entire human experience in a historical sense, and hence historical materialism has become a synonym for Marxism. We are so used to the contemporary division between 'theorists' and 'practitioners' in academic history that it is all too easy to ignore the connections between these two dimensions of the work of Marx and Engels. With this in mind, Chapter 2 seeks to outline the Marx and Engels's theory of history. It expands on the summary outline of the earlier part of this introduction. The constituent elements of this discussion are the intellectual background of Marx and Engels, the **dialectic**, the role of labour, class struggle, gradualism and revolution, progressive phases of development, and structure and **agency**.

Chapter 3 addresses the other side of the theory/history equation: the historical writings of Marx and Engels. The connection between the theory and practice of history that their work embodies is an often neglected but germane fact. All too often critics and sympathisers concentrate on one aspect in isolation from the other.

Perhaps one of the reasons for the impasse of Marxist history is the way in which a generation has used the British Marxist historians, in particular E.P. Thompson, as the starting point. In so doing, that generation avoided a more thorough knowledge of Marxist theory and its application to the practice of history. Seeing how theory transcribed to historical practice is essential to understanding Marx and Engels's approach to history. Unlike many of their followers, despite many other distractions, the work of the two founders of historical materialism embodied both the theory and practice of history. Both men expressed the desire to write more history and, but for their all-consuming political work and Marx's treatise on economics, we might have been endowed with much more substantial historical writings. Measured thus, rather than by selective quotation, much of the vulgar criticism of Marxism simply melts into the ether. This chapter selects Marx's *Eighteenth Brumaire of Louis Napoleon*, volume I of *Capital*, Engels's *Peasant War in Germany* and his late correspondence concerning Marxism and history, collected together as the *Letters on Historical Materialism*. These are chosen because they constitute the most significant cases of Marx and Engels's historical writing. This is far from an exhaustive list and a wider study would have to include Marx's *Class Struggles in France* and his writings on India, Ireland and America, and Engels's writings on Germany, military history and Christianity. This body of work indicates that Marx and Engels did not just meditate abstractly upon history but applied their theory to historical writing and research; indeed, these two aspects developed hand in hand. History was not simply a distant past but also a contemporary process which Marx and Engels sought to shape. Confronting the past that 'hangs like a nightmare on the minds of the living' and dispelling inherited inhibitions was necessary for the revolutionary transformation of the present.

In Chapter 4, the best of the second generation of Marxist historians are discussed. Those selected – Leon Trotsky (1879–1940), Antonio Gramsci (1891–1937) and Georg Lukács (1885–1971) – dealt with new areas of historical inquiry and refined key elements of Marx's original vision of history in the light of their experiences of war and revolution. There were others – such as Plekhanov (1856–1918), V.I. Lenin (1870–1924), Rosa Luxemburg (1871–1919), Walter Benjamin (1892–1940), C.L.R. James (1901–89) and W.E.B. Du Bois (1868–1963) – who also made original contributions to Marxism during this period that have not been included. The three to be explored were chosen on the grounds that they have the greatest present-day relevance to history, both in terms of their continuing legacy and their insights into the issues that dominate the current agenda of history. Even when we consider these three, we have to be ruthlessly selective, not being able to discuss for example Trotsky's contemporary historical writing of the 1930s or his discussion of culture and everyday life. Perhaps most pertinently, this generation had to confront the rise of Stalin which has become a theoretical and historical issue that cannot simply be wished away. All three had a different relationship with Stalinism; all in different ways avoided its worst distortions. Gramsci made a vital contribution to theoretical issues such as class consciousness, anthropology and culture. Lukács's *History and Class Consciousness* (1923) and *Lenin* (1924) constitute major contributions to the Marxist theory of history and collectively form a systematic philosophical treatment of the history of ideas. Trotsky's *History of the Russian Revolution* (1930) was the most impressive piece of historical writing within the Marxist tradition up to that point, and (some would argue) even to the present.

In Chapter 5, we encounter the third generation of Marxist historians, those who emerged from the ashes of the Second World War. In 1946, the Communist Party Historians' Group was formed. It assembled some of the most talented historians of both their generation and the Marxist tradition as a whole. Their fertile imaginations would enrich social history with novel approaches and methods. Here we concentrate on two of the most prominent members of the group, Christopher Hill and Edward Palmer Thompson. Both played a formative role in the development of **history from below**; both achieved unparalleled status in their respective fields. Both this and Chapter 6 devote considerable, perhaps disproportionate, attention to E.P. Thompson. This is a necessary misfortune. In English-speaking academia, the consideration of Marxist history in the past few decades has been reduced in large part to a discussion of Thompson. Despite Thompson's own intentions, and admitting his individual brilliance as a Marxist historian, it is unfortunate that the great mass of Thompson criticism has been substituted for a serious engagement with Marxist history as a whole. For Marxist history to move beyond the current impasse, clarity on the questions raised by the E.P. Thompson debate is essential. I try to be fair to the issues and offer my own solution. This is not a consensus position in all its details but many would at least share my objection to the widespread slide from Thompson to **poststructuralism**.

Chapter 6 examines the debate that emerged amongst British Marxist historians. Thompson and **socialist humanists** (the proponents of history from below) measured themselves against the structuralism inspired in part by Louis **Althusser**. These arguments surfaced first in the mid-1960s only to be rekindled in more dramatic fashion in the late 1970s. The contested positions have had formative consequences upon the writing of Marxist history since and a retrospective evaluation is made of the major issues involved. It would be tempting to think that the current malaise in Marxist history can be directly traced to these vituperations. The episode certainly scarred Marxist history but grander reasons contributed to its loss of momentum. The principal reason must be detected in the cooling of the intellectual and academic climate towards Marxism which turned to bleak winter conditions during the years of Thatcher, Reagan and the New Right. The **structuralist-humanist** collision acted as a prelude to a much greater assault on Marxist history in the 1980s and 1990s in the shape of postmodernism.

Chapter 7 reviews the Marxist response to the postmodern challenge to history. From the 1970s, poststructuralism has influenced the historical agenda with its greater concern for the role of language, representation and a scepticism about the possibility of historical knowledge. Sometimes this new agenda is described as the **linguistic turn**. It combines bold, seemingly menacing, statements from theorists with the new conceptual approaches of several practising historians. In an ironic twist of ideas, Marxism is both a major target of postmodernism and one of its major progenitors. But postmodernism's field of fire is much wider than Marxist history alone; history as a discipline is caught in the crossfire. Such Marxists as Alex Callinicos and Bryan D. Palmer have sprung to the defence of realist approaches to history (Marxist history included). Indeed, possibly because they have so often been the targets, it is Marxists who have mounted some of the most effective counter-thrusts to postmodernism's theoretical claims.

▶ Conclusion

In the quest for historical knowledge, nothing can be taken for granted. At the beginning of an inquiry into Marxist historical writing the most fundamental question can yield some of the most interesting fruit. Given the time-scale, geographical diffusion and scope of research, we should question the value of talking of a Marxist historical school or **classical Marxism** at all. That utility has to be proved. It also has to be demonstrated that the school has some degree of internal coherence and is not a motley fleet flying a flag of convenience. Clarifying what this common core is, and whether it has continuing relevance, are the foremost tasks of this book.

1 The Wide Panorama of Marxist History

'There is no document of civilisation which is not at the same time a document of barbarism. And just as such a document is not free of barbarism, barbarism taints also the manner in which it was transmitted from one owner to another. A historical materialist therefore dissociates himself from it as far as it is possible. He regards it as his task to brush history against the grain.'

Walter Benjamin, *Theses on the Philosophy of History* (1940)[1]

▶ Old and new history

To survey the Marxist historical writing is to demonstrate the persistence of Marx in twentieth-century historical inquiry. For a school of history so often accused of **reductionism** and **determinism**, Marxism more than any other (only the **Annales** is nearly comparable) embodies a wide range of approaches and subjects. Because the British Marxist historians of the post-Second World War era have been associated with '**new history**', there is the temptation to think that Marxism rejects traditional forms such as biographical, political, intellectual and narrative history. Marxist historians have excelled at the conventional forms of history as well as the innovative. Isaac Deutscher's *Stalin* (1967, 1st edn 1949) and his multi-volume work on Trotsky provide a model for Marxist biographies.[2] A host of Marxist biographical portraits could be assembled: Paul Frölich's Rosa Luxemburg, Tony Cliff's Lenin, Christopher Hill's Cromwell or Milton, and Georges Lefebvre's (1874–1959) Robespierre or Napoleon. In the preface to the final volume of his Trotsky trilogy, Isaac Deutscher explained the interaction between the great events and individuals: 'It was as if a huge historical conflict had become compressed into a controversy and feud between two men [Trotsky and Stalin].' Deutscher carefully drew out the tragic story of the persecutions of Trotsky's family based on the revolutionary's letters to his loved ones which 'added a sombre depth to the drama'.[3] Far from Marxism rejecting biography, what distinguishes Marxist biography is a greater theoretical clarity about the role of the individual in history, which always presents the greatest puzzle for every biographer to solve. In fact, the non-Marxist Ian Kershaw borrowed from Marx on the role of the individual in

9

history in writing his biography of Hitler. Kershaw was in effect following Tim Mason's advice that every biography of Hitler should begin with the following passage from Marx's *The Eighteenth Brumaire of Louis Bonaparte*: 'Men do make their own history, but they do not make it just as they please; they do not make it under circumstances chosen by themselves, but under circumstances directly encountered, given and transmitted from the past.'[4]

As for narrative style, a concern of traditional history, both the story-teller's art and an eloquent literary flow are present in many Marxist works. C.L.R. James's *Black Jacobins* (1938) or Leon Trotsky's *History of the Russian Revolution* (1930) could hardly be accused of sacrificing literary sensibilities on the altar of jargon. Like the narrative art or biography, Marxist history also contains shining examples of the study of high politics and history from above. In their different ways, Tim Mason's *Social Policy in the Third Reich* (1977) and John Saville's *1848* (1987) take the elite perspective to throw light on to the character of class struggles under Hitler and at the apogee of Chartism respectively. Again, as with biography, these are also distinct from traditional approaches in their conceptual framework. They are less concerned with statesmanship and more with the actions of rulers, states and governments as protagonists in a battle of wits, ideas and strategy between classes.

One of the most commonplace accusations levelled at Marxism is that it overplays economic history. It should be no surprise then that Marxism produced works of great importance and popularity in this field. Explaining the seemingly inexplicable depression of the 1930s, Leo Huberman's *Man's Worldly Goods* (1936) provided a widely read Marxist economic history and critique of the 'natural laws' of bourgeois economics. Harry Braverman's highly influential *Labor and Monopoly Capital* (1974) charted the de-skilling and **alienating** processes of capitalist mass production in both the factory and office. Both of these works owe a great debt to Marx's *Capital* which sought to lay bare the workings of the new world of capitalism in terms of political economy and history. An impressive body of Marxist scholarship has evolved within economic history.[5] Marxist historians have intervened in several major debates about economic aspects of history, most notably the **transition** from feudalism to capitalism (of which more later) and the **standard of living debate**.

Whilst not rejecting traditional approaches, Marxist history has during the last century also provided some of the most innovatory ones. **History from below** subjected ordinary people and their struggles to historical scrutiny. George Rudé's *The Crowd in the French Revolution* (1959), E.P. Thompson's *Making of the English Working Class* (1963), Christopher Hill's *The World Turned Upside Down* (1972) and Rodney Hilton's *Bond Men Made Free* (1973) are major examples of this approach. A host of other studies accompanied these major works and these collectively had a profound effect on the direction of social history. Battling against the victor's intentional suppression of past struggles in the popular memory, John Saville summarised the task of history from below in relation to Chartism:

A radical movement draws essential   n the inspiration of its past struggles and its past heroes; but who   the poor half-mad O'Connor on Kennington Common, leading his   rs to ridicule and execration? What was quite forgotten was the   ntinued in Chartism in the months that followed the events of   ven the memory of the mass arrests and jailings were wiped from   The contemporary agencies of the media were extraordinarily eff   ing this greatest of all mass movements of the nineteenth century; but when all is said the almost complete obliteration of Chartism from public consciousness in the middle decades of the century remains a remarkable phenomenon.[6]

Despite fierce criticism of Marxism from feminist and black nationalist historians, Marxists were consequently amongst the pioneers of women's and black history. Sheila Rowbotham's *Hidden from History* (1973) helped to open up the field of radical women's history, while Marxists C.L.R. James, Eric Williams and Eugene Genovese's work on black slavery and Peter Fryer's *Staying Power* (1984) on the black experience in Britain played a similar role in black history. W.E.B. Du Bois stood out as an early historian of the black experience in the USA.[7] Du Bois's *Black Reconstruction* (1935) examined the anti-racist dynamic that the American Civil War unleashed. At that time white American historians opined that radical reconstruction (1867–77) when blacks got the vote in the South was a period of corrupt northern vindictiveness, an era of the 'carpetbagger' and the 'scalawag' ending with the restoration of 'home rule' of the South. Du Bois tore apart the racist premises of this work. In their place he explained that the North won the Civil War because of the role of American blacks, that their activities cemented the union after the War, that the enfranchisement of free blacks was one of the greatest steps towards democracy in history and that the counter-revolutionary disenfranchisement of the southern blacks made race the great social problem of twentieth-century America. The work was a classic and an inspiration to Marxist historians such as Herb Apetheker and Eric Foner. Marxists also played their part in the development of oral history, which grew out of history from below. Marxist historians Ronald Fraser and Luisa Passerini used oral history to bring freshness and new insight to the conventional thinking on the Spanish Civil War and Italian Fascism through reviving the emotional flux of experience in the former and exposing the complex boundary between consent and dissent in the latter.[8]

Both sides of the Atlantic took up the history from below approach.[9] Civil rights agitation and Vietnam radicalised a generation of historians. Many of these were non-Marxist, others were explicitly Marxist, others still Marxist-influenced but preferring the American label 'radical'. Howard Zinn, a participant in and educationalist of the civil rights movement, wrote *A People's History of the United States* (1980), a general history which was 'disrespectful of governments and respectful of people's movements' to counter existing histories that 'understate revolt, overstate statesmanship, and thus encourage impotency in citizens'.[10] Perhaps the most noted of these Marxist historians is Eugene Genovese whose work on black slavery mirrored Thompson's stance towards **base and superstructure**, **hegemony** and **class**. His *Roll, Jordan, Roll* (1974), a history of slavery in the USA, is one of the early examples of how history from below could be extended beyond the confines of the traditional labour movement. Herbert Gutman's *The Black Family in Slavery and Freedom 1750–1925* (1976) is another case of a path-breaking history written by an American Marxist of the Thompsonian stripe. Arguing against American exceptionalism, David Montgomery's *Fall of the House of Labor* (1987) charted the American working class's rise in militancy during the late nineteenth and early twentieth centuries and its fall after 1920–2.

The cultural dimension of history, encompassing everything from art to everyday life, has since the 1960s occupied an increasingly central position in historical research. Here again Marxists have made their mark. F.D. Klingender's *Goya and the Democratic Tradition* (1947) is a fascinating account of Goya's paintings and their context of **Enlightenment** and revolution. Paul Siegel and Victor Kiernan are among a number of Marxists who have interpreted William Shakespeare from a historical perspective.[11] Both E.P. Thompson and Christopher Hill have examined the great poets – Milton, Marvell, Blake – as a sensitive barometer of their times. In 1958, Hilton re-examined the legend of Robin Hood, making this motif of English folklore a legitimate area of scholarship and provoking a lively debate. Anticipating today's concern for myth and representation in history, Hilton argued that what mattered more was not that Robin Hood existed but that 'one of England's most popular literary heroes is a man whose most endearing activities to his public were the robbery and killing of the landowners, in particular church landowners, and the maintenance of guerrilla warfare against established authority represented by the sheriff'.[12] In the feverish agrarian discontent of the thirteenth and fourteenth centuries, English peasants dreamed of Robin Hood. They aspired to the egalitarianism of Robin's band, which chose its own leader and lived outside the backbreaking routine of agrarian toil. More recently Christopher Hill's *Liberty against the Law* (1996) connected the seventeenth-century revival of Robin's popularity with those who saw the law and the enclosure movement trample on their liberties and rights.

E.P. Thompson has been prominently associated with greater concern for and wider definition of culture. With his studies of eighteenth-century **plebeian** customs such as wife sales and rough music, he helped (via a dialogue with anthropology) to construct the bridgehead of new cultural history. Michel Vovelle, the French Marxist historian, also engaged with the **history of mentalities** in his studies of death, revolutionary festivals and the dechristianisation campaign during year two (1793–4) of the French Revolution. His *Mentalities and Ideologies* (1990) made the case that a productive dialogue can take place between Marxism and the history of mentality. As Vovelle remarked, the Marxist Georges Lefebvre's *Great Fear* (1932), which looked at the advancing wave of anti-aristocratic hysteria in 1789, was one of the earliest examples of a history of popular belief or mentality. From the theoretical point of view, the French ***Annaliste*** Robert Mandrou's definition of ***mentalité*** as 'visions of the world' bears some remarkable similarities to Gramsci's notion of popular and folkloric 'conceptions of the world'. Marxist history has proved itself able to innovate and engage in a productive dialogue with new historical approaches. In the relationship between Marxism and new history, Guy Bois struck the right note when he said: 'It is a matter of union, it is also a matter of combat.'[13]

▶ The long and short of It

If some Marxists have turned towards cultural history and the micro-study, others have continued to focus upon the longer time-frame and long-run processes. These distinctions have contributed in part to the perceived (and at times exaggerated) differences between '**humanist**' and **structuralist** versions of Marxist history. Marx's concept of the **mode of production** has played a tremendously suggestive role in these latter studies. Owing much to Engels's *Origin of the Family, Private Property and the State* (1884), the archaeologist Gordon V. Childe's *What Happened in History* (written in 1942) provided the classic text on the origins of civilisation, the development of agriculture and the rise of class society. Chris Harman tackled the even more ambitious project of a world history from a Marxist perspective in *The People's History of the World* (1999). D.D. Kosambi's *An Introduction to the Study of Indian History* (1956) applied the Marxist approach to history to the broad sweep of social development on the sub-continent. Geoffrey De Ste Croix's *Class Struggle in the Ancient Greek World* (1981) elaborated a Marxist interpretation of Ancient Greece and Rome. His themes – the importance and definition of class and class struggle, a comparison of Marx and Weber, the nature of slavery, the dynamics of particular modes of production, and the explanatory power of Marxism – single it out as a work of relevance beyond its own particular period of study.[14] The thesis that he advanced returned to Edward Gibbon's great question of the eighteenth-century classic, *The Decline and Fall of the Roman Empire* (1776–88). Rome, according to De Ste Croix, fell into crisis because of the limits of its slave system of exploitation. Over time the available reserves of new slaves had become exhausted with the result that the cost of slave labour spiralled. This undermined the Roman ruling class's principal source of wealth and power. The whole edifice of Roman civilisation started to crumble.

From the decline of one civilisation to the rise of its successor, Chris Wickham, Perry Anderson and Guy Bois have written important works on the genesis of

European feudalism.[15] As well as his discussion of Marx's concept of the **Asiatic mode of production**, Chris Wickham played a notable part in the 'Feudal revolution debate' in the journal *Past and Present* in the 1990s.[16] In two review articles, he has appealed for a greater engagement on the part of Marxist historians with the kinds of long-run and comparative issues addressed by the historical sociologists Michael Mann and W.G. Runciman.[17] But it is Rodney Hilton more than any other Marxist who has made the study of medieval Europe his own. His investigations range from the peasant revolts and the character of the feudal mode of production, to the crisis of feudalism (an often neglected ingredient in the rise of capitalism). Guy Bois, too, has attempted to explain the feudal crisis in classical Marxist terms as a clash between the forces and relations of production in his study of fourteenth- and fifteenth-century Normandy.[18] In these works he contested demographic (or 'Malthusian') and monetarist interpretations of the collapse of fourteenth-century European society.[19]

Since Maurice Dobb's path-breaking *Studies in the Development of Capitalism* (1946), many Marxist historians have discussed the transition from feudalism to capitalism. Concentrating on the state, Perry Anderson's *Lineages of the Absolutism State* (1974) built on Marx's perceptive comments about absolutism and outlined an explanation of the historical function of absolutism, the role of Roman law and the key differences between absolutism in Eastern and Western Europe.[20] Whilst Marx and Engels referred to absolutism as a state that balanced the interests of the bourgeoisie and the aristocracy, Anderson stressed its defence of the nobility. Continuing these themes with a narrower focus, David Parker applied a Marxist view of absolutism to the French state in *The Making of French Absolutism* (1983).

A Marxist debate on transition emerged in earnest with Paul Sweezy's challenge to Maurice Dobb's account. Sweezy, an American Marxist, equated **capitalism** with the rise of the towns and markets, disputing Dobb's emphasis on the relations of production. Rodney Hilton, the Marxist medieval specialist, edited a volume that brought together some of the major contributions to this debate.[21] Robert Brenner, another American, rekindled the discussion, arguing that the differential pattern of lord–peasant class struggles in Europe played a determining effect on the pace and location of capitalist development (the **Brenner debate**). In Brenner's account, class struggle displaced other elements of Marxist accounts of transition, taking particular issue with the idea of productive forces driving the transition.[22] He also wrote a major account of the role of the London merchants in the English Civil War as a revolutionary moment within the larger process of transition.[23] Marxists, such as Peter Kriedte and Hans Medick, have also contributed to the notion of proto-industrialisation (a first phase of pre-factory mass industry). Immanuel Wallerstein sought to understand the expansion of capitalist markets as an emerging world system with an advanced Western European core and concentric geographical peripheries. All these scholars had an impact well beyond the ranks of Marxist historians.

Whilst modes of production and social formations have prompted a host of works, the idea of the **forces of production** (or aspects thereof) has also induced Marxist historical study. In part many of the studies already discussed employ the forces and relations of production as a couplet. Other studies, such as histories of science, bring the forces of production to the fore. The eventual discovery and publication of the Engels's *Dialectics of Nature* in the 1920s provoked a long-running argument on science and Marxism. *Dialectics* posited that nature itself was dialectical and attempted to comment on recent scientific discoveries and thought in order to demonstrate their theoretical shortcomings. This encouraged Marxists to study the history of science. The popular science writers of the British Communist Party provide two classic examples of these in J.D. Bernal's *Science in History* (1954) and Joseph Needham's *Science and Civilisation in China* (1954). For a history of the debate over science within Marxism itself, Helena Sheehan's *Marxism and the Philosophy of Science* (1993) summarises the arguments up to the Second World War. Controversies have beset these themes. Some have maintained that the forces of production inevitably leads to a vulgar deterministic Marxism and try to distinguish between Marx and Engels or different faces of Marx on this point. Others, Marxists included, have disputed the scientific status of Marxism or history.

▶ Revolutions

For reasons all too apparent, Marxist historians have gravitated towards history's great revolutions. Chris Harman and Pierre Broué have both written on the failed revolution in Germany in the years 1918–23.[24] Trotsky's most important historical work took 1917 as its subject. C.L.R. James brought the Haitian slave revolution (1791–1804) to life. Christopher Hill and Brian Manning have developed rich and varied writings on the English Civil War. Marx himself wrote some of his greatest work on the revolutions of his day: the revolutions of 1848, the Paris Commune of 1871, the Spanish revolution of 1854 and the American Civil War. Friedrich Engels's *Peasant War in Germany* (1850) discussed the revolutionary events of 1525 and is tackled in Chapter 2. The French Revolution has attracted more interest on the part of Marxist scholars than any other historical event. It is not difficult to comprehend why. The French Revolution was a great historical turning-point, an event with global implications, a continuing contemporary reference point for French identity and for the analysis of subsequent revolutions. Marx devoted considerable time to the study of this revolution and wished to write his own history of the Convention (the revolutionary assembly). This study acquainted him with historians, such as Adolphe Thiers (1797–1877), François Mignet (1796–1884), Augustin Thierry (1795–1856) and François Guizot (1787–1874), who analysed the great events of 1789–1815 as class struggles. In a letter to Weydemeyer, Marx acknowledged that it was not he who discovered the classes and **class struggle** but these bourgeois historians.

For much of the twentieth century, the social interpretation of the French Revolution – which stressed the intractable crisis of the rulers, class character of the events and profound consequences of these revolutions – dominated the historical literature. Though the social interpretation was widely subscribed to, some of its leading practitioners were Marxists and its analytical categories owed much to Marx. Georges Lefebvre and Albert Soboul (1914–82) (both members of the French Communist Party) elaborated what was considered, from the 1920s, to be the authoritative 'social' account of the revolution. In the preface to the 1964 English translation of Lefebvre's *The French Revolution*, he could even be described as the leading scholar of his generation and 'seldom the subject of controversy among historians'.[25] The history of the Revolution was no longer simply determined by the actions of great men – the Robespierres, Dantons and Napoleons – but by the evolving balance of social forces. The urban poor, the peasants, and the crowd were not a 'swinish multitude', as British conservative Edmund Burke (1729–97) believed, but were a real force behind the revolutionary events.[26] But this social interpretation is now subject to a fierce counter-attack. The revisionist onslaught began in earnest in the mid-1970s.

Reaching across more than six decades of scholarship, Georges Lefebvre, Albert Soboul, George Rudé and Michel Vovelle have written general histories of the French Revolution from an explicitly Marxist perspective. Each has also made his own contribution to the narrower issues within the revolutionary period. Georges Lefebvre is famed for *The Great Fear* (1932), his study of the panic that radicalised the countryside in 1789. Under the supervision of Lefebvre, Albert Soboul wrote an account of the revolutionary urban poor in *The Parisian Sans Culottes and the French Revolution* (1964). Soboul succeeded his mentor as the leading historian of the revolution. George Rudé scrutinised the role of the crowd, the *sans culottes* being the title given to the urban poor in revolutionary Paris. Rudé and Hobsbawm asserted that Lefebvre pioneered history from below and it could be argued that via this route Rudé's work on the crowd in France and on John 'Liberty' Wilkes (1727–97), along with Hobsbawm's *Primitive Rebels* (1959), were the first major applications of this perspective within English-language Marxism.[27] From another British Marxist, Richard Cobb's *People's Armies* (1961–3) was a monumental study of the popular revolutionary armies as instruments of terror created during the most radical phase of the revolution, 1792–4. In *Police and People* (1970), Cobb looked at the interaction between protest and repression, the popular movement and the repressive forces of the state, and the movement from below and the evolving economic situation; or, as he puts it, 'dearth, famine and the common people'. *Police and People* also tried to clarify the way in which 'popular history' had opened up new research materials and changed the relationship between the historian and the sources. *Paris and its Provinces* (1975) examined the difficult and complex relations of banditry, geography, administration, food supply and terror between the nation's revolutionary capital and its hinterland. In addition to a standard history of the Revolution *The Fall of French Monarchy 1787–92* (1972), Michel Vovelle has attempted to analyse the dechristianisation campaign of 1793–4 and the widespread popular festivals that characterised the revolutionary period.[28]

From the 1970s, François Furet led a revisionist counter to the Marxist-influenced orthodoxy. This shifted the focus from a social interpretation to the political one, from 1789 as a bourgeois revolution to a series of accidents. The attacks on the Marxist history of the French Revolution reached a falsetto pitch as the 200-year anniversary approached. Jonathan Clark, the conservative historian, noted with unconcealed delight the return of the political interpretation of the revolution: 'Meanwhile the tumbrils roll through the street to collect the old guard [of historians] and Marx's head is carried aloft by the mob, stuck on a pike.'[29] (It is worth noting in passing that Christopher Hill and the social interpretation of the English Civil War were subjected to analogous revisionist critiques.) Eric Hobsbawm's *Echoes of the Marseillaise* (1990) assessed the place of the French Revolution in world history and responded to the revisionist critique of the Marxist interpretation of these events. McGarr and Callinicos's *Marxism and the Great French Revolution* (1989) also sounded a Marxist counterpoint to the revisionist consensus through reaffirmation of the social interpretation and a theoretical and comparative defence of **bourgeois revolution**.

The French Revolution also acted as the starting point for Eric Hobsbawm's unfolding history of Europe. From the 'dual revolution' of the late eighteenth century (the Industrial Revolution and the French Revolution) to the present, this work constituted one of the great feats of modern historiography. Hobsbawm tried to capture the character of the successive ages of European and world capitalism: the ages of revolution, of capital, of empire, and the age of extremes.

Whilst revolutions occupy a special place in the Marxist account of history, Marxist historians have also sought to understand their obverse both in the sense of counter-revolutionary defeats and when class struggle was at a lower pitch. In terms of the former, Christopher Hill's *Experience of Defeat* (1984) examined the defeated hopes of the radical Levellers and the religious millenarians after the high point of the English revolution had passed. Likewise, John Saville's *1848* charted the last great upsurge of Chartism when the English state was able to mobilise its considerable military forces for the defeat of that movement. As for when class struggle is not so obviously out in the open, much of the work of history from below, which has already been mentioned, has been to conceptualise and uncover this.

▶ Concepts and theory

All Marxist history is informed by an array of concepts such as **social relations of production**, class struggle, mode of production and hegemony. With the development of academic Marxism since the Second World War, the boundaries of Marxist and non-Marxist history have blurred considerably. By the 1960s even some conservative historians had adopted Marxism as a useful instrument. It is on the conceptual level that eclectic borrowings from Marx are at their greatest. Many historians selectively adopted certain Marxist categories as fruitful tools for formulating hypotheses or for use in historical explanation. The 'mode of production' category provides one such illustration. The French Marxist, Guy Bois, described mode of production as the 'key concept' of Marxist history and noted that this idea had had a profound effect upon the great medievalists of the Annales school, George Duby and Jacques Le Goff. R.S. Neale also viewed the mode of production as the chief category of Marxist history. Others, notably E.P. Thompson and Robert Brenner, have asserted that the concept of class struggle should be accorded conceptual primacy. Thompson even argued that class struggle was more important than classes *per se*. Selection is even more pronounced with the exclusion of certain concepts. Several of those historians who privileged class struggle also rejected base and superstructure (the view that the socio-economic relations are more important than, and have an influence on, the realm of politics and ideas).

Marxist concepts have helped historians to ask new questions, sometimes in old fields of inquiry. But this conceptual agenda has not been static. Innovation can be observed, for example, in the studies of nationalism from the 1980s. Benedict Anderson, Victor Kiernan and Eric Hobsbawm's work on the birth of nationalism and the creation of nationalist myths projected into the distant past broke new ground in the study of national identity. This 'invention of tradition' located the way in which modern nation-states sought legitimacy through giving new and old institutions the mystique of permanence through a series of seemingly ancient symbols, ceremonies and practices, such as coronations, anthems and flags.[30]

Marxists have continued to make a lively contribution to the theory of history. Marx and Engels's writings on this subject were both extensive and highly suggestive. *The German Ideology* (1845–6), the *Preface to the Critique of Political Economy*, the *Communist Manifesto* (1848), *Socialism: Scientific and Utopian* (1880), *The Eighteenth Brumaire of Louis Bonaparte* (1852) and their correspondence all prominently feature historiographical issues, questions of historical theory and method. The middle generation of Marxists took up these questions with Lukács providing the most systematic treatment in *History and Class Consciousness* (1923), an often underestimated classic of Marxist philosophy of history. More recently, this element of investigation has been rejuvenated at various levels. Several historians have reflected on the utility and continuing relevance of Marxist theory. R.S. Neale, Christopher Hill and Victor Kiernan, amongst others, have attempted to restate the value of Marxism as a tool of historical research and analysis.[31] These historians have also sought to clarify the contribution of Marxism to twentieth-century historiography. Eric Hobsbawm's *On History* (1997) constituted a more substantial attempt to explore historiographical questions ranging from postmodernism to the Russian Revolution. For Hobsbawm, Marx provided the 'essential base' of historical investigation, because of his unique attempt 'to formulate a methodological approach to history as a whole, and to envisage and explain the entire process of human social evolution'.[32] Likewise Geoffrey de Ste Croix observed the utility of Marxism in the unlikely context of Ancient Greece and Rome:

> Marx's analysis of society although devised in the course of an effort to understand the mid-nineteenth-century capitalist world, resulted in the construction of a set of concepts which work remarkably well when applied even to the Greek and Roman world and can be used to *explain* many of its features and developments – the total destruction of Greek democracy over some five or six centuries, for example, and even the age-old problem of 'the decline and fall of the Roman empire' or let us rather say 'the disintegration of quite a large portion of the Roman empire between the fourth and the eighth centuries'.[33]

Theoretical discussions have at times taken a polemical turn as with E.P. Thompson's 'humanist' indictment of **Althusserianism** and structuralism in the *Poverty of Theory* (1978) and in his public dispute with Richard Johnson in the pages of *History Workshop Journal*. This debate uncomfortably straddled the theorist–practitioner division of labour with Thompson showing that he could take on the theorists at their own game. Despite this, Thompson articulated a certain scepticism towards theory, at one point describing himself as a 'Marxist empiricist' and implying that Marxist historians should be happiest on the practitioner's side of the fence. Perry Anderson, one of Thompson's protagonists, has more than anyone else combined the theorist and the practitioner. Alongside his long time-frame structural histories of the rise of feudalism and the absolutist state, he has written several major theoretical works on the Marxist philosophy of history.

Distinguishing between practising historians who write history and Marxist theorists who write on the philosophy of history, there is a voluminous literature of this latter type and only a small sample can be cited here. In the middle generation of Marxism, Lukács, Gramsci and Benjamin are three such examples. Benjamin's *Theses on the Philosophy of History* (1940) were an amazingly poetic and provocative attack on social democracy and **historicism**. Benjamin contended that Marxist history's purpose was to offer the working class 'a memory as it flashes up at a moment of danger'. These dangers were all too apparent in Benjamin's Germany of lost revolutions and Hitler's consolidation of power. Non-Marxists have engaged in great contests with the Marxist theory of history. Karl Popper's *Poverty of Historicism* (1957) was a thoughtful empiricist critique of Marxism, and Geoffrey Elton's *Practice of History* (1967) launched a broadside against 'new' and Marxist history. Other Cold War critics were less impressive. More recently Marxist theory of history has been criticised by historical sociologists such as Anthony Giddens, W.G. Runciman and Michael Mann, and postmodernists such as Hayden White, Jacques Derrida and Michel Foucault. Stephen Rigby's *Marxism and History* (1987) was perhaps the most important specific critique of Marxist history, borrowing as it did from techniques of literary criticism and subjecting Marxism to sharp scrutiny. For Rigby, there were many 'textually authorised Marxes'.[34] He implored us to abandon the attempt to discover 'what Marx actually thought'. Marxists might reply that this is to ignore that Marx's work was indisputably purposive: it was a guide to the drama of human emancipation. From within the Marxist camp, G.A. Cohen's *Karl Marx's Theory of History – A Defence* (1978) attempted to reconstruct a coherent singular view of Marx's theory of history. This orthodox position engendered a considerable debate in academic journals where Cohen was taken to task for technological determinism and doctrinaire defence of Marx. Perry Anderson's *Arguments within English Marxism* (1980) turned to the questions raised by the aforementioned Thompson–Johnson debate. In *Arguments*, he raised the pivotal issues that have emerged for Marxist (and non-Marxist) historians: questions of structure and **agency**, base and superstructure amongst others. His *Considerations of Western Marxism* (1976) sought to delineate a genealogy of **classical Marxism**, carefully excluding the pretenders of the late Second International and Stalinism. Alex Callinicos also pondered the major theoretical objections to the Marxist view of history in *Making History* (1987). He surveyed both the trends within Marxism, from Cohen to analytical Marxism, as well as the major rival theoretical schools (empiricism, historical sociology and postmodernism). Callinicos revisited this last preoccupation in *Against Postmodernism* (1989) and *Theories and Narratives* (1995), which were timely and trenchant ripostes to an increasingly confident historiographical trend. Others – Bryan D. Palmer, Frederick Jameson, Perry Anderson and Terry Eagleton are examples – have also intervened in these debates from a Marxist (though not always historical) perspective.

▶ Distortions of Marxism

Marxist history is all too often misrepresented through a theoretical caricature: one that bears little semblance to Marxist historical writing. For the English Tudor scholar Geoffrey Elton, Marxism as a doctrine 'stultifies the study of history by reducing history to a repository of examples selected or distorted to buttress the scheme'.[35] Across the Atlantic, Gertrude Himmelfarb worried that Marxists were yoked to the 'formidable burden of ideology' which acted as a 'predetermined schema that applies to all periods and all events'.[36] From empiricist to postmodernist quarters, Marxism is accused of economic reductionism, determinism, schematism, and even (in the case of the postmodernists) of **empiricism**. Opponents deduce their criticisms from what they take to be Marxist theory, which is usually based on a handful of vulgarised assumptions. They do not assess the way in which Marxism's most able historians have sensitively applied and refined that theory. Such criticism amounts to little more than, as Michel Vovelle succinctly observed, 'vulgar critics of vulgar Marxism'. Thus, analysis of Marxist historical writing is an indispensable and neglected part of the relationship between Marxism and historiography.

Increasingly, Western Marxism has provided its own framework of reference. Reassessments of the founders of Marxism are too easily brushed aside as dogmatic exercises in holy scripture. Some thinkers, following this dismissal of what Marx actually said, have metamorphosed into the butterfly of '**postmarxism**'. In part, this is an adaptation to the '**fall of communism**'; in part the climate for left-wing academics began to change after the **enthusiasm of 1968** began to wane in the mid-1970s. For two decades those working within an explicitly Marxist framework have been under attack. **Postmodernism**, **historical sociology** and empiricism all provide serious challenges to Marxist historiography, and when historical journals produce special editions on 'the crisis of social history' or 'the end of labour history', it is the influence of Marxist history that is implicitly challenged. Some trends of 'Marxism' have abandoned its core defining characteristics, both in terms of political practices as well as in historical method. Dismayed by the self-proclaimed Marxists of his day, Marx exclaimed, 'All I know is that I am not a Marxist!' A crucial dimension of the Marxist historical tradition has been to reassert Marx's method in order to reject the advances of false friends.

Assessing the Marxist tradition immediately poses a methodological problem. It would seem natural to adopt a 'history of ideas' approach, to look at the level of pure thought and its development unsullied by the complications, accidents and contingencies of historical events. Such an **idealist** approach to history is unable to explain the evolution of an intellectual tradition and this is especially pronounced where Marxism is concerned. The temptation is to disconnect intellectual history from the evolving historical context, to link one thinker to the next in a daisy chain of thought. Just as Charles Darwin (1809–82), the originator of the notion of biological evolution, cannot be held responsible for Herbert Spencer (1820–1903), who transposed the evolutionary idea of the survival of the fittest to human society, so should we be aware that Marx cannot be culpable for Stalin's part in history, or at least not without a fair trial. Hindsight dangerously equates original thinkers with those that vulgarise and distort their ideas. With this counsel of caution, it is necessary to authenticate, as the art expert would a great painting, the provenance and consistency of an intellectual tradition. This approach allows us to assess Marxism's contribution to historical writing. It is my contention, though I am not alone, that Marxism is only a viable intellectual tradition if one defines criteria that exclude some self-styled 'Marxisms' (notably Stalinist approaches). The practices of Stalinist regimes, parties and historians fundamentally contradict the basic propositions of Marxism. For Marxism to be meaningful, these approaches should be excluded from it.

Here the politics and the history walk hand in hand, if not necessarily in step. Political deviations from Marx have habitually entailed deviations from his historical method. The most telling examples are the degeneration of the Second International, the period after the Russian Revolution and then the emergence of postmarxism. As Marx and Engels' influence on the Second International faded, a biologically or technologically deterministic version of historical materialism spread through the socialist parties of Europe through such thinkers as H.M. Hyndman (1842–1921), Karl Kautsky (1854–1938) and Eduard Bernstein (1850–1932). With the rise of Stalin, Marx's original historical vision became an indecipherable blur. Trotsky described this development as the 'Stalin school of falsification'.

▶ Stalinism and Marxist history

What passed for Marxism became the official religion of the Soviet Union and in turn Eastern Europe, China and various other parts of the globe. From being the inspiration of the labour movement or persecuted revolutionaries it was transformed into its opposite, a state ideology. George Orwell, the English socialist, wrote in *1984* (1949) a withering critique of the Soviet Union. Nothing encapsulated the social function of history under Stalinist rule so accurately as his words, 'Who controls the past controls the future: who controls the present controls the past.'

A sharp antithesis exists between the best Marxist works and the history most influenced by Stalinism. Though the pace differed, the decline of Marxist history in the Soviet Union coincided with the rise of Stalin. During the 1920s, when the question of Lenin's successor was not settled, history in the Soviet Union flourished. During the years of the New Economic Policy, intellectual and cultural life recovered from the devastation of war, revolution and civil war. The situation was very different from the intolerant dogmatism associated with Stalin's 1930s. In the 1920s, party historians were willing to work with non-Marxist historians. As Russia's leading Bolshevik historian, Mikhail Nikolaevich Pokrovskii, stated, non-Marxist hands would help to construct a communist culture. Despite this, as early as 1922, Pokrovskii was drawn into the factional struggle that was ultimately to consolidate Stalin as Russian dictator. The target of Pokrovskii's intervention was Trotsky, with whom he disagreed over the character of Russian absolutism. Close to Bukharin and the 'right' faction of the Central Committee, Pokrovskii again stepped into the debate over the relationship between Lenin's theory of revolution in Russia between 1905 and 1917 and Trotsky's thesis of **permanent revolution**.

In late 1924, Pokrovskii confirmed Stalin's fraudulent assertion that Lenin believed socialism could be built in one country. The following year, the Central Committee asked Pokrovskii and the Institute of Red Professors to work on a history of the Russian Revolution which was published in 1927. His relatively sympathetic biographer highlighted the contradictions within the account. Its interpretation of Lenin was 'dubious' and 'questionable', and its remarks about Trotsky 'scurrilous'. In trying to reconcile Lenin to both anti-Trotskyism and to Stalin's 'socialism in one country', Pokrovskii obscured the considerable evolution of Lenin's attitudes between 1905 and 1917. He ignored the intellectual watershed that Lenin crossed in 1917 when the Bolshevik leader finally decided on the possibility of *socialist* revolution in Russia and failed to explain the sharp disagreements that this produced within the Party in 1917.[37] In order to create the impression of continuity between Lenin and Stalin, Pokrovskii also omitted all Lenin's passages on the necessity of revolution in the West for the survival of socialism in Russia.

The debate over the October Revolution lasted until 1931 and exhibited the symptoms of Stalin's tightening grasp on power. Increasingly, the slightest questioning of Stalin's distortion of Lenin was identified as Trotskyite heresy. It ended with Stalin's personal invective against historical debate, which he equated with 'rotten liberalism' and which he wanted 'gagged'. The target of Stalin's outburst was the unfortunate Slutskii, who had dared to state the obvious fact: Lenin had underestimated the moderation of pre-war German Social Democracy. Stalin's tirade ranged against the fundamentals of history itself and marked the effective death-knell of anything resembling the classical Marxist approach to history:

> Is it not perfectly clear that by his talk of the inadequacy of the documents Slutskii is trying to cover up the utter inadequacy and falsity of his so-called conception? Let us assume that, in addition to the documents already known, a mass of documents were found containing, say more resolutions of the Bolsheviks urging the necessity of wiping out centrism. Who save the hopeless bureaucrats can rely on documents alone? Who, besides archive rats, does not understand the necessity that a party and leader must be tested primarily by their deeds, and not by their declarations?[38]

In line with the dictator's preferences, the masses vanished from 1917 as makers of their own history, now visible only when being herded like the sheep in George Orwell's fable *Animal Farm* by Lenin and the Party. Photographs were doctored, histories falsified, and historians were tightly controlled. Stalin personally censored historical works and wrote falsified accounts of events. Historical interpretation became a blunt instrument in factional disputes or to find historical precedent for the vilification of the *kulaks* (the richer peasants). Even more astonishingly, Soviet historians eulogised the 'great men' of Russian history, Peter the Great and Ivan the Terrible, as they had under Tsarism. This reversion to Russian nationalism can be illustrated by the case of the great film-maker Sergei Eisenstein (1898–1948). His earlier works *Battleship Potemkin* (1925), *Strike* (1925) and *October* (1927) lionised the people and documented the revolutionary actions of workers, sailors and the Petrograd masses. In his later epic works, *Alexander Nevksy* (1938) and *Ivan the Terrible, Part One* (1945), old nationalist myths were resurrected for the purposes of the 'Great Patriotic War' and the personality cult of Stalin. Like fidgeting Bolshoi ballerinas, historians had to toe an inconsistent and shifting party line. They had to beware of, and avoid, a multiplying catalogue of heretical deviations: objectivism, romanticism, cosmopolitanism, bourgeois methodology and idealism. To err was human; 'to the Gulag' was the General Secretary's response. During the 1930s the orthodoxy of Pokrovskii was overturned and denounced to the extent that it was officially described as anti-Marxist.

As the Stalinist system spread across Eastern Europe, similar mutilated versions of Marxist history developed. For example, the German Democratic Republic (DDR) demanded that historians wrote material that was politically relevant, using history to legitimise the regime and to promote a national consciousness that highlighted historical episodes which took Germany progressively closer to its socialist future. The promulgation of scientific laws of history became a substitute for historical explanation. The DDR historians also sought to challenge West German interpretations of national history and to influence the West German working class, at which they were spectacularly unsuccessful.[39] What resulted was a dull rigid teleology in which the major issues were the fine-tuning of socio-economic periodisation and the positivistic elaboration of the laws of history. Equally in Communist China, rulers have taken an intense interest in the past, disseminating a form of world history that charts the inevitable victory of socialism over capitalism and the necessity of the Chinese revolution. Shifts in historical interpretation match policy turns, rationalising, for example, the Sino–Soviet split and the events of the cultural revolution.[40] Even with the *glasnost* period in the Soviet Union, old habits died hard, as the rehabilitation of the Bolshevik leader and economist Nicholai Bukharin (1888–1938) offered historical precedent for Gorbachev's market socialist reforms.

Whilst a few Eastern European Marxist historians, such as Witold Kula and Boris Porshnev, established reputations beyond the Iron Curtain, the best examples of Marxist historical writing in the twentieth century – from Trotsky's *History of the Russian Revolution* (1930) to E.P.Thompson's *Making of the English Working Class* (1963) – took as their methodological starting point the rejection of Stalinism. Sometimes the Stalinist–Marxist distinction is less clear cut when the influence of Stalinism is present, if not total, as with the British Communist Party Historians' Group or such individuals as Georges Lefebvre or Eric Hobsbawm. At the very least, these historians, by their failure to provide an adequate analysis of the class character of the Soviet Union, leave Marxist history without a response to the charge that Marxism is dead after the events of 1989–91. Even Thompson, whose moral denunciation of Stalinism was particularly vociferous, was guilty of this. His designation of the Soviet Union as a form of 'parasitism' was hardly a robust explanation. Some have attempted to trace residual distortions in the work of such Marxist historians. For instance, some have stressed the link between history from below and the popular front strategy of the Communist International (1935–9), and others have seen the connection between Stalinist determinism and Althusserian structuralism.[41]

The exclusion of Stalinism from Marxism is not to deny that there are disagreements within Marxism and that there has not been an evolution of Marxism itself (or even that there are historians who uneasily combine elements of the two). Marxism's theoretical and empirical frontier, like that of science, advances over a broad front. It does not furnish absolute truth but it approximates reality; it is provisional. Lukács aptly described the relationship between innovation and tradition within Marxism:

> Orthodox Marxism, therefore, does not imply the uncritical acceptance of the results of Marx's investigations ... It is the scientific conviction that dialectical materialism is the road to truth and that its method can be developed, explored and deepened only along the lines laid down by its founders. It is the conviction, moreover, that all attempts to surpass and 'improve' it have led and must lead to over-simplification, triviality and eclecticism.[42]

It is possible to maintain that the classical Marxist tradition contains both examples of historical writing and the philosophy of history which allow a convincing alternative to current historical fashions. Marx and his followers have plenty to say on some of the chief historiographical questions facing us today: culture, language, idealism, total history and class. That is why Marxism has been one of the most influential bodies of theory in historical investigation. What is more, Marxism can mount telling critiques of empiricism, postmodernism, and neo-**Weberianism**. History itself is under attack. As Richard Evans observed in the poignantly entitled *In Defence of History* (1997):

> Such has been the power and influence of the post-modernist critique of history that growing numbers of historians themselves are abandoning the search for truth, the belief in objectivity, and the quest for a scientific approach to the past. No wonder so many historians are worried about the future of their discipline.[43]

How have Marxist historians coped with the experience of Stalinism? First, some historians formally accepted Stalinism but were able to write Marxist history in spite of this. The ability to do so depended on circumstances and the areas of study. The British Communist Party historians in the 1940s and 1950s were able to fall within this category because of particular factors (discussed below). Gramsci might also be included under this heading. He never broke from Stalin but because of his imprisonment was able to work beyond the influence of Stalin. However, there were areas where Stalinism and writing Marxist history were evidently incompatible, Russian Revolution and the Hitler–Stalin Pact being cases in point. Second, there are some Marxist historians who explicitly reject Stalinism but who have not developed a rigorous explanation of this phenomenon. Many of those historians associated with history from below would be included in this camp. Thompson could say:

> I was, of course, very active in the Communist Party and remained so until 1956. This didn't mean that one didn't have many inner doubts and also wasn't guilty of many casuistries explaining away what one should have repudiated in the character of Stalinism. But also I am not prepared to accept a Trotskyist interpretation of a whole past that dismisses an entire phase of historical development and all the multiform popular initiatives and authentic areas of self-activity and heroism as 'Stalinist'. The popular dimensions of Communist activity, then and in many cases still today, are such as to prevent this kind of intellectualisation.[44]

Here Thompson conflated his sympathy with the communist rank and file (one shared by many of the very Trotskyists he takes issue with) and the need for a root and branch break with the intellectual and political tradition of Stalinism and the communist parties. David Montgomery, the American Marxist labour historian who, like Thompson, had been a Communist Party member, had a similar ambivalence. One the positive side of the scale, the American Communist Party put its members in touch with the real struggles of black and white working-class America and, on a day-to-day level, members tried to make sense of things through some form of Marxism:

> The negative side is also important. The real flowering of creative work among the people you are thinking of came after they had left the Party. The official intellectual life of the Party ... was stifling. In spite of the familiar slogan 'Marxism is a guide to action, not a dogma,' theory appeared at that level of the movement in the form of explanations of official texts or even *ex post facto* justifications of actions taken, and not as a rigorous method of analysing and changing social realities. In this sense, both the roots and the breaking away were very important.[45]

Third, there are those Marxists who have rejected Stalinism and formulated a systematic explanation of the character of the Soviet Union. Leon Trotsky would be an obvious candidate for this category. The significance of this typology is that it explains the complex relationship between Stalinism and Marxism in historical writing, but, more than this, it also helps to account for the way in which Marxist historians have been affected by the collapse of communism and the ability of Marxist history to renew itself. To speed renewal there are Marxist historians whose work provides a historical materialist explanation of the rise of Stalinism. Hobsbawm may dismiss such issues in his *Age of Extremes* (1994) as forgotten and irrelevant arguments, but if there is to be a new generation of Marxists this question is paramount. What Hobsbawm finds unpalatable is that those who provide the clearest analysis of these events come from the Trotskyist camp so long reviled by the communist parties across the world as Hitler's agents. In this tradition, Moshe Lewin's *Lenin's Last Struggle* (1968) charted Lenin's growing opposition to Stalin, which was hampered by a fatal combination of assassination attempts and strokes. Isaac Deutscher's biographies of Stalin and Trotsky demonstrate the way in which their struggle was more than a clash of personalities: it embraced political principle and far-reaching socio-economic forces. Though there is not the time to go into the case here, the isolation of the revolution, the defeat of promising revolutionary situations in Europe, the destruction of the Russian working class through war, civil war and famine and the counter-weight of the rising ruling bureaucracy all contributed to this process.

Ironically those who equate Stalinism and Marxism employ a teleological logic akin to Orwell's account of *Animal Farm*. If totalitarianism was inscribed in Lenin's *What is to be Done?* (1902), then the need to search for an explanation in the twist and turn of the actual historical events is redundant. The most extreme version of this teleology can be witnessed in Talmon's *Origins of Totalitarian Democracy* (1966) in which the ideas of the Enlightenment and Rousseau are blamed for the terror and dictatorship in Russia. As well as a historical materialist account of the rise of Stalinism, there have also been class analyses of the Soviet Union which clarify the reasons for excluding Stalinism from Marxism proper. These again started with the works of Leon Trotsky and embody a number of writers and positions. Amongst these, Leon Trotsky's *Revolution Betrayed* (1937) and Tony Cliff's *Russia: Marxist Analysis* (1947) stand out.[46] For a class analysis of Eastern Europe from different non-Stalinist perspectives one might consult Rudolph Bahro and Milovan Djilas.[47] Chris Harman's *Class Struggles in Eastern Europe* (1988) applied the techniques of history from below to the revolts of workers, students and peasants in Eastern Europe against their rulers: East Germany 1953, Hungary and Poland 1956, Czechoslovakia 1968, Poland 1980–1. For these Marxists, such revolutionary episodes, more than any Cold War propaganda, exposed the humbug and brutality of the Eastern European ruling classes. On the revolutions of 1989, Alex Callinicos's *Revenge of History* (1991) provided a positive and sharply perceptive analysis in line with the state capitalist view of the Soviet Union and its satellites.

▶ Conclusion

Despite the fact that the impact of Marxist historians is now somewhat dissipated, their body of work is considerable and still influential upon wider ranks of historians. Their endeavours raise two questions. First, what were the insights of Marx that so animated these authors? Second, why has the project of Marxist history come to an impasse? These questions underscore this text.

That Marxism encompasses such a broad range of historical subjects and approaches is no accident. Old and new approaches, long- and short-run history, theory and empirical research all feature in Marxist history's panoramic perspectives. It was one of Marx's convictions that an understanding of history must embrace its entirety and its opposing poles. His **dialectical** method, as we shall see in the next chapter, is premised on the conviction of the connectedness of opposites acting together in a greater whole. Despite the diversity of Marxist historical writing, it is clear from the case of Stalinism that Marxism is not an openly inclusive label. The incompatibility of Stalinism and Marxist history reveals that Marxism's core principles and methods can be understood negatively: what Marxism is not. The following two chapters on Marx and Engels positively outline the elements that underpin the classical Marxist tradition and the historical writing that is derived from it.

2 Marx and Engels's Conception of History

'The class struggle, which is always present to a historian influenced by Marx, is a fight for the crude and material things without which no refined and spiritual things could exist. Nevertheless, it is not in the form of the spoils which fall to the victor that the latter make their presence felt in the class struggle. They manifest themselves in this struggle as courage, humour, cunning and fortitude. They have retroactive force and will constantly call into question every victory, past and present, of the rulers. As flowers turn towards the sun, by dint of a secret heliotropism the past strives to turn towards that sun which is rising in the sky of history. A historical materialist must be aware of this most inconspicuous of all transformations.'

Walter Benjamin, *Theses on the Philosophy of History* (1940)

▶ Introduction

Harold Wilson, the former Labour Prime Minister, once boasted that he had not got beyond the first page of *Capital*, implying that Marx was both impenetrable and no longer relevant. The impression that Marx is difficult to read is widespread. However, core propositions of Marxism are reasonably straightforward. After all, they were written for, and assimilated by, millions of working-class people in their most popular form, *The Communist Manifesto* (1848). This chapter seeks to explain Marx's conception of history without recourse to unnecessary jargon. At the same time, it addresses the key technical terms which Karl Marx (1818–83) and his life-long collaborator Friedrich Engels (1820–95) themselves employed.

Marx's view of history, **historical materialism** as he termed it, consists of a number of overarching concepts that need to be considered. These include the **forces** and **social relations of production**, **materialism**, **class struggle**, **base and superstructure** and the **dialectic**. Marx set out to answer the following questions: what are the common features of all human history? Is history scientific? How does progress come about? He employed these concepts to help answer these problems. But in order to understand why Marx should tackle such an ambitious task it is worth examining his intellectual background.

▶ History and the Enlightenment

Karl Marx can be described as a second-generation product of the European **Enlightenment**. His views emerged from a critical engagement with three major viewpoints that grew out of the Enlightenment: French utopian socialism, British political economy, and German philosophy. The Enlightenment also provided a number of histories and philosophies of history that were encountered by the young Marx.

It was in the eighteenth century that the horizons of historians began to lift from the narratives of battles, royal houses and the Church to more fundamental questions such as why civilisations flourished and eventually collapsed. Even though they were quite different, these works shared a desire to understand civilisations from the perspective of their social dynamics in much the same way that Newton (1642–1727), Galileo (1564–1642) and Copernicus (1473–1543) before them had sought to reveal the laws of motion of the universe. The era of the Enlightenment bequeathed historical masterpieces such as Giambattista Vico's *New Science* (1725–44) and Edward Gibbon's (1737–94) *The History of the Decline and Fall of the Roman Empire* (1776–88).[1] Vico believed that the history of all gentile peoples passed through common developmental phases (in which culture was 'poetic' or 'theological', then 'heroic' and finally 'human').[2] History was viewed by Enlightenment thinkers as cyclical because, whilst it witnessed the gradual growth of reason at the expense of the imagination, ultimately the moral corruption of the rational human age brought decline and returned a people to their initial state. Gibbon, on the other hand, sought to explain the collapse of the Roman Empire through the corroding influence of Christianity on the imperial state. His broad sweep of history, his attempt to understand the underlying processes of the long run of ancient history and his interweaving of narrative and explanation mark out *The History of the Decline and Fall of the Roman Empire* as a historiographical classic. In these works we can see where Marx might have gained his desire to explain change over time.

The Enlightenment also saw eager discussion of the encounter between Europeans and non-Europeans in the exotic reaches of the globe. Some Enlightenment thinkers speculated about the 'state of nature' of the first men and women: the 'noble savages' who lived in simple societies according to nature's laws. Others, such as Adam Ferguson (1723–1816) and Georg F.W. Hegel (1770–1831), viewed these societies as the dawn of human history and European society, having passed through a number of intermediary stages, as its setting sun, although Hegel's conception of 'World Historical Peoples', while sharing Vico's cyclical view, ascribed no great importance to the civilisations of Africa. Ferguson believed that different races belonged to different historical epochs: hunting, pastoralism, agriculture and commerce. Despite his racial categories, here was an attempt to chart human history by means of different stages in the process of production, *pace* Marx. Likewise, Adam Smith (1723–90), the Scottish political economist and author of *The Wealth of Nations* (1776), adopted the same stages of society and argued that the mode of subsistence shaped the character of warfare and justice.[3]

Hegel, the German idealist philosopher, was particularly influential on the young Marx. Indeed, having adapted it from Hegel, the dialectic became the cornerstone of Marx's method. Hegel and then Marx utilised the dialectic to describe and explain the complex processes of human history. This method rests on the following premises:

1 All things are in themselves contradictory. (See the **unity of opposites** in the Glossary.)
2 Contradiction is at the heart of all change.
3 If we concentrate on individual things we can only see the differences between them not the relationships between them.
4 The world can only be understood by seeing things as processes. Changes in quantity lead to changes in quality. .
5 Things only acquire meaning when understood as instants in a process of change. (See the **negation of the negation** and **mediation** in the Glossary.)
6 Things must be understood as part of a wider whole, a **totality**.

The failure to appreciate the centrality of the dialectic has led many to lapse into deterministic or crude versions of Marxism. Whereas for Hegel history developed through the ideas and the mind, through the increasing human consciousness of our world and ourselves, Marx preferred to view human history as developing in relation to the material world. He 'turned Hegel on his head' and, having appropriated the dialectic, rejected **idealism** for a materialist conception of history.

Finally, the social historians of the French Revolution profoundly influenced Marx in his reading of history. In the early part of the nineteenth century, French social historians interpreted the events of 1789–1815 as the result of class conflict, as the rise of the bourgeoisie and its antagonism to the old regime dominated by the feudal aristocracy.[4] Marx inherited much from the Enlightenment but his view of history was both distinctive and more elaborate. Like Enlightenment thought, Marx was concerned with the connection between history and science. He sought to discover the hidden laws or variables that underpinned human history which could uncover the great riddles of history: why did civilisations rise and fall? What were the distinctive features of different historical epochs? What fuelled historical progress? What made humans differ from the rest of the animal kingdom? Can history be scientific?

▶ Can human history be scientific?

Both Marx and Engels believed that their socialism rested on scientific, not utopian, foundations. Engels credited Marx with discoveries akin to Charles Darwin's
(1809–82) in the field of evolution. While Marx and Engels believed that their
conception of historical change (historical materialism) *was* scientific, whether or
not the study of history or society can be scientific has long been a subject for
debate. Most recently, postmodernists have maintained that science and the whole
rationalist tradition is a grand narrative, a fictional account of the long view of
human history, and should treated with 'incredulity'.[5]

Marx often employed the language of the natural sciences to underline the
scientific character of his work. He spoke of the laws of historical development just
as Newton wrote of the laws of motion of the universe. This rhetoric has led many to
accuse Marxism of **determinism** (formulating immutable laws that deny free will
and openness in history). At the same time, both Marx and Engels were well aware
that natural and human histories were not simple equivalents. Though the dialectic
operates in both, in human history it is not blind as it is composed of conscious
human beings capable of choice.[6] As a result, the level of determination is lower in
human history and the sharpness of alternatives is more acute: there are more
either/or dilemmas, such as the tussle between revolution and counter-revolution.

Marx hailed the progress of modern science but was also one of its sharpest
critics. He noted that it brought spectacular progress in human wealth but
condemned the majority to poverty; it raised the potential of human production
but diverted vast resources into the weapons of destruction; it promised human
liberation from drudgery but enslaved millions in underpaid and exhausting toil
(in subscribing to this final point, Marx and Engels would formulate a critique of
their own age, not least the British 'Industrial Revolution'[7]). Marx and Engels's
claim to have developed a *scientific* socialism relied on a number of elements:
empirical observation and research, scientific scepticism, and **dialectical materialism**. Marx believed that scientific revelation was progressive, with discoveries
widening the frontier of human understanding. Therefore in every epoch there
were boundaries to scientific knowledge that could be by-passed in the future.
Engels argued that Marx made two such discoveries: the real character of **exploitation** under capitalism and the materialist conception of history.

The limits of scientific knowledge result from the fact that direct observation –
empiricism – alone was incapable of explaining natural phenomena. The
explanatory limits of observation also provide the material basis for religion,
mysticism and animism; the task of the scientist is to prise open the inner secrets of
matter. Marx's science stands or falls on his assertion to have uncovered the inner
workings of human history. According to this proposition, the development of
human society is not inexplicable (i.e., either random or mystical) but is within our

grasp if viewed from the correct scientific standpoint. In the same way that new branches of sciences had unlocked the mysteries of, for example, the earthquake, so historical materialism explained the character of human society.

Marx firmly believed that the study of history could be scientific, and he constantly endeavoured to base his ideas on the most up-to-date thinking. Allied to this was Marx's prodigious empirical investigation in whatever field he was studying. He was also keenly aware of the need for a critical approach to new work and acknowledged that demonstrable proof was the necessary companion of scientific advance (one of his favourite mottoes was 'doubt everything'). Similarly, Engels upbraided 'so-called Marxists' who toyed with theory as a way of avoiding serious historical research.[8] For Marx, the dialectic suggested that theory and evidence, though opposites, must be intimately connected. Despite the current fashion for denying the scientific character of history, it does have accepted procedures of verification or falsification and methods allowing us to point to the firmest conclusions reasonable.

More fundamentally, Marx's philosophy was the culmination of the long struggle of science against religion and magic, which had itself provided the **epistemological** basis for a scientific study of society. Theology had previously overshadowed science in the universities and monasteries as well as the latter being heavily censored by the Church. Scientific knowledge remained, as Engels put it, the 'humble handmaiden' of the Catholic Church.[9] For science to emerge in its own right, a battle of ideas took place which closely reflected the fortunes of the battles against the old feudal order. Scholarship and learning gradually escaped the confines of the monastery as the reformation and bourgeois revolutions created the space for scientific inquiry beyond the control of Rome. Protestantism, with its rejection of the miracles and magic of Catholicism, took the first step towards the seventeenth-century **materialism** of Sir Francis Bacon (1561–1626) and Thomas Hobbes (1588–1679). This materialism reflected the desire to explain matter without recourse to religion or mysticism and therefore went hand in hand with the great discoveries of the age in Newtonian physics, anatomy and chemistry. Yet this materialism was a limited, static, intellectual system: science and materialism were not concerned with the *historical process* of the universe, the unitary and the evolving character of matter. With Darwin's discovery of evolution, Engels declared 'Nature is the proof of the dialectic.' He and Marx lived in an age when science and philosophy recognised the historical or evolutionary character of life and the universe. Dialectical materialism is therefore not a method in the sense of a laboratory procedure or a statistical correlation, though it does provide insights into these and it is a scientific paradigm (it has been adopted by a small number of present-day working scientists).[10]

Perhaps the most persuasive support for Marx's argument that his view of history is scientific is the predictive quality of his laws of capitalist development as outlined in *Capital* (1867). Many natural sciences have, as a defining characteristic, a predictive quality for their laws. Chemists know the reaction that will occur if they add an acid and an alkali long before they mix the two. However, critics of Marx place too much emphasis on his supposed role as prophet. Marx himself acknowledged the limits of second-guessing the future and some of his forecasts were indeed off the mark. He was particularly prone to telescoping economic crises and underestimating the powers of the recovery of the capitalist system. However, Marx outlined many features of the capitalist world that are familiar to us today (the generalisation of wage-labour, the concentration of capital, its internationalisation, the boom-slump cycle, etc.). His insights into industrial capitalism made at a time when the fledgeling factory system affected little more than Lancashire, parts of Belgium, and small pockets of the Franco–German borders are quite remarkable.

▶ The distinctiveness of human labour

Marx and Engels reacted enthusiastically to Darwin's theory of evolution and sought to apply it to humanity. According to Engels's pamphlet, *The Part Played by Labour in the Transition of Ape to Man* (1876), conscious labour, the unique physiology of the hand and tool-making provided the impetus for the development of the human species: 'Hundreds of thousands of years ... certainly elapsed before human society arose out of a troupe of tree-climbing monkeys. Yet it did finally appear. And what do we find once more as the characteristic difference between the troupe of monkeys and human society? *Labour.*'[11] As our human ancestors descended from the trees, they underwent a series of metamorphoses: their front legs became free so that the hand became more dextrous; they stood increasingly upright; they became omnivores and, as a result of increasing protein intake, their brains expanded; their vocal cords developed, and they ultimately acquired speech. These physiological developments were necessary for the course that human history was eventually to take.

Even before Engels's adaptation of Darwinian theory, he and Marx had privileged labour and production as the distinguishing characteristic of human nature. The role of labour constituted their grounds for the refutation of idealism. Labour, for Marx and Engels, is what makes us human, because material needs, not human thought, are the mainsprings of our development, with consciousness itself a necessary condition of human production. Marx and Engels, however, rejected the crude materialism of Feuerbach (1804–72). For Marx and Engels, the mind does not passively reflect the material world, through labour, *we* change the world around *us*. During this process mind and matter interact, transforming subjective plans into objective artefacts. The comparison of human labour and the animal kingdom illustrates this distinction. Even the most elaborate works of an animal species, the spider's web or the caterpillar's cocoon, are made instinctively; they are uniform attributes of those species and of their paths of evolution. Unlike other animals, humans, whether building a shelter or weaving cloth, are able to conjure pictures in *their* minds, to design, to innovate, to anticipate nature: in short, consciously to produce. Because of labour, human society is dynamic, whereas other species adapt slowly and blindly to changing circumstances.

It is hard to explain the success, or even the survival, of the human species without an appreciation of the contribution made by labour. Gordon V. Childe, the Marxist archaeologist, pointed out that on the face of it humans have a multiplicity of evolutionary disadvantages: we are naked and cannot naturally survive in cold climates; we are not equipped with the fangs or claws of a predator; we cannot graze as we have only one stomach; and because of the size of the mature human brain, we are exceptionally vulnerable during our long infancies. The pattern of human evolution and our achievements as a species are only explicable by the distinctive quality of human production.[12] Once Marx and Engels had established the primacy of production to human nature they began to detail its historical characteristics: they initially made the distinction between the forces and **relations of production**.

The forces of production

The forces of production are an aggregate of the knowledge, tools, and (natural and human) resources of production in any given society.[13] These forces enable production to take place, and indeed to expand. They encompass various aspects of life: the development of technology or skills and the ability to harness nature for productive ends. Generally, the productive forces develop cumulatively and progressively because the satisfaction of human needs gives rise to new needs. History's most common example of expanded requirements placed on production is the growth in the number of mouths to feed.

The advances in technology, in skills, in travel, in modes of language and thought – in sum, the gathering forces of human production – are quite astonishing. One sound indicator of the amazing expansion in the productive forces over the long run of human existence is population growth.

Those living in Victorian Britain witnessed ample demonstration of the development of the forces of production; they, Marx included, marvelled at the feats of engineering that dwarfed the most spectacular achievements of antiquity and the Middle Ages. Steam power signalled the age of the railway, the steamship and the factory, which within a century had conquered the entire globe.

Human history has been characterised by an unending struggle with the natural environment. Floods, tempests, droughts, man-eating predators and poisonous vegetation reveal our frailty, but we have also transformed these potentially destructive forces of nature into forces of human production. Each new manipulation of nature has advanced the forces of production: the ability of human beings to satisfy their material needs. Consider fire: capable of destroying the sources of food, shelter and human life itself, the fire gods in ancient religions were suitably threatening, dangerous and capricious. But by trial and error, imitation, and eventually conscious design, fire has been transformed from a threat to survival to something which enhances our lives: fire renders indigestible meats edible, it facilitated some of the earliest forms of agriculture through the slash-and-burn techniques, it allows humans to inhabit cold and dark climates, and it ultimately enabled the early technological advances of industrial capitalism through the burning of fossil fuels. The progressive harnessing of nature massively expanded the productive forces at our disposal. Over time human societies were less at the mercy of nature and more its master: damming or diverting rivers, irrigating barren lands, constructing sailboats, waterwheels and windmills, and erecting buildings from mud, rock, slate or brick.

These changes affect human social behaviour. The growth of the productive forces might bring about a fall in the death rate, an increase in leisure time or a greater division of labour, thus altering the character of society. As the forces of production mount up, human societies are transformed or as Marx put it, the relations of production are altered: a village may become a city and dense forest may become agricultural land. This all results in an evolution in the social relations between people.

▶ The social relations of production

In the process of production, humans interact with each other and with nature. Marx termed these interactions the relations of production. The relations of production vary from one society and stage of historical development to another. As specific social relations of production, gold and silver become money, tidal currents become trade routes, black men and women are enslaved and land becomes tribal hunting territory or privately owned wheat fields.

The interactions between humans are social relations of production. But unlike the beehive with its complex yet static division of labour, human society has the capacity to evolve rapidly. These relations may develop into **class** relations, though most of human history consisted of small egalitarian hunter-gatherer bands with rudimentary technology, few possessions, and often a nomadic existence. In the last 10 000 years, various **class** societies (based on larger social groups, social inequality, enhanced technology and economic advances) have emerged. Over time, the division of labour increasingly separated mental and material production, allowing the creation of **surplus** produce, private property, and groups that can live off the labours of others, through religious consent and physical coercion.

In each class society, the social relations of production entail exploitation whereby the ruling class have special functions, authority and privileges and live off the fruits of the labours of the majority.

This pattern of class relations varies across history. It may be the ancient Roman master and slave, the feudal lord and the serf, the guild master and the journeyman in the workshops of medieval Europe, or the capitalist and the wage-labourer. These relationships of exploitation give rise to class conflict and provide one of the principal driving forces of human history, an 'uninterrupted now hidden, now open, fight', as Marx famously put it in the *Communist Manifesto*.[14]

Taken as a whole, a society is constituted by its social relations of production. Human societies are shaped by their relationship to natural resources (plants and animals, climate and terrain); this relationship implies specific, though evolving, social relations that may over time enter into crisis. Where once settled agriculture first flourished in the Fertile Crescent of the Middle East, now arid desert is found. The combination of the exhaustion of natural resources, deforestation, soil erosion and climatic change has denuded human history's Garden of Eden. These clashes between the forces and relations of production hold the clue to the collapse of great civilisations and the seemingly inexplicable timing of revolutionary crises.

In this respect, there are some interesting parallels with the pioneering demographer, the Reverend Thomas Robert Malthus (1766–1834), who wrote an enormously influential treatise, *An Essay on the Principle of Population* (1798).[15] He maintained that populations tended to grow more rapidly than food production, and that population, would precipitate a crisis point of catastrophic famines and epidemics (the 'positive check' on population). Both Marx and Malthus explained the evident cycle of development and crisis in materialist terms. They differed in that Malthus treated population and agriculture as two isolated ahistorical variables, whilst Marx understood the transition to new **modes of production** and their revolutionary changes in productivity. Malthus, unlike Marx, did not account for the improvements in technology and agricultural efficiency which enable modern societies increasingly to avoid the famines that he foresaw.

▶ The clash between the forces and the relations of production

The combination of the forces and relations of production holds the key to Marx's explanation of great epochal transformations of civilisations: either catastrophic decline or progressive surges forward. As the forces of production develop, changes occur in the relations of production, both in the division of labour and in human environments. Just as the use of iron tips on spears could make killing big game easier and safer and therefore alter hunting patterns, or irrigation could increase the numbers of mouths fed by a given piece of land, so today medical advances and contraception have transformed sexual mores. New social relations of production can enable the acceleration of the productive forces. During certain periods, however, the existing social relations of production can act as a barrier to the advance of the productive forces:

> At a certain stage of development, the material productive forces of society come into conflict with the existing relations of production or – this merely expresses the same thing in legal terms – with the property relations within the framework of which they have operated hitherto. From these forms of development of the productive forces these relations turn into their fetters. Then begins an era of social revolution.[16]

This may be in the form of environmental constraints, or societal constraints or a combination of these factors. When the productive forces and the social relations of production clash, the existing structure of society stifles progress, hampering humanity's ability to provide for its material needs. In these periods social systems enter into a crisis which may lead to 'the revolutionary recomposition of society or the mutual ruination of the contending classes'.[17] The ruins of once great civilisations attest to this recurring historical problem. With the fall of Ancient Rome, such a clash between the forces and relations of production resulted not in a more advanced phase of human history but a stagnation, fragmentation and retrogression: 'The last centuries of the declining Roman Empire and its conquest by the barbarians destroyed a number of productive forces; agriculture had declined, industry had decayed for want of a market, trade had died out or been violently suspended, the rural and urban population had decreased.'[18]

We can observe that this pattern has been repeated many times: in ancient Egypt, Islam and China, and in the civilisations of the Amerindians and Africans. Ruined monuments in the wilderness attest to this process the world over: on Easter Island, in the Andes or at the site of the Great Zimbabwe. After a phase from 1000 to around 1350, when European feudalism brought some technical innovations and slowly increasing output, it entered a succession of crises until ultimately industrial capitalism rose in its place. From the early sixteenth to the late eighteenth centuries, three great conflagrations – the Reformation, the English Civil War and the French Revolution – allowed the forces of production to break loose from the shackles of the feudal relations of production. The interaction between these two features explained for Marx the great transformations of the past, the rise and fall of civilisations, the new stages of development, progress, regression and the conflicts at the heart of human history.

According to Marx, the development of the forces of production corresponded to a particular stage of economic development, which he called the mode of production. The determining characteristic of human epochs was the character of production and exploitation: slavery in the Ancient world, serfdom in feudal society, wage-labour under capitalism. In Marx's writings the five major historical modes of production are:

- Primitive communism
- The ancient mode of production
- The **Asiatic mode of production**
- Feudalism
- **Capitalism**

Socialism and communism were conceived of as future modes of production that would liberate humanity from exploitation and oppression, using the general increase in the productive forces for the general good.

▶ Base and superstructure

Marx's rejection of idealism and his view of labour and production demonstrated that his conception of history was materialist. Ideas, politics and the state were not written out of history but judged to be a superstructure that rested on material foundations. This superstructure does not develop independently but is constrained in any given epoch by what is economically desirable or at least possible. Marx outlined this in the preface to *A Contribution to the Critique of Political Economy* (1859):

> In the social production of their existence, men inevitably enter into definite relations, which are independent of their will, namely relations of production appropriate to a given stage in the development of their material forces of production. The totality of these relations of production constitutes the economic structure of society, the real foundation, on which arises a legal and political superstructure and to which correspond definite forms of social consciousness. The mode of production of material life conditions the general process of social, political and intellectual life. It is not the consciousness of men that determines their existence, but their social existence that determines their consciousness.[19]

The character of the ideal, legal and political superstructure corresponds to the stage of economic development. For example, ideas that seem abhorrent to modern minds (such as infanticide and cannibalism) were viewed as quite normal in societies that relied for their survival on such practices.[20] Racism is another set of ideas that developed for material reasons. It became widespread in the eighteenth century as a result of the contradiction between the general proclamations of the universal rights of man in Europe and America on the one hand, and on the other, the great profits and cheap commodities of European commerce drawn from the slave trade and empire which was based on the denial of these rights to black Africans.[21]

The base and superstructure relationship explains the Marxist understanding of the state. In the first instance, states evolved because of the existence of classes with irreconcilable material interests. Engels linked the rise of the state with the emergence of the first class societies in *The Origin of the Family, Private Property and the State* (1884). The public authority (religion and weapons) of chiefs and their officials and 'bodies of armed men', seemingly standing above society, regulated those divided interests:

> Because the state arose from the need to hold class antagonisms in check, but because it arose, at the same time, in the midst of the conflict of these classes, it is, as a rule, the state of the most powerful, economically dominant class, which through the medium of the state, becomes also the politically dominant class, and thus acquires new means of holding down and exploiting the oppressed class.[22]

Without the superstructure of the state and 'the ruling ideas' in society, the exploiting minority could not maintain their rule. As Marx and Engels wrote:

> The ideas of the ruling class are in every epoch the ideas of the ruling class, i.e. the class which is the ruling *material* force of society is at the same time its ruling *intellectual* force. The class which has the means of material production at its disposal, has control at the same time over the means of mental production, so that thereby, generally speaking, the ideas of those who lack the means of production are subject to it.[23]

States are fashioned in the image of the economic base. The European absolutist monarchies of early modern Europe, for example, corresponded to a phase in the transition from feudalism to capitalism in which the state balanced between the feudal aristocracies and the rising bourgeoisie in order to respond to sharpening international military and economic rivalry.[24]

Marx and Engels also explained the relationship between ideas and society through the base and superstructure metaphor. The history of religion illustrates how Marx conceived the relation between the material base and ideas.[25] Initially religion reflected not the existence of deity but human ignorance and inability to explain nature, death and moral codes. According to this mystical explanation of the unknown, the grain ripened because of the providence of God and our dead ancestors had passed to a spiritual realm. Marx pointed out that religious ideas adapted themselves to changing material and social circumstances, otherwise the bewildering inconsistencies and reversals in religious thought would be inexplicable.

In *On The History of Early Christianity* (1894), Engels sketched the changing character and historical context of Christianity. In its early years this new religion fused together various traditions: stoic, Judaism, pagan. Originally it was a religion of the rebellious Jews of Roman-controlled Palestine and then of the passive urban **plebs** of Rome. Christianity faced periods of peace with the authorities and periods of persecution, until it ultimately became the official religion of the Roman ruling class. With each change in its social context, Christian religion transformed itself. It was able to prophesy the apocalyptic destruction of the Roman state at one time, or social harmony and 'render unto Caesar' at another. In the Middle Ages, the Church was yet again transformed as it firmly entrenched itself as part of the hierarchy of feudal society, its main ideological support and the largest landowner in Europe. The growth of the towns and the challenge that they constituted to feudalism spawned the fragmentation of Christianity with the emergence of the successive heresies. Protestantism, based on individualism, hard work and the rejection of existing religious authority, became, according to Engels, 'the religious disguise' for the interests of the bourgeoisie. Calvinism inspired bourgeois revolution in Holland and the English Civil War donned the 'ideological costume' of Puritanism.[26] The religious banner had led thousands into the battles of the bourgeois revolutions, without which the transition to capitalism could not have taken place.

The example of Christianity also demonstrates that Marxism does not conceive of the economic base as the only active ingredient in history unaffected by change in the superstructure. In the case of the bourgeois revolutions, ideas (Protestantism, liberalism and nationalism) through practical activity reshaped the productive base of society. Criticising the inactivity of left-wing followers of Hegel, Marx spelt out the relationship between ideas and reality: 'The weapon of criticism cannot, of course, supplant the criticism of weapons, material force must be overthrown by material force. But theory, too, will become a material force as soon as it seizes the masses.'[27] The base and superstructure relationship is not a one-way process and it is only at the most general level or 'in the last hour' that the base becomes determining.

Critics of Marx have accused him of being reductionist (the idea of matter being determined exclusively by one of its constituent parts, in this case the economic). For classical Marxism, **reductionism** is alien to this particular approach because the dialectic is based on the concept of the unity of opposites (i.e., the dynamic interaction of the economic and the non-economic) and the concept that the whole (society) is greater than the sum of the parts (one being the economic). The static or 'unilinear' materialism sometimes attributed to Marx and Engels was precisely what the two young revolutionaries explicitly rejected and superseded in the work of the English seventeenth-century materialism (Hobbes, Bacon and Newton), the French eighteenth-century materialism – Diderot (1717–84),

Helvetius (1715–71) and d'Holbach (1723–89) – and the German nineteenth-century materialist (Feuerbach).

▶ The role of the individual in history

In early modern Europe, powerful social, cultural and historical forces increasingly suggested that the role of the individual in history was paramount. The French and American revolutions proclaimed the inalienable rights of the individual just as Protestantism before them had expounded each individual's personal relationship to God. Eighteenth- and nineteenth-century Scottish and English political economists mirrored this individualism in their view of economic life. Focusing on personal development and relationships of individuals, the modern novel became the dominant literary genre from the late eighteenth century. Historiography evolved from propaganda and myth for royal houses to the history of great men, with biography and the history of events becoming the main genres of bourgeois history. Historians marvelled at the work of exceptional individuals: at the great inventions and scientific discoveries, at feats of exploration, at the great battles and campaigns, at the statesmanship of politicians and rulers. Samuel Smiles, who embodied the spirit of the Victorian middle-class world, based his popular moral philosophy of self-improvement on these examples of personal achievement.

Marx's views stood in sharp contrast: 'how absurd is the conception of history held hitherto, which neglects the real relationships and confines itself to high-sounding dramas of princes and states'.[28] The 'great men' view of history was a part of a pervasive individualism. Marx observed that this 'great illusion of the age' sprang from 'the anticipation of bourgeois society which began to evolve from the 16th century . . . The individual in this society of free competition seems to be rid of natural ties.'[29] As all aspects of life were transformed into commodities, people provided for themselves not through their traditional intercourse with nature and with customary, often personal, patterns of obligation and consumption but as individuals through the impersonal market. Marx ridiculed members of his generation who believed themselves to be self-made, self-sufficient, independent 'Robinson Crusoes' (a criticism of the Enlightenment's cult of the individual, as characterised by the eponymous hero of Daniel Defoe's novel of 1719, *Robinson Crusoe*). In his *Theses on Feuerbach* (1845) Marx argued that human nature is not inherent in each single individual but is social, and therefore individual consciousness is the 'ensemble of social relations'.[30] Marx posited that history is incomprehensible if based on the abstraction that it is comprised of isolated individuals. Every human being, great or small, not only shapes history but is shaped by it; as Marx put it in *The German Ideology*, 'Circumstances make men just as much as men make circumstances.'[31]

This did not mean that Marx and Engels regarded the actions of individuals as irrelevant. They stressed the role of human activity in history whether in invocations of working-class self-emancipation or in various statements such as:

> History does *nothing*, it 'possesses *no* immense wealth', it 'wages *no* battles'. It is *man*, real, living man who does all that, who possesses and fights; 'history' is not, as it were, a person apart, using man as a means to achieve *its own* aims; history is *nothing but* the activity of man pursuing his own aims.[32]

Marx recognised that the aggregate of individual actions constitutes history but he did not believe that individuals are an all-powerful historical force. Historical circumstances raised individuals such as Napoleon I (1769–1821) or Bismarck (1815–98) to greatness but also humbled and humiliated them in turn. Napoleon swept the whole of Europe before him but ended his life broken and defeated on the island of St Helena. The events that govern the changing fortunes of even great men result from a host of other human acts. Studying the motivations and intentions of individuals can only provide limited insights into history because of the unintended consequences and numerous accidents that occur when a host of other individuals' actions combine.[33]

Such is the apparent importance of accidents that some historians – for example, A.J.P. Taylor (1906–90) – have ascribed historical primacy to accident or contingency. Marx, however, saw order not chaos in historical events, because accident and the interaction of individuals were constrained and structured. Although sometimes motivated by caprice, humans more normally act on ideals, particular goals or ambitions. Marx was interested in discovering the historical forces that shaped the intentions of the masses and their leaders. The social position of individuals affords certain opportunities and capacities to act. Their material interests shape their ideas, whether they are conscious of it or not. The different material class interests produce class struggle but this is not necessarily an obvious or automatic process because they go through a series of intervening stages: interests have to be transposed into contemporary ideas, and ideas are formulated into motives and conscious goals propelling individuals to act in the real world. In the aggregate, individuals follow ideas that articulate their class interests and act in a fashion similar to others in their class.

▶ Class and history

Class struggle is central to the Marxist view of history. When asked his favourite figure in history, Marx named the leader of the greatest slave rebellion of Roman antiquity, Spartacus. Although inequality – the existence of haves and have-nots –

is common sense to anybody living in the modern world, class is not as straightforward as it may at first appear. Huw Beynon, the Marxist sociologist, suggested that class is 'the most useful and problematic concept' for historians.[34] According to Marx, an individual's class position shapes his or her seemingly random ideas and actions because classes constantly enter into conflicts with other classes and engage in internal disagreements.

For Marx, class is a feature of the social relations of production and exploitation. Because exploitation in its most basic form in any given society is a two-way relationship between exploiter and exploited, Marx believed in the existence of the major distinct classes with particular material interests, and he maintained that this led to class conflict. Imagine the life of the peasant on a Polish estate in the eighteenth century: exploitation took the form of compulsory and unwaged labour on the lord's land. For possibly three days a week peasants were obliged to leave their own plot of land and work on their master's. When performing the *robot* (the labour service to the lord), serfs worked at a much lower pace than they did in their own time; they would 'drag their feet' and perhaps feign injury or illness. The lord obviously had an interest in making his serfs work harder and used agents, threats, incentives, custom and religion to achieve this.[35] Although the forms of exploitation differ, these kinds of relentless unspoken conflict are woven into the fabric of all class societies. The very process of exploitation – extraction of surplus labour by the ruling class from the labouring majority whether through taxation, profits, obligatory labour, rents, tribute or payment in kind – demonstrates an inherent clash of interests. As, according to Marx, class is not in the first instance subjective but entrenched in the material process of exploitation, class is not about particular lifestyles, perceptions, consumption or attitudes, although these may indeed be symptomatic of a particular class. This contrasts with mainstream sociology's preference for the idea of social stratification: that societies are composed of a multiplicity of layers from the most to the least powerful. Marx's rejection of this latter view of class based on culture or status has engendered much subsequent debate amongst social historians.

Resistance to exploitation has taken many forms, whether as a feature of everyday life or erupting in great revolutions.[36] The first recorded strike in history took place 3000 years ago amongst skilled craftsmen who were building a pyramid for Rameses III. Strikes and industrial action over pay in modern industry are an example of conflict over the rate of exploitation, but the eighteenth-century food riot in Western Europe in which rioters seized bread and sold it at what they saw as a fair price is essentially part of the same process. Although historians have questioned the extent to which earlier forms are, in fact, class activities, history is littered with tax riots, mutinies, slave rebellions and revolutions. Clearly in some of these cases, class struggle moves beyond bartering over the individual rate of exploitation to wider political and ideological questions. For instance, food riots in India during British imperial control relate in complex and reciprocal ways to nationalist awareness and struggles among the peasantry and urban poor.

Whilst class is therefore primarily objective, the degree to which a class becomes aware of its own interests and consciously struggles to achieve them is obviously subjective. With this in mind, Marx made the distinction between a class-in-itself – a class in the objective sense – and a class-for-itself that had achieved an appreciation of its own material interests. The existence of a superstructure of ruling-class ideology and its state allows the process of exploitation to be conducted under the guise of the common good. The class conflict and the experience of exploitation undermine the prevalence of ruling-class ideas and the popular legitimacy of the state.

During revolutions, this awareness is raised to new heights, and a revolutionary class becomes increasingly conscious of its own potential and presents its interests as the interests of the whole of society. Revolutionary crises draw the class struggle into open ground for all to see, and success or failure of the revolutionary class either drives society forward or, as Marx saw it, into the mire of historical stagnation or regression. Thus Marx viewed the English revolution of the seventeenth century as a successful bourgeois revolution that allowed the unfettered development of commercial, agrarian and eventually industrial capitalism in England. The revolution was, according to Marx's analysis, able to sweep away the social relations that had frustrated these productive forces: the stifling hand of the Stuart state on commercial activities, its archaic foreign policy, the slow transition to capitalist property relations on the land, and tax structures and privileges that favoured the aristocracy.

As well as philosophising about socialism, Marx and Engels were actively engaged in efforts to create workers' organisations (principally the Communist League and the International Workingmen's Association) with the goal of socialist revolution. This upheaval would take place as the capitalist system aged and itself blocked the progressive development of the productive forces. Their vision of socialism was not based on a design of the perfected human beehive as with earlier utopian socialists, but through the exercise of the revolutionary power by the working class (what they dubbed the dictatorship of the proletariat) which Marx had caught a brief glimpse of during the Paris Commune of 1871. Given these experiences Marx and Engels spelt out that socialism would be democratic, 'a movement of the immense majority', and would replace the competitive chaos of capitalism with planned rational production for human need rather than profit. Ultimately, a classless society, communism, would develop in which the principle of 'from each according to their abilities, to each according to their needs' would operate, and humans would pass from the realm of necessity to the realm of freedom.

▶ Conclusion

The reason for the controversy and importance of Marx and Engels's view of history is that they claimed that Marxism could scientifically explain the dynamics of all human history and that this understanding made real human emancipation possible.

It is an understatement to say that the task that Marx set himself was bold and ambitious. This intellectual audacity gave a scope to Marx's horizons that other thinkers did not attempt and it is as a result of this that he remains intellectually difficult to ignore even by the bitterest of opponents. Even acknowledged adversaries such as Weber or Braudel owed a great deal to Marx's thought and many have borrowed his categories and insights. At the same time others, haunted by the revolutionary conclusions of his work, have dismissed or caricatured his thought.

Dialectical materialism may be summarised as follows:

1 Labour is the secret of human distinctiveness and production implies a certain level of productive forces and certain social relations.
2 These forces and relations of production allow us to discern different epochs in human history and to understand the progressive unfolding of these epochs. The clash between the relations and forces of production provokes revolutionary crises.
3 The material base of society gives rise to, and is of greater overall significance than the superstructure of law, politics, ideas and the state, though there is an interaction between the two.
4 Class struggle, itself a product of the exploitative social relations of production, is endemic to human history and plays a determining role in historical outcomes, in particular in the case of revolutionary crises.

This conception informs the historical writing of the two founders of Marxism, and this in turn allows us to sharpen our understanding of how their intellectual framework applied practically to the writing of history. How the pair translated their philosophy of history into actual histories tests the proposition that Marxism provides a singular and coherent view of history which is neither determinist nor reductionist. It also raises the standard by which other Marxist historians can be measured, and allows the comparison between Marxist and non-Marxist history.

3 The Historical Writings of Marx and Engels

'He studied slavery, he studied the middle ages, he studied commercial capitalism, and eventually he studied the capitalism of his own day. With all that in the past he was able to look forward to what was to going to take place during the next generation. The most marvellous piece of writing that I know is the chapter before the last in Capital volume I – "The Historical Tendency of Capitalist Accumulation." It's a masterpiece of summing up and pointing out the implications for the future. I tried to do the same.'

C.L.R. James, in an interview[1]

Although neither was a historian in a conventional sense, Marx and Engels's historical writings constitute a substantial opus.[2] Moreover, their work as a whole is suffused with historical analysis. For instance, discussions of the **transition** from feudalism to **capitalism** reappeared time and again in their popular works (*German Ideology, Communist Manifesto, Socialism: Scientific and Utopian*). For them the transition was both an index of historical development of their day and a pointer to subsequent world-historical transitions. Even *Capital,* which is usually conceived of as a work of dense political economy, periodically turns to historical circumstances to bring its analysis of capitalism to life.

Marx was consumed by an interest in history. He praised some historians and was caustic about others. His collected works are littered with references to contemporary and classical historians. Marx's dialogue with historians is fascinating. He pronounced on Gibbon, Livy, Ranke, Guizot and Thiers. He admired the French restoration historians of the French Revolution who identified it as a class conflict. In contrast, he scorned Leopold von Ranke (1795–1886), the **empiricist** and father of professional bourgeois history, as 'a mere root-grubbing historian' who attributed great events to 'mean and petty causes'. Though these are often scattered remarks, a picture emerges of Marx's attitude to what history is, and how it should be written. From studying Marx's view of history, we can cast further light on his social theory itself, to visualise more than the simple outlines suggested by his theoretical elaboration. From these writings a number of conclusions are clear. History was centrally important for the development of Marx's thought. This was not a formal or abstract acknowledgement (as with Hegel, for example), but a commitment to discover the real workings of history through serious scholarly research. For Marx and Engels, philosophy or economics were not able alone to provide a deeper understanding of the human condition: they both required historical contexts. This chapter will examine four cases of historical writings by the originators of the Marxist tradition: *The Eighteenth Brumaire of Louis Bonaparte, Peasant War in Germany, Capital,* and Engels's late letters which address historical materialism.

▶ Marx's *The Eighteenth Brumaire of Louis Bonaparte*

Of Marx's works, *The Eighteenth Brumaire of Louis Bonaparte* came closer than any other to conventional historical writing. It dealt with the relatively short episode in French history between the February revolution of 1848 and Louis Bonaparte's *coup d'état* of 2 December 1851 (the event Marx called the Eighteenth Brumaire after the date in the revolutionary calendar when Bonaparte's more illustrious uncle had seized power in 1799). Despite the narrow time span, *The Eighteenth Brumaire* elaborated these events within the long-run context of French history. These events signalled another phase in the development of the bourgeois revolution that began with the storming of the Bastille in 1789. Unlike much of Marx's work, in which history was used to illustrate and give flesh to his historical materialism or the rise of capitalism, here the reverse is true: **historical materialism** was employed to explain a series of specific events. As such it has ranked alongside Engels's *The Peasant War in Germany* or Trotsky's *History of the Russian Revolution* as a model for subsequent generations of Marxist historians.

The Eighteenth Brumaire divides into three sections: the introductory chapter, summarising the subject and establishing Marx's general approach to it; the following five chapters, skilfully interweaving a narrative of events with insightful class analysis; and the final chapter, which discusses the social character of the Bonapartist regime. For someone so often accused of determinism and usually dealing with historical generalisations, this study of individuals and events provided a crucial test of Marx's view of history itself. His introduction offered arguably unique insights into the role of the individual in history, the question of symbolism and language. These questions remain so close to the heart of current historiographical debate that it is difficult for historians to ignore these passages.

Marx's opening remarks immediately awakened the reader to the parallels between the protagonists of 1848–51 and those of 1789–99: the revolutionary leaders, the treacherous and facilitating centre and the budding dictator were repeated. Employing a witticism to make a serious point, the cast's costume changed from tragedy in the first instance to farce the second time around. Marx observed that this very repetition of roles raised a question mark over free will in history.

But it was not fate that handed out these roles. Individuals did exercise choice, but they were also constrained by historical circumstance. This formulation has been a central expression of the non-deterministic character of Marxism: 'Men make their own history, but they do not make it just as they please; they do not make it under circumstances chosen by themselves, but under circumstances directly encountered, given and transmitted from the past.'[3]

It is instructive that H.C.G. Matthew, who was no Marxist, should quote this in his biography of Gladstone because it articulated so perfectly the tension in biography between individuals and their historical context. Matthew wrote:

> Of few can Marx's truism be truer than of William Ewart Gladstone. His epic public career – first in office in 1834, last in 1894 – confronted the prime of Britain as the first industrial nation. The agenda of free trade and imperialism was dictated by forces far beyond the control of individuals acting as such. Yet the interpretation and execution of the agenda was achieved by the decisions and actions of individuals and explained through their speeches and writings. In this interpretation, execution, and explanation, Gladstone's career holds a central place. In the process through which the British governing class came to terms with its new commercial and industrial destiny, Gladstone was its vital agent.[4]

After confronting the role of the individual in history, Marx broached the paradox that the revolutionaries of 1848 appeared to be trapped in the language and symbolism of the past:

> The tradition of all dead generations weighs like a nightmare on the brain of the living. And just when they seem engaged in revolutionising themselves and things, in creating something that has never yet existed, precisely in such periods of revolutionary crisis they anxiously conjure up the spirits of the past to their service and borrow from them names, battle-cries and costumes in order to present the new scene of world history in this time-honoured disguise and this borrowed language. Thus Luther donned the mask of the Apostle Paul ... and the revolution of 1848 knew nothing better to do than to parody, now 1789, now the revolutionary tradition of 1793 to 1795. In like manner a beginner who has learnt a new language always translates it back into his mother tongue, but he has assimilated the spirit of the new language and can freely express himself in it only when he finds his way in it without recalling the old and forgets his native tongue in the use of the new.[5]

Here again this hits the nerve of current historical debate. Historians, such as William Sewell and Gareth Stedman Jones, have argued that language held the revolutionaries of the 1840s back in France and Britain respectively. Their work was a cornerstone of the **linguistic turn** away from Marxist-influenced social history, which has created a new concern with language, symbols, icons and rituals. It is ironic that in his study of the revolution of 1848, Marx anticipated this focus 150 years ago. Not only did the revolutionaries of the 1848 take up the symbols of the past but so too did those of 1789, who 'performed the task of their time in the Roman costume and with Roman phrases, the task of unchaining and setting up modern bourgeois society'.[6] This paradoxical allusion to classical antiquity found its origin in the contradiction between the heroic efforts needed to achieve bourgeois society and the inherently unheroic character of that society: 'Bourgeois society in its sober reality had begotten its true interpreters and mouthpieces in the Says, Counsins, Royer-Collards, Benjamin Constants and Guizots; ... Wholly absorbed in the production of wealth and in peaceful competitive struggle, it no longer comprehended that ghosts from the days of Rome watched over its cradle.'[7]

Looking forward to workers' revolution, Marx argued that it would have to go beyond the limits imposed by these images of the past. In 1848 the words of the bourgeois revolutionaries echoed more thunderously than their deeds because they needed the rhetoric of former times to conceal the real content of their movement. In contrast, workers would need to combine practical activity with explanations of the real content of their revolution in order to win.

The very opening lines of Marx's *Eighteenth Brumaire* underlined the constraints that the language and symbolism of the past placed on the revolutionaries of 1848:

> The social revolution of the nineteenth century cannot draw its poetry from the past, but only from the future. It cannot begin with itself before it has stripped off all superstition about the past. Earlier revolutions required recollections of past world history in order to dull themselves to their own content. In order to arrive at its own content, the revolution of the nineteenth century must let the dead bury their dead. There the words went beyond the content; here the content goes beyond the words.[8]

Marx sought to achieve two further goals: an analysis of the events and to reflect upon the social character of Louis Bonaparte's Second Empire. The revolution of February 1848, which promised a 'social republic', appeared to offer a new world for the working class. But in June 1848, when the Parisian working class rose in defence of the right to work, that phrase 'was drowned in the blood of the Paris proletariat'. But that treachery 'haunts the subsequent acts of the drama like a ghost', being followed by successive betrayals and a repeated narrowing of the base of the regime.[9] Marx identified the ironic reversal by which bourgeois scaremongering conjured the fear of anarchy only to have these very same reactionary practices and phrases turned against them by Bonaparte. Where the bourgeoisie had banned juries and meetings, transported opponents, disbanded sections of the National Guard and curbed the press, Bonaparte used these methods against them. Where they had called for 'Property, family, religion, order' to oust the left, Bonaparte did so to them:

> It [the bourgeoisie] repressed every stirring in society by means of state power; every stirring in its [bourgeois] society is suppressed by [Bonaparte's] the state power. Out of enthusiasm for its purse, it rebelled against its own politicians and men of letters; its politicians and men of letters are swept aside, but its purse is being plundered now that its mouth has been gagged and its pen broken.[10]

Due to the bourgeoisie's fear of the workers, they unwittingly allowed Bonaparte's **lumpenproletarian** movement to seize power. Marx then asked the question that must have been on the lips of the European left: how was it that the Parisian working class allowed the coup to succeed? In part, they had been betrayed by the middle-class allies, by the 'grocer and the bourgeois'; in part, repression had taken its toll; and finally the leading cadres of the working class, its barricade commanders, had been decimated by Bonaparte's wave of arrests and demoralised by previous defeats.

Having discussed Bonaparte's coup of 2 December 1851, Marx then tried to analyse the unique and novel characteristics of his regime. This elaboration of Bonapartism has been richly suggestive for Marxists trying to grapple with exceptional state structures, and in particular in the interpretation of fascist regimes.[11] The first feature of the regime was that it seemed to be independent of a class base. The bourgeoisie and the proletariat had succumbed to military repression and, exhausted, appeared incapable of exercising state power. 'The struggle seems to be settled in such a way that all classes equally impotent and equally mute, fall on their knees before the rifle butt.'[12] The legislative function of the state withered in the face of an all-powerful executive personified by Bonaparte himself. His executive authority was upheld by the soldiers, the bureaucratic machine of the state and the priests. The coup's 'immediate and palpable result was the victory of Bonaparte over parliament, of the executive power over the legislative power, of force without words over the force of words'.[13] The state seemed independent and without a social base. In reality, Bonaparte was able to mould a social foundation for the state from his movement – centred on the lumpenproletariat – and the conservative small-holding peasantry. He turned these social forces to his own reactionary ends. Marx reserved particular bile for the lumenproletariat, which has led to the mistaken criticism from some quarters that the disdainful Marx had no sympathy for the poor.[14] Describing the small-holding peasants, Marx gave one of his most famous sociological descriptions. They acted not as a cohesive class, but more akin to potatoes emptied out of a sack:

> Insofar as millions of families live under economic conditions of existence that separate their mode of life, their interests and their culture from those of other

classes, and put them in hostile opposition to the latter, they form a class. Insofar as there is merely a local interconnection among these small-holding peasants, and the identity of their interests begets no community, no national bond and no political organisation among them, they do not form a class.[15]

For Marx, both the small-holders and Bonaparte provided each other with their deepest psychological need: the former with a national saviour, the latter with the chance to emulate his glorious uncle. Bonaparte appealed not to the class awareness of the peasantry – their revolutionary side – but to their stupefied seclusion. He played on the baser part of their character: their superstition, their prejudice, their harking back to the past. Small-holding property ownership, which had opened up new possibilities and enriched the peasants after the first revolution, now resulted in the redivision of land and heavy mortgage debts. Because the peasants were unable to represent themselves they needed a representative, which came in the shape of Bonaparte. This passive, historically doomed, social base gave the Second Empire the illusion of independence. As a consequence of the regime's weak foundations, Bonaparte attempted to be all things to all classes:

> This contradictory task of the man explains the contradictions of the government, the confused, blind to-ings and fro-ings which seeks now to win, now to humiliate one class and then another and arrays all of them uniformly against him, whose practical uncertainty forms a highly comical contrast to the imperious, categorical style of the government decrees, a style which faithfully copied his uncle.[16]

Whilst the bourgeoisie had ceded political power to an adventurer, it had done so to preserve its rule over the economy: 'After the coup d'etat, the French bourgeoisie cried: Only the chief of the Society of December 10 can save bourgeois society! Only theft, can still save property; only perjury, religion; only bastardy, the family; disorder, order!'[17] Marx's fullest history therefore brought together in an impressive manner the heterodox elements of the process of revolution: silhouette biography, long-term national development, a discussion of language and symbolism, the narrative of events and a sophisticated class analysis of the Second Empire.

▶ Engels's *Peasant War in Germany*

The defeat of the German revolution of 1848–9 prompted Engels to pen *The Peasant War in Germany* for the *Neue Rheinische Zeitung*. Outside Russia and the Iberian peninsula, a revolutionary tide had swept across the entire continent in early 1848. Within six months however, the retreat had begun and, one after another, the revolutionary institutions (such as the Frankfurt assembly) collapsed. The Great

Peasant War of 1525 provided pertinent insights into the situation faced by the defeated revolutionaries of Europe. The author added a further preface at the time of German unification, underlining the importance of these events to the under-standing of the long-term fate of capitalist development in Germany. Equally, the brilliant and inspiring flashpoint of 1525 was contrasted with the demoralisation among revolutionaries in 1850: 'It is time once more, as a counter-weight to the present slackening evident almost everywhere after two years of struggle, to present to the German people the clumsy yet powerful and tenacious figures of the great Peasant War.'[18]

Then, as in the mid-nineteenth century, the German bourgeoisie had failed to act as resolutely as revolutionary events demanded. In a country with apparently such a weak revolutionary history, the radical ideas and actions of the urban poor and peasantry in 1525 constituted a rich revolutionary antecedent. Amid pessi-mistic conclusions drawn by others, Engels explained that the failure of 1849 lay with the compromising character of the German bourgeoisie and not any inherent weakness in the German working class. Engels also insinuated that the mass of the German peasantry had historic grievances that the German working class could address, thereby winning over a powerful ally (which he explicitly outlined in an appendix on the German village).

Even non-Marxist historians cite Engels's work as 'a starting point for all modern debate on the revolution'.[19] Another historian of the Peasant War, Janos Bak, described it as 'a classic example of the application of the principles of social science to a particular event but also an important piece of evidence for the development of a dialectical and historical materialism itself'.[20] Engels was aware that he and Marx rarely wrote purely historical works. He noted that *The Eighteenth Brumaire of Louis Bonaparte* and *Class Struggles in France* applied historical material-ism to produce historical studies.[21] *The Peasant War in Germany* demonstrated Engels's view that historical materialism fused together science and partisanship, an incompatible combination according to conventional wisdom. Engels's attitude to Zimmerman, a left-wing historian of the Peasant War, illustrated this feature of the Marxist approach to writing history. Marx's companion praised Zimmerman for both his empirical rigour and his revolutionary enthusiasm for his subject:

> If, nevertheless, Zimmerman's presentation lacks inner connections; if it does not succeed in showing the politico-religious controversies of the times as a reflection of contemporary class struggles; if it sees in these class struggles only oppressors and oppressed, evil folk and good folk, and the ultimate victory of the evil ones; if its exposition of the social conditions which determined both the outbreak and the outcome of the struggle is extremely defective, it was the fault of the time in which the book came into existence. On the contrary, for its time, it is written quite realistically and is a laudable exception among German idealist works on history.[22]

By Engels's own admission, it was his theoretical framework and methodology, not any new empirical research, that distinguished his *Peasant War* from Zimmerman's work. Engels sought to demonstrate the 'inner connections' between millenarian ideas and class struggles, and to describe accurately social conditions in the early sixteenth century. The Peasant War provided lessons for the embryonic workers' movement. For Engels, their education should be informed by historical material-ism, so he wrote neither a chronicle of romantic heroism nor a morality tale. The scrutiny of material life alone could provide scientific historical insights. Engels was therefore concerned with long-term socio-economic development, and with the different classes, their situations and struggles.

In similar fashion to Trotsky's chapter on Russia's 'combined and uneven' development in *The History of the Russian Revolution*, Engels's first chapter skilfully outlined Germany's long road of development. In the fourteenth and fifteenth centuries industry developed through the flourishing urban guilds that supplied wider markets. Augsburg and Nuremburg became centres of luxury production with fine cloths and gold- and silver-smiths. Commerce simultaneously increased in the shape of the Hanseatic League (a federation of northern commercial towns led by Hamburg, Lübeck and Bremen). These towns thrived until competition from the Dutch and English resulted in their loss of Baltic and North Sea markets. In contrast, the southern commercial centres of Germany traded mainly with Italy and the Levant. This industrial and commercial progress encouraged agriculture and the production of raw materials (mining and dye crops) in the environs of the towns. However, to the east and west of these growing commercial and industrial centres, small towns were by-passed and remained in a state of parochial torpor. Whilst com-merce had brought political and economic centralisation in France and England, the regional character of development increased the centrifugal forces inside Germany. When compared to the Netherlands, France and England, provincialism and stagnation scarred German history and the development of its bourgeoisie.

Bourgeois revolution was the major theoretical issue of *The Peasant War in Germany*. For Engels, the Peasant War highlighted the great paradox of German unification. Whereas in France a great social revolution – in which the monarchy was destroyed and the old ruling class driven from political power – unified and modernised the state, in Germany, bewilderingly, the reactionary forces of the Prussian monarchy and the Junkers performed these tasks. The Peasant War of 1525 illuminated the historic bargain struck between the Junkers and the big bourgeoisie in the course of Bismarck's unification of Germany (1866–71), in which the bourgeoisie timidly subordinated itself to the Kaiser and the aristocrats. The German bourgeois class remained, at the great turning points of German history, hostile to those social forces below them and reliant on those above them. This stemmed from the stunted and parochial character of their formation as a class, which stretched back to the late Middle Ages.

The European bourgeois revolutions sprang from the same general long-run crisis of feudalism and involved similar social forces (though in different stages of maturity and different configurations). Despite counter-revolutionary reverses and recoveries in the *ancien régime*, the action of the gathering forces of capitalist production meant that the effects of these revolts were cumulative and linked. A variety of civil and international wars, dissenting religious movements and revolts played their part in the bourgeois transformation of Europe and should be considered as part of the **bourgeois revolution**:

> Even the so-called religious wars of the sixteenth century involved positive material class interests; those wars were class wars, too, just as the later internal collisions in England and France. Although the class struggles of that day were clothed in religious shibboleths, and though the interests, requirements, and demands of the various classes were concealed behind a religious screen, this changed nothing and is easily explained by the conditions of the time.[23]

The entangled outcomes of these events added to the complexity of bourgeois revolution. The result of the German Peasant War was highly contradictory: the monasteries were burnt to the ground, their lands taken and the clergy humbled; the peasants were decisively defeated with many ruined and some in the east were driven into serfdom; the opposition and independence of the towns was broken. The German princes were the only clear winners, resulting in provincial royal centralisation. The **Thirty Years' War** (1618–48) also had paradoxical consequences, confirming the independence of the economically advanced Dutch Republic but holding back development in parts of central Europe as well as accelerating the restoration of serfdom east of the Elbe. The subtlety of Engels's case, it is worth noting in passing, contrasted with the schematic account of East German historians of the German Democratic Republic, for whom the Peasant War set in motion the inexorable process that culminated in the 'socialist paradise'.[24]

Engels also described the complexities of the social structure at the time of the Peasant War. He examined the social orders (nobility, clergy, townsfolk and peasantry). He probed each of these estates in turn, revealing their inner fissures. Within the nobility, the princes had become increasing powerful through wars, taxation and extortion. They impoverished the middle nobility through their military exactions. The knights and barons therefore attempted in turn to maintain their lifestyles by increased burdens on the peasantry. Von Hutten's and von Sickingen's Swabian League revolt (1524), in which sections of the nobility clashed with the princes, gave military expression to the waning fortunes of the nobility. Likewise the clergy were socially divided between the aristocratic bishops, arch-bishops and abbots who lived in luxury and the **plebeian** urban and rural preachers who stood outside the wealth of the Church. Amongst these plebeian clerics, the

Peasant War found its most radical leader, Thomas Münzer. In the towns, the richest layer formed an urban elite with aristocratic status, the rich to middling burghers formed a moderate opposition and the poorest formed a more radical opposition. In the areas affected by the Peasant War, these fractures broke apart the seeming harmony between and within the social orders. Noting that the social classes were much more complex and less cohesive than in nineteenth-century Germany, Engels nevertheless considered the Peasant War to be a **class struggle**. In contrast to Zimmerman, Engels sought not to romanticise the peasantry but to give a scientific analysis of their situation:

> Although gnashing their teeth under the terrible burden, the peasants were difficult to rouse to revolt. They were scattered over large areas, and this made every agreement between them extremely difficult; the old habit of submission inherited by generation from generation, lack of practice in the use of arms in many regions, and the varying degree of exploitation depending on the personality of the lord, all combined to keep the peasant quiet.[25]

The Peasant War also constituted a narrative history of the dynamics of that most complex of historical events, **revolution**. Engels pieced together the interrelation of social forces, traced the social content of religious heresies; he outlined the evolving relationship between ideology and the war and described the social base of the insurgents and their military achievements. With the Reformation, German society turned inwards on itself and in the course of the peasant rebellion three camps emerged: a Catholic reactionary camp headed by the wealthy strata of the Church, a moderate reformist Lutheran camp of burghers, and a plebeian revolutionary camp of urban poor and peasants. Engels fiercely criticised those historians who could only see a religious conflict:

> In spite of the latest experiences, the German ideology still sees nothing except violent theological bickering in the struggles that ended the Middle Ages. Should the people of that time, say our home-bred historians and sages, have only come to an understanding concerning divine matters, there would have been no reason whatever for quarrelling over earthly affairs. These ideologists are gullible enough to accept unquestioningly all the illusions that an epoch makes about itself, or that ideologists of some epoch make about that epoch.[26]

Having charted the history of medieval heresies, Engels demonstrated their social content. In a world intellectually dominated by the Church, it was unsurprising that peasant and plebeian demands should express themselves in religious terms. In Münzer's case, this was in the form of a millenarian communism, which rejected the authority of the Bible and instead proposed that reason was the real and living revelation. Through religion, the radical leaders of the revolt were able to provide a resolute ideology and leadership to the conflict. This was all too often lacking as the peasants were time and again beguiled and betrayed during duplicitous negotiations with their opponents.

With admirable narrative skill, Engels intertwined the various elements of the war and the revolutionary process: the interaction between the balance of military forces and fortunes, the sharpening ideologies, and the cycle of radicalising victory to despairing defeat. These changing circumstances explained Luther's metamorphosis from critic of the existing religious order to violent counter-revolutionary. Through the shifting balance of social forces, Engels made sense of the turning fate of the peasant cause as the rapid succession of victories was halted and ultimately suppressed by the renewed alliance between the nobility and the princes.

In his conclusions, Engels again returned to the long-term effects of the conflict. The war's end signalled the brutal crushing of the peasantry. Many peasants were ruined and driven into a more servile position. The clergy also lost out with the seizure of Church lands and the burning of the monasteries. The impotence of the nobility was confirmed as their castles stood in ruins, and finally burgher opposition was broken. Surveying the scarred landscape of battle, the princes emerged as the real victors, concentrating power in their regional strongholds and, in contrast to the modernising impulse of royal centralisation elsewhere in Europe, reinforcing the disunity of German lands.

▶ *Capital*, volume I

Karl Marx is famed for his monumental analysis of the nascent capitalist system, *Capital: A Critique of Political Economy*. The first volume was finally published in 1867, nearly two decades after he had embarked on the project. It has an undeserved reputation for being impenetrable, abstract and dull. Harold Wilson, three times Labour Prime Minister, boasted that he could not get past the first couple of pages of the book. On closer inspection, however, one discovers considerable sections of this work that are principally historical narratives of the rise of capitalism. Given the centrality of this effort to Marx's life and the importance of the subject, it would be an error to overlook *Capital*; it should be seen, if not as a work of history, then certainly as a work with considerable historical content. This has not gone unnoticed by Marxist historians. Several have returned to the first volume of *Capital* to understand the process of capitalist development in Britain. Maurice Dobb's groundbreaking *Studies in the Development of Capitalism* (1946) owed much to *Capital* for its rejection of the **vulgar Marxist** versions of capitalist origins. John Saville and E.P. Thompson praised its neglected historical riches. David McLellan described the historical part of volume I as 'a masterly historical account of the genesis of capitalism which illustrates better than any other writing Marx's approach and method'.[27] Indeed, William Morris (1834–96), the designer and English revolutionary socialist, admitted that he 'even tackled Marx, though I must confess that though I thoroughly enjoyed the historical part of *Capital*, I suffered agonies of confusion of the brain over reading the pure economics of that great work'.[28]

In the first volume of *Capital*, Marx described in some detail the process by which capitalist agriculture established itself in England. Here, serfdom had disappeared by the late fourteenth century. Over time, some small-holding free peasants evolved into richer peasants (or yeomen) who became tenant farmers, and others formed a special class, small at first, of rural wage-labourers. During the reigns of Henry VII and Henry VIII, the big English landowners dismissed their retainers, and their tenants drove the cottagers off the land. As the old relations of clientship, **villeinage** and service had been eroded, a large number of the poor were now without land or property and had only begging, vagabondage or labouring as a means of making a living.

In chapter 28, 'Bloody legislation against the expropriated', Marx detailed the methods that the English state used to coerce the landless into waged work. From Henry VII to Anne, the law gave the authority to imprison, whip, brand, enslave and even execute the 'sturdy vagabond':[29]

> These men, suddenly dragged from their wonted mode of life, could not suddenly adapt themselves to the discipline of their new condition. They were turned *en masse* into beggars, robbers and vagabonds, partly from inclination, in most cases from stress of circumstances. Hence the end of 15th and the whole of the 16th century, throughout Western Europe a bloody legislation against vagabondage [was written]. The fathers of the present day working class were chastised for their enforced transformation into vagabonds and paupers. Legislation treated them as 'voluntary' criminals, and assumed that it depended on their own good will to go on working under the old conditions that no longer existed.[30]

The Reformation accelerated this rural metamorphosis through the dissolution of the monasteries, during which monastic lands were seized and one of the bulwarks of rural traditionalism was destroyed. England's integration into the European economy also played its part. Large quantities of raw wool were produced for the Flemish textile industry, and this gave landowners with increasingly vast sheep flocks greater incentives to evict peasants or enclose common land. These flocks disrupted and transformed the social relations of the countryside. By the sixteenth century, the English had become producers of woollen textiles rather than simply producers of raw materials, a definite index of English economic progress. Marx observed that at the time of the English Civil War the majority of the rural population were still yeomen (independent peasants). One hundred years later, the yeoman had virtually disappeared, as had the common land of the villagers.

In the intervening years, enclosure and the clearing of estates had spread apace. The clearances drove the cottagers off the land, conducted in most dramatic and systematic form against the clans of Highland Scots after the defeat of the Jacobite cause in 1745. Marx summed up the overall process by which capitalism had conquered the British countryside:

> The spoliation of the church's property, the fraudulent alienation of the State domains, the robbery of the common lands, the usurpation of feudal and clan property, and its transformation into modern private property under circumstances of reckless terrorism, were just so many idyllic methods of primitive accumulation. They conquered the field for capitalist agriculture, made the soil part and parcel of capital, and created for the town industries the necessary supply of 'free' and outlawed proletariat.[31]

Marx's *Capital* furnished Marxist history with the greatest realisation of his approach, method and science. The pulsating heart of his method mixed the abstract (i.e., theory) and the concrete (empirical evidence and research). Evidence was not selected simply to fit the theory, like feathers stuffed into a pillowcase, as empiricists would have it. Instead the continuous dialogue of theory and evidence yielded a successively more subtle and refined analysis of capitalism. The sheer scope of evidence embodied in the work is quite staggering, being the product of years of voracious reading in the British Museum. Government Blue Books, ancient and modern historical works, and major and obscure political economists informed the analysis. His attention to detail, to earnest empirical research, to the conviction of the mutual dependence of theory and evidence, indicated Marx's understanding of how knowledge was produced; namely, the writing of *Capital* discloses his **epistemology**. In *Capital*, Marx was at pains to avoid both the speculative approach in which theory begets knowledge as well as the empiricist approach in which knowledge results from the objective accumulation of evidence. Marx tested and refined his theories and concepts by a sceptical dialogue with evidence. In this respect, he followed the **Enlightenment** conviction that scepticism, reason and science provided a universal path to knowledge and truth. Latter-day postmodernists and some feminists, amongst others, have rejected the universality of this scientific/realist epistemology, alleging that it is a partisan weapon of the powerful in a male, white, Western capitalist dominated world. Marx's *Capital*, it could plausibility be argued, demonstrated the opposite. The Enlightenment epistemology of reason could equally be wielded by and for the victims of domination. Indeed Marx viewed those in his day who mounted similar epistemological criticisms as reverting to a pre-Enlightenment mysticism or idealism.

It is one thing to note Marx's commitment to scientific principles, but it is quite another to say that he espoused in the name of objectivity a pose of scientific neutrality. Integral to his method was the combination of research and tigerish partisanship. The cruelty of members of the ruling classes was subjected to scathing denunciation. The Duchess of Sutherland's crimes were spelt out in detail, including 3000 Highland families being forced off their land at gunpoint, their villages burned and sacked, so that Glasgow could have labourers and the rich have open countryside to hunt deer and raise sheep. His unconcealed hatred for the Duchess was matched by his contempt for the British MPs 'who could not be reproached with being excessively endowed with genius', the supposed cream of the British ruling class.[32]

Neither did his science imply a rejection of art, or more precisely an appreciation of the narrative quality of history. Judging from this text, it is clear that he approached historical writing as both science and literary art. Marx's metaphoric imagination was a carnivalesque world stocked with figures from gothic fiction and classical mythology. With the lengthening of the working day, capitalism was overtaken by its 'blind unrestrainable passion, its were-wolf hunger for surplus-labour'.[33] Elsewhere, he portrayed capitalism as a rapacious Dracula figure preying on the last ounce of the worker's blood: 'Capital is dead labour, that, vampire-like, only lives by sucking living labour, and lives the more, the more labour it sucks.' And at its birth, 'capital comes dripping from head to foot, from every pore with blood and dirt'.[34] Elsewhere capital is the Juggernaut, the mystical rolling structure that crushed victims beneath its wheels. In addition to the metaphor and mordant wit touched on above, Marx consciously deployed various literary techniques – metaphor, oxymoron, leitmotif, epigram, alliteration – to underscore his most important points. Liverpool's rich, who amassed their wealth through the slave trade, lived the oxymoron of 'respectable hypocrisy'. In the following extract, he employed several of these techniques as he rounded on the system that claimed to bring civilisation to the world:

> The discovery of gold and silver in America, the extirpation, enslavement and entombment in mines of the aboriginal population, the beginning of the conquest and looting of the East Indies, the turning of Africa into a warren for the commercial hunting of black-skins, signalised the rosy dawn of the era of capitalist production. These idyllic proceedings are the chief momenta of primitive accumulation. On their heels treads the commercial war of the European nations, with the globe for a theatre. It begins with the revolt of the Netherlands from Spain, assumes giant dimensions in England's Anti-Jacobin War, and is still going on in the opium wars against China, etc.[35]

▶ Engels's *Letters on Historical Materialism*

Towards the end of his life, amid the growth of the socialist movement in Europe, Engels found the need to restate and clarify Marx's (and his) view of history. He wrote a series of letters to socialist colleagues outlining the Marxist theory of history on questions of causation, the role of the individual, and the role of economics in history. Collected together, these letters provide some of the richest insights into the historical method of Marxism. He, like Marx before him, noted the danger of false friends. Supposedly using historical materialism as their guide, such people speculated, rationalised and deduced from a few Marxist phrases 'as an excuse for not studying history'. This was impermissible for Engels because theory must be tested against real historical evidence. Marxists, he insisted, could not deduce everything from abstract principles. In so doing, Engels was reasserting the unity of the theory and practice in Marxist history. In a letter to Conrad Schmidt he wrote in August 1890, he insisted: 'But our conception of history is above all a guide to study ... All history must be studied afresh, the conditions of existence of the different formations of society must be examined in political, civil-law, aesthetic, philosophic, religious, etc., views corresponding to them.'[36]

Engels was therefore concerned by the totality of societies in all their different aspects, and not just the economic dimension. The economic determinism of a new generation of Marxists obviously concerned Engels. This after all was the era in which the leaders of the socialist parties of the Second International, be it Kautsky in Germany, Hyndman in England, or Guesde in France, subscribed to a deterministic view of history, a vulgarisation of Marxism. In a letter to Joseph Bloch, Engels ridiculed the attempt to find an economic cause for everything from a subtle linguistic change to the formation of each of the small states of medieval Germany. Likewise, in correspondence with Conrad Schmidt, he indicated that it would be pedantic to try to find economic causes for particular ancient religious beliefs. This idea of economic causation for everything in every circumstance was nonsense. He argued that Marx and he had had to overemphasise the economic factor of history in the process of winning a polemic with **idealists** at the level of theory. When, however, it came to actual historical writing, namely theory applied to the practice of history, it was a very different matter, and such an overemphasis was an impermissible error.

These two letters also revealed a much more sensitive notion of causation. The historical stream was a complex process with multiple causes, the manifold actions of individuals resulting in each historical event. Restating human and individual agency, he paraphrased Marx's quote from *The Eighteenth Brumaire*, 'We make our history ourselves, but first of all, under very definite assumptions and conditions.'[37] Human **agency** is underlined. But our actions take place within a very specific historical context. Like a skilled and quick-fingered seamstress, history knits together flawlessly agency and structure. In one sense history aggregates the actions of many individuals:

> history proceeds in such a way that the final result always arises from conflicts between many individual wills, and every one is in turn made into what it is by a

host of particular conditions of life. Thus there are innumerable intersecting forces, an infinite series of parallelograms of forces which give rise to one resultant – the historical event.[38]

The individual acts but in concert with a host of others; the consequence is often an unintended consequence of any of them. Pressure at one point of the system may cause strain at a distant part of the 'parallelogram of forces'. This should not be considered simply as a random chaos of unrelated parts but as constituting a dynamic whole, which develops according to certain principles that are indecipherable in the random appearance of the individual parts:

> This may in its turn again be regarded as the product of a power which operates as a whole *unconsciously* and without volition. For what each individual wills is obstructed by everyone else, and what emerges is something that no one intended. Thus history has proceeded hitherto in the manner of a natural process and is essentially subject to the same laws of motion.[39]

These 'laws of motion' exist because individuals act within constraints set not only by the actions of others but also their own physical needs and material situations:

> But from the fact that the wills of the individuals – each of whom desires what he is impelled to by his physical constitution and external, in the last resort economic, circumstances (either his own personal circumstances or those of society in general) – do not achieve what they want, but are merged into an aggregate mean, a common resultant, it must not be concluded that they are equal to zero. On the contrary, each contributes to the resultant and is to this extent included in it.[40]

Engels made the distinction between the complexity of the actions of individuals at the level of the immediate, the short term or small scale, and the materialist laws of motions that operated in the last resort. The 'production and reproduction of real life' (much wider than conventional notions of economics) is the '*ultimately* determining factor in history': 'Neither Marx nor I have ever asserted more than this. Hence if somebody twists this into saying that the economic factor is the *only* determining one, he transforms that proposition into a meaningless, abstract and absurd phrase.'[41]

Production explained the development of human history ultimately or, as Engels put it in a letter to Borgius in January 1894, 'more nearly parallel to ... economic development the longer the period considered and the wider the field dealt with'. This distinction between the immediate and ultimate is crucial for a defence of Marxist historical method. Engels reasserted the value of the **base** or the 'economic situation' **and superstructure** which included:

political forms of the class struggle and its consequences, such as: constitutions drawn up by the victorious class after a successful battle, etc., juridical forms, and even the reflections of all these actual struggles in the minds of the participants, political, juristic, philosophical theories, religious views and their further development into systems of dogma.

But in so doing he attempted to clarify their relationship. Their relationship is not simply base as cause and superstructure as effect, but an interaction of all these elements taking place within 'an endless host of accidents'. Far from the superstructure passively reflecting the base, it influences and often determines the *form* of historical struggles. It is in terms of the long run and the *content* of history that the 'economic movement is finally bound to assert itself'.[42]

These letters provide an invaluable summary of the Marxist historical approach, addressing some criticisms levelled at Marxist history. Engels's formulation, 'study all history afresh', is a far cry from the criticism of empiricists such as Popper or Elton that Marxism is a preconceived scheme into which evidence is found to fit. It is hard to resist making the point that Engels here anticipated some of the most notable historical trends of the twentieth century. The material basis of life and the long-run perspective were the chief concerns of the non-Marxist **Annales** school, and in particular Fernand Braudel. But where Braudel diminished the role of events and the individual as 'froth on the surfaces of the waves', Engels coupled these insights about long-run material development to the understanding of the significance of the immediacy and human agency. Furthermore, his defence of the materialist conception of history was hardly a rigid mechanism with no room for chance, accident and individual choice. His notion of the interactions of multiple actors resembling a 'parallelogram of forces' has affinities with chaos and complexity theories' attempts to deal with causation in complex systems, the most popularised version of which is the butterfly effect. The unity of the theory and practice in history that Engels propounded is lacking today in the hostile debates between 'theorists' and 'practitioners' over postmodernism. The epigram that we make history but in definite circumstances, repeated time and again by both Marx and Engels, was deceptively simple. Not only does it propose a relationship between **intentionalism** and **structuralism** – that is, between the individual and the structural constraints that confront him or her (issues that have plagued twentieth-century historiography) – but also between individuals and their time. Marx and Engels are in essence saying that, because people make history, they can, to some extent, transcend their own circumstances. Marxism proposes that history is therefore concerned with the connections between continuity and change, between **diachrony** and **synchrony**, between the past, the present and the future. These issues are highly relevant in a historiographical context where the influence of linguistics, **historicism** and anthropology are asserting the importance of the disconnection between the present and the past, of synchrony over diachrony.

▶ Conclusion

All too often the neglect of these historical writings of Marx and Engels has impoverished discussions of Marxism. These writings allow us to observe how Marx and Engels applied their theories to the practice of history, just as their political activities give indispensible insights into their politics. These writings have little in common with subsequent vulgar Marxism, or with the frequent caricatures of their work. It is no wonder that Engels sought to rescue Marxism from those who vulgarised it in the Second International, and that Marx declared his exasperation with false friends. There were already cuckoos in the nest. With this in mind, E.P. Thompson was wrong to identify a 'bifurcation' (a separation into two camps) within Marxism in the 1970s since Marx and Engels had witnessed it within their own lifetime and sought to distinguish their own work from alien influences. But these distortions are minor in comparison with what was to come in the shape of both the Second International revisionism of Bernstein and Kautsky and the Stalinist perversion of Marxism. Like the pigs' inversion of the teachings of Old Major after his death in George Orwell's *Animal Farm*, Stalinism turned each element of Marx's teaching upside down. There is a striking consistency within the Marxist pioneers' historical writings on a range of such issues as human agency, the rich and varied paths of capitalist development and the interconnections of the long run and short run. This coherence makes a persuasive case for a rejection of the fashionable view that there was more than one Karl Marx or that there were some unbridgeable differences between him and Engels. This unanimity between Marx and Engels furnishes us with basic principles against which to judge subsequent Marxist writings.

4 The Second Generation and the Philosophy and Writing of History

'In every era the attempt must be made anew to wrest tradition away from a conformism that is about to overpower it. The Messiah comes not only as the redeemer, he comes as subduer of the Antichrist. Only that historian will have the gift of fanning the spark of hope in the past who is firmly convinced that *even the dead* will not be safe from the enemy if he wins. And this enemy has not ceased to be victorious.'

Walter Benjamin, *Theses on the Philosophy of History* (1940)

Dearest Delio,
'I feel rather tired and can't write a long letter. Go on writing to me about everything that interests you in school. I think you like history, as I liked it at your age, because it concerns living men; and everything that concerns them – as many men as possible, all the men in the world, insofar as they unite in society and work and strive to improve themselves – must necessarily interest you more than anything else. But is this the case for you? A hug.'

Antonio.
Gramsci's deathbed letter to his son[1]

From Marx and Engels's groundwork, subsequent Marxists have built an impressive body of historical work. This chapter selects those second generation Marxists – Gramsci (1891–1937), Trotsky (1879–1940) and Lukács (1885–1971) – who made the most original contribution to Marxist historiography. These Marxists dealt with new areas of historical inquiry and refined key elements of Marx's original vision of history in the light of their experiences of world war and revolution. Gramsci made important theoretical contributions on class consciousness, hegemony and culture. His perceptive application of Marxism to the problems of the twentieth century have been used by many Marxist historians since. Lukács's *History and Class Consciousness* (1923) and *Lenin* (1925) are major contributions to the Marxist view of history and collectively a systematic philosophical treatment of the history of ideas. Trotsky's *History of the Russian Revolution* (1930) provided the greatest example of historical practice within the Marxist tradition up to that point, and possibly to the present.

Within Marxism, a long-standing tension emerged between a classical dialectical approach and crude mechanistic views. This inevitably was a reflection of political differences between those who claimed Marx's inheritance and how they responded to great historical events. The figures on which this chapter focuses are those Marxists intellectuals who opposed the stale orthodoxies of the late Second International and the Stalinised Comintern. It is no accident that these have proved most useful to subsequent Marxist historians and more consistently continue the method of Marx and Engels.

▶ Trotsky's *History of the Russian Revolution*

Lev Davidovitch Bronstein grew up in a Ukrainian Jewish peasant household. Due to the relative prosperity of his parents, he received a good education. While still in his teens he became a revolutionary, being first arrested and imprisoned in Siberia at the age of 19. There he adopted the alias Trotsky from one of his jailers. After 18 months' captivity, he managed to escape to London where he moved in the circles of the Russian émigré Marxists including Lenin, Martov and Plekhanov. When the 1905 Revolution broke out in Russia, Trotsky returned to play a leading role in events as the President of the St Petersburg Soviet. Despite his early acquaintance with Lenin, he was not to join the Bolsheviks until the outbreak of the Revolution of 1917. From his experiences during that revolution he wrote the historical masterpiece, *The History of the Russian Revolution*.

Isaac Deutscher, the Marxist historian and Trotsky's biographer, considered *The History of the Russian Revolution* 'unique in world literature': 'No other Bolshevik has or could have produced so great and splendid an account of the events of 1917; and none of the many writers of the anti-Bolshevik parties has presented any worthy counter-part to it.'[2] A.L. Rowse, the English historian, believed that Trotsky matched Carlyle and Churchill for vividness and descriptive powers, but surpassed them in his theoretical grasp of the historical process.[3] Certainly, as chairman of the Petrograd Soviet and its military revolutionary committee and member of the Bolshevik central committee from the summer of 1917, Trotsky was uniquely placed to survey the events. *The History of the Russian Revolution*'s monumental size also allowed Trotsky to combine detailed empirical research with Marxist analysis. As a historian Trotsky was exceptional among the leaders of the early Marxist movement. Lenin, Luxemburg, Kautsky, and Marx and Engels before them, had not achieved such a feat of history writing. Important continuities nevertheless exist between *The History of the Russian Revolution* and *The Peasant War in Germany* or *The Eighteenth Brumaire of Louis Bonaparte*. *The History of the Russian Revolution* fitted the political requirements of the day as Trotsky saw them: to defend the revolution against its bourgeois detractors and to correct Stalinist falsification, including the distortion of Trotsky's own role. Exiled in Turkey, he accomplished this Herculean task of half a million words within a single year.

Trotsky, like his predecessors, set the revolutionary events within the peculiarities of Russian history. This path of development revealed the enigma of the Russian Revolution: how Europe's most underdeveloped country could witness the most developed and conscious working class. Trotsky's first chapter elaborated the riddling paradoxes of Russian 'combined and uneven development', juxtaposing the most backward conditions in the countryside with islands of equally advanced and highly concentrated industry. This contradiction unravelled as war matched Russian society against more advanced European rivals. Like the founders of the Marxist tradition, Trotsky prioritised the concrete explanation of the path of Russian development rather than a general model of modernisation to which all countries conformed.

This point of departure allowed Trotsky to engage in 'a scientific conscientiousness, which for its sympathies and antipathies – open and undisguised – seeks support in an honest study of the facts, of determination of their real connections, an exposure of the causal laws of their movement'. Trotsky refused to write about the revolution as 'a series of adventures' or as if 'strung along a thread of some preconceived moral'.[4] Again, like Marx and Engels, he insisted on the complementary character of science and partisanship and derided the 'treacherous impartiality' and artificial objectivity of the historian who sought to stand on the wall of a threatened town and mediate between besiegers and besieged. Such impartiality about the Russian Revolution turned out to be 'a cup of conciliation with a well settled poison of reactionary hate at the bottom'.[5]

Responding to the criticism that the selection of facts and texts proved that the historian could not be scientific, Trotsky argued that the 'coefficient of subjectivity' – the degree of subjective latitude – was not determined by the politics or temperament of the historian, but exclusively by their method. **Intentionalism**, or what Trotsky called the psychological approach to history, which viewed history 'as the interweaving of the free activities of separate individuals or groupings offers . . . a colossal scope for caprice'.[6] Materialism minimised this distortion because it began with the objective not the subjective, with the social not the individual, with the fundamental not the incidental, and thus strictly limited the personal fancies of the author.

For Trotsky, the first fundamental aspect of Russian development was its backwardness: 'the slow tempo of her development, with the economic backwardness, primitive social forms and low level of culture resulting from it'. Climate, geography, the character of production, the social system and external relations determined this late modernisation. The Russian plain stood at the mercy of the winds during its cold winter and dry summers. Agriculture, the long-run basis of Russian progress, advanced primitively via extensive methods; in the north the forests were cleared and in the south the steppes were drawn into cultivation. The expanding frontiers of Russian agriculture dissipated the forces of production: towns remained underdeveloped, agriculture remained antiquated, even the artisanal industry of the guilds failed to emerge, and social differentiation – the division of labour – scarcely existed. Standing between Europe and Asia, Russia incorporated elements of each. The incompleteness of the feudalism, which only emerged in the sixteenth century, and cultural poverty characterised the Russian social system. Serfdom arrived late and was accompanied by the absolutist state, in which the nobility ceded power to the monarch in return for feudal rights over the servile peasantry. The Russian Orthodox Church never commanded the degree of land and sovereignty of the Papacy. Cities on the scale of the European Middle Ages did not emerge; there was no guild-based urban industry; the few cities were exclusively administrative or commercial, and their trade was directed externally. The social consequence was that no significant burgher class emerged, and hence there was no Reformation, no 'third estate', and no **bourgeois revolution**. Religious dissent thus took the form of purely peasant sects such as the Old Believers. The Pugachev peasant rebellion (1772–5) could find no echo in the towns and its defeat reinforced absolutism and serfdom. Other threats to Tsarism failed to bring fundamental change. The Decembrist conspiracy (1825) rapidly collapsed. Led by a modernising section of the nobility, it would not have found allies amongst the peasantry that it exploited.

Russia was locked in military competition with Europe and this forced attempts to make good the gap between East and West. Peter I's (1682–1725) military and industrial policies to modernise Russia spurred the state to assimilate features from the advanced countries. This imitation, however, did not mean that Russia followed the pattern set down by the pioneers. Applying the dialectic to the history of capitalist development, Trotsky hypothesised scientific laws:

> The laws of history have nothing in common with a pedantic schematism. Unevenness, the most general law of the historic process, reveals itself most sharply and complexly in the destiny of backward countries. Under the whip of external necessity their backward culture is compelled to make leaps. From the universal law of unevenness thus derives another law which, for the lack of a better name, we may call the law of *combined development* – by which we mean a drawing together of the different stages of the journey, a combining of the separate steps, an amalgam of archaic with more contemporary forms. Without this law, to be taken of course in its whole material content, it is impossible to understand the history of Russia, and indeed of any country of the second, third or tenth cultural class.[7]

This combined development was reflected in the highly advanced nature and rapid development of Russian industry immediately before the First World War. At the same time, modern industry complemented and strengthened the antique character of Tsarism and the Russian countryside, at least temporarily. The social structure reflected this paradox. The bourgeoisie was small, isolated, highly reliant on foreign capital and confronted with a highly concentrated, militant class of first-generation proletarians. Though the tasks of the bourgeois revolution had not yet been achieved, unlike England in 1640 or France in 1789, the great cities of Russia were not composed of artisans and small owners. Instead, during the revolution of 1905, whilst a revolutionary working class drew support from rebellious sections of the army and peasantry, it terrified the bourgeoisie. In the revolutionary upsurge, the Russian working class created Europe's most advanced forms of political organisation: the soviet and the revolutionary party. Like Russia's place in the industrial world, her proletariat occupied a paradoxical position in the international working-class movement in which, despite its youthfulness and its smallness, it nevertheless developed greater levels of class consciousness than its European brothers and sisters.

Trotsky sought to reveal the relationship between revolution and the changing consciousness of the mass of participants. Revolution was more than anything else the entry of the masses on to the stage of history. They were driven there not by the gradual development of their ideas but by extraordinary circumstances. These material circumstances of revolutionary crisis were independent of the will of participants, who initially were only aware of the conviction that they could no longer endure the regime as it was. The pattern of development and economic and social facts forged this crisis. Further changes in the objective situation could not resolve this impasse; instead, this was achieved by the 'swift, intense and passionate changes in the psychology of the classes which have already formed themselves before the revolution'.[8] Soviet scholars criticised Trotsky's narrative for an overestimation of the fickle psychic process: in other words, the question of consciousness. They preferred to explain events through economic crisis alone. Trotsky rejected 'the vulgarly economic interpretation of history which is frequently given out for Marxism' in his preface to the second volume: 'It would be the crudest mistake to assume that the second revolution was accomplished eight months after the first owing to the fact that the bread ration was lowered during the period from one-and-a-half to three-quarters of a pound.'[9]

Before him, in *The Eighteenth Brumaire*, Marx had noted the conservative and backward-looking character of revolutionary ideas and the way in which consciousness lagged behind revolutionary events. Where Trotsky's work marked an advance on what had been written before in the Marxist tradition was that he formulated the methodological difficulties of writing a **history from below**. Recording the changing consciousness in the factories, barracks, villages and streets was far from straightforward. The people had little time or inclination to write down their experiences and therefore the evidence was fragmentary, accidental and incomplete. The pace of events and the hardships of 1917 prevented calm contemplation or reflection. Therefore the historian had a difficult task that was in some ways analogous to that of the revolutionary party. The Bolsheviks had to make these very same estimations of mass consciousness in order to formulate its tactics. This assessment, which was also the crux of writing a history of the revolution, was not an impossibility; after all, as the October Revolution had proved: 'If this can be made by a revolutionary leader in the whirlpool of the struggle, why not by the historian afterwards?'

Where Marx and Engels had theoretically explained the relationship between mass consciousness, political leadership and events, Trotsky diligently interwove these elements in an unfolding narrative of the revolution. Unlike his Stalinist historian-critics, Trotsky's elaboration of scientific laws of history did not exclude the individual from events. Part of the vivid colour of *The History of the Russian Revolution* is Trotsky's incisive and pithy pen-portraits of character and personality. He summed up Woodrow Wilson, the American President, as a 'mixture of knavery and democratic piety'. His observations on Kamenev were equally biting: 'a revolutionary conception without a revolutionary will is like a watch with a broken spring'. Stalin was a 'strong, but theoretically and politically primitive, organiser ... inseparable from the soil ... inclined to defend practical conclusions which he adopted without any mitigation whatever uniting insistence with rudeness'. Trotsky was also concerned to show the role of individual initiatives within the revolutionary masses. At the beginning of the February Revolution a handful of workers went to the barracks and convinced a single non-commissioned officer of the fourth company of the Pavlovsky regiment of their cause, and he in turn led the soldiers' mutiny. This was a crucial event. Who was this officer? Nobody knows; his identity lost 'forever among the hundreds and thousands of equally heroic names'.[10] In another example, one Bolshevik and two sympathisers won the Second Corps of Guards of the Romanian front to the side of the October Revolution.[11] Trotsky pointed out that the historian's task was to bring to life the actions of the people who made the revolution. 'Let us not forget that revolutions are accomplished through people, although they be nameless. Materialism does not ignore the feeling, thinking and acting man, but explains him.'[12]

The chief actors of 1917 were an essential aspect of the explanation and narrative of events. Their actions could not be understood by their personality alone. Using the French Revolution as an analogy, Trotsky remarked that it was only the evolving circumstances that made people heroes or figures of fun. The once eminent Girondins became ludicrous and pitiful when confronted with the Jacobins. In 1792, Jean-Marie Rolland, the respected factory inspector of Lyons, became a living caricature. In other words, the Jacobins measured up to the most radical phase of the revolution, but their opponents did not. Changing circumstances sapped the powers of those who had once led the revolution, leaving them tragically impotent. These people suffered from what Trotsky described as a 'fatal lack of correspondence between means and end'.[13] Lenin had likewise been isolated and ridiculed in the Petrograd Soviet on his return to Russia for his slogan 'All power to the soviets'. This correlation of the individual and the circumstances alone explained the failure of the Provisional Government to retain power:

> To explain the passive policy of Kerensky before the uprising solely by his personal qualities, is merely to slide over the surface of things ... All of them [the members of the Provisional Government], however, jointly and singly, turned out to be paralyzed, fell like Kerensky into a kind of heavy half-sleep – that sleep in which, in spite of the danger hanging over him, a man is powerless to lift a hand to save himself.[14]

If personality did not explain the pendulum swing of the revolution, then it was certainly one indispensable element of that process. The role of Lenin in 1917 demonstrated this and, as Trotsky indicated, 'The role of personality arises before us here on a truly gigantic scale. It is necessary only to understand that role correctly, taking personality as a link in the historic chain.'[15] Lenin was neither, as his opponents and Stalinist sycophants alike presented him, 'the demiurge of the revolutionary process', nor was he an independent factor in the revolutionary process; instead he embodied an expression of the past struggles, as did his party. Without Lenin, however, the two great Bolshevik Party crises – over support for the Provisional Government and the October insurrection – would have been more protracted and difficult to resolve. Trotsky waived judgement as to whether the Party would have overcome them in Lenin's absence. Elsewhere, he stated that October would not have happened but for Lenin.[16]

Individuals, both the most famous leaders and the anonymous masses, were for Trotsky an expression of the classes to which they belonged. The revolution itself was the process by which the working class realised its opportunity to seize power. Its actualisation was a complex process. Class consciousness was uneven and ever changing; as Heroclitus, the originator of the **dialectic**, observed, 'Everything flows'. Trotsky described class consciousness as a molecular process of mass psychology of dazzling kaleidoscopic complexity. It was characterised by the unevenness and contradictions of the working class, between the capital city and the provinces, between the soviet and the factory committees, between the committees and the rank and file, and between the soldiers and the workers: 'Such is the inevitable dynamic of a revolutionary process, which creates thousands of contradictions only in order accidentally and in passing, as though in play, to resolve them and immediately create new ones.'[17]

The Stalinists produced a simplistic caricature of the actual relationship between the Party and the class. Trotsky stressed the way in which the Party for much of the time lagged behind the workers. If the Party generally agitated against the government, on occasions it had to calm the workers in Petrograd to avoid premature and disastrous engagement with Kerensky. For Trotsky, what distinguished the Bolsheviks from other socialists was that they did not talk down to the masses but they were willing to learn from the people as well as patiently explaining the revolutionary opportunities to them: 'The growth of the Bolshevik influence, which took place with the force of a natural historical process, reveals its own contradiction upon closer examination, its zig-zags, its ebbs and flows.'[18] The October Revolution signified the culmination for the working class of the psychological process of self-realisation. They were now ready to seize the opportunity presented to them by the objective situation that opened up in February. The Bolshevik Party was their instrument, the piston-box driven by the kinetic energy of the workers, soldiers and peasants. The success of the revolution was for Trotsky the most dramatic and momentous event in history. Within eight months, Tsarist rule had been replaced by a socialist government in a country of 150 million based on a new form of direct democracy: the soviet. And even if the besieged revolution lasted only a short time, its mark on history would nonetheless be immense.

The History of the Russian Revolution provided a remarkable exemplar of Marxist historical writing, one that has rarely if ever been surpassed. Equally remarkable was the relative neglect of this masterpiece, which is an indication of Trotsky's political isolation from the mid-1920s onwards. As Deutscher observed, Trotsky was 'the only historian of genius that the Marxist school of thought has so far produced – and so far rejected'.[19] In many ways this three-volume work broke new ground in terms of the scope of its empirical research, the theoretical contribution on the questions of class consciousness and combined and uneven development, its history from below, and the application of Marx's method to a major historical subject. Perhaps most importantly for us today, Trotsky's book challenged the Stalinist distortion of the Marxist historical method. The events of 1989 have signalled a defensiveness and retreat on the part of former Western Marxists. Trotsky's *History of the Russian Revolution* rejected the equation between Stalinism and Marxism in terms of political practice, ideas and the historical method even before the completion of the first five-year plan.

▶ Gramsci's contribution: hegemony, folklore and anthropology

One of the commonest criticisms of Marxist history is that it offers an unsophisticated explanation of the realm of ideas, in particular that its approach to language, belief and mentalities is **reductionist**. According to the critics, Marxism relies on a crude correspondence between the material or economic **base**, and the **superstructure** of ideas. The thinking of Antonio Gramsci not only demonstrates the subtleties of the Marxist approach to popular consciousness, but also directly addressed some of the principal concerns – language, anthropology, popular belief and folklore – of contemporary historians.

Antonio Gramsci was born into an impoverished petty-bourgeois family in under-developed Sardinia. Eventually he won a scholarship to the University of Turin in 1911. While studying literature and linguistics he engaged with the ideas of Benedetto Croce (1866–1952), the liberal idealist philosopher, Antonio Labriola (1843–1904), the Italian socialist thinker, and Marx. Gramsci, who had become a little-known journalist, was enthused by the Russian Revolution and was a founding member of the Italian Communist Party. Italy was in the grip of a profound social crisis with rural and industrial unrest, known as the *bienno rosso*, 'the two red years'. This culminated in factory occupations across Italy which brought the government to its knees. Gramsci played an active role within the factory councils movement which organised the occupations. With the ultimate defeat of this movement and the king's invitation to Mussolini to take power, the Italian Communist Party suffered a series of setbacks ending in its destruction and the imprisonment of several leaders, including Gramsci himself. From 1926 to the end of his life, Gramsci was captive in a fascist jail or in hospital under guard.

Gramsci, like Lukács, took issue with some of the intellectual developments associated with the rise of Stalin's brand of Marxism in the Comintern of the 1920s. In particular he objected to the catastrophist view of the inevitable and terminal collapse of capitalism. But for one fact, he, like Lukács, might have made his peace with the intellectually sterile supposed Marxism of the Russian dictator. Gramsci's incarceration had perverse effects on his writing. In many respects, his *Prison Notebooks* were his most important work. However, he had to write in an obscure language to evade the censor's pen. For example, he was unable to use the terms 'working class' or 'proletariat', and therefore had to write of the subaltern class in its place. His language is as a result more opaque and difficult than most Marxists, which, by the way, gives him a certain cachet in academic circles. Notwithstanding the need to deceive the authorities, the language he used was not merely decorative. It contained real insights into popular consciousness not fully elaborated up to that point in the Marxist tradition. His jail spell also had the fortunate consequence of isolating him from the distorting influence that Stalinism exerted on the Communist International. Whilst Trotsky broke with Stalin through conscious choice, in Gramsci's case Mussolini kept Stalin at bay. As a result, Gramsci's writings retained a vitality and independence of mind at a time when the intellectuals of the Comintern became a slavish chorus to the General Secretary.

Gramsci's notion of **class consciousness** was very far from the caricatured image of the Marxist position, a mechanistic linear progression from false to true class consciousness. He deployed a number of useful concepts and suggestions that Marxist historians have subsequently adopted and that have added to the analytical sharpness of their work. E.P. Thompson's writings on the eighteenth century, for example, were heavily influenced by Gramsci's analysis of folklore. Gramsci built on Marx's writings on class consciousness, making them central to his investigation and developing a greater conceptual clarity over this particular question. Gramsci introduced a number of new categories – **hegemony, common sense** and **good sense, contradictory consciousness, organic intellectual** – that allow a more subtle analysis of popular ideas.

▶ Gramsci on hegemony and popular consciousness

Gramsci elaborated and modernised Marx's notion of ideology. One of the contemporary problems facing Marxists after the Russian Revolution was the need to explain the failure of revolutions in the West. Gramsci proposed that part of the answer lay in the differential character of the state and ruling class power. Adducing as an analogy the centaur, a mythical beast that was half-man and half-beast, Gramsci asserted that ruling classes maintained their position both via state coercion and the consent of civil society. In Russia, because of its backwardness, the repressive apparatus of the state was the principal mechanism of ruling class domination because civil society was, in embryonic form, 'primordial and gelatinous'. The role of the revolutionary party was therefore to overturn state power in a **class struggle** that he characterised as a rapid and fluid **war of movement**. In the West, by contrast, civil society was much more developed and therefore the ruling class could count on consent to a much greater extent, resulting in a class struggle which was much more difficult, slow and different in character. This **war of position**, as Gramsci called it, had to contend with an arduous struggle within civil society because 'in the West, there was a proper relation between the State and civil society, and when the State trembled a sturdy structure of civil society was at once revealed. The State was only an outer ditch, behind which there stood a powerful system of fortresses and earthworks.'[20]

The state and the ruling class were much more entrenched through its long-established moral and intellectual leadership, or hegemony, of civil society. The task of the revolutionary party was therefore to contest moral and intellectual leadership over the working class and other oppressed classes and sections of society. The coercion–consent dialectic and the notion of hegemony provided historians with sensitive tools for the analysis of class struggle in a whole range of settings.[21]

Gramsci's starting point for his discussion of popular consciousness was its philosophical character. Unlike bourgeois philosophers, Gramsci rejected the premise that philosophy should be considered the timeless pursuit of specialists. Instead, philosophy had to be critically assessed from the historical and social point of view and seen as a component of the ideas of a society. Philosophy, like all thought, responded to contemporary problems and developed from existing modes of thought. Where philosophers differed from ordinary people lay in the greater systematisation, rigour and coherence of their thought. Philosophy did not exist in a separate realm but was projected throughout society in fragmented and refracted forms. Philosophy was therefore one aspect of the historical consciousness of each generation. For Gramsci, then, everyone was a philosopher as language, common sense, religion and folklore all entailed particular conceptions of the world. As he wrote in his *Prison Notebooks*, 'One's conception of the world is a response to certain specific problems posed by reality, which are quite specific and "original" in their immediate relevance.'[22]

For the masses, this philosophy was constrained by local dialects, with their limited power of expression, by a largely uncritical acceptance of folklore and common sense, and therefore by the inability to shape these elements into a coherent unitary conception of the world. Accordingly, popular consciousness was a 'strangely composite' contradictory consciousness with class conscious fragments alongside archaic ones: 'it contains Stone Age elements and principles of a more advanced science, prejudices from all the past phases of history at the local level and intuitions of a future philosophy which will be that of a human race united the world over.'[23]

In some respects, a worker might be a 'walking anachronism, a fossil', while in others he or she might express the most modern and progressive ideas, and it was this lag that rendered the working class incapable of acting with 'complete historical autonomy'.[24] Rather than the speculative and mechanical versions of class consciousness on offer in the Comintern at the time, Gramsci's account was deeply imbued with his experiences of immersion into the class conflicts of the Turin factory workers. The basis for the development of popular consciousness was an awareness that our own consciousness, our identity, was the product of the historical process 'which deposited in you an infinity of traces, without leaving an inventory'. According to Gramsci, philosophy moved forward not through the brilliant insight of individuals but via the wide diffusion of a critical awareness that could become the basis of political action:

> For a mass of people to be led to think coherently and in the same coherent fashion about the real present world, is a 'philosophical' event far more important and 'original' than the discovery by some philosophical 'genius' of a truth which remains the property of small groups of intellectuals.[25]

The contrast between what a worker said and did, between thought and action, was another contradictory element of popular consciousness. This could not be simply ascribed to self-deception or false consciousness, particularly as this was a feature not only of the individual but of social groups and classes. It reflected deep-seated historical contradictions of the social order. Because of the ideological domination or hegemony of the ruling classes, the worker or 'active man-in-the-mass' had no clear understanding of his or her practical activity, or the political consequences of his or her actions. Despite this, these actions transformed the world. In this sense the individual worker's theories about the world stood in opposition to his or her activity resulting in a split, composite or contradictory consciousness:

> One might almost say he has two theoretical consciousnesses (or one contradictory consciousness): one which is implicit in his activity and which in reality unites him with his fellow-workers in the practical transformation of the real world; and one, superficially explicit or verbal, which he has inherited from the past and uncritically absorbed.[26]

This verbal conception of the world, which the worker uncritically received, acted as an impediment to action, even resulting in a moral and political impotence. The ability to overcome this passivity depended upon the development of a critical self-awareness, through the internal contest of contradictory ideas which the worker measured against external experience. The first stage in this development consists of an awareness of class, namely a sense of estrangement or otherness from the hegemonic power. The capacity critically to appraise the world – good sense – allowed for the development of class consciousness. This process, beginning with the fragmentary sense of class difference, ultimately culminated in a single coherent conception of the world that has overcome common sense. For Gramsci, this process was not a purely intellectual procedure; it was tied to practical experience. Practical activity and experience of the world shaped conscious development through the friction between the two sides of contradictory consciousness. This evolution, however, was not automatic as it required the creation of institutions to consolidate its advances and an intellectual minority to embody them. Gramsci here was alluding to the organisations of the working class, and principally the revolutionary party. Through these institutions a dialogue between intellectuals and the masses could take place, drawing the former into practical struggles and widening the elemental class awareness of the latter. The mutual development of these groups formed a layer of 'organic intellectuals' who were not specialist philosophers but were organically entwined and growing with the masses, an expression of the working class in its ascent to a common and independent conception of the world. This implied raising

> the intellectual level of ever growing strata of the populace, in other words, to give a personality to the amorphous mass element. This means working to produce *élites* of intellectuals of a new type which arise directly out of the masses, but remain in contact with them to become, as it were, the whalebone in the corset.[27]

This said, Gramsci again asserted the dialectic of theory and practice, or praxis. He envisaged no separation between theory and practice. The ideas of the network of organic intellectuals were not arbitrary but were tested against the practical requirements of the age. These ideas had to contain a rationality fitted to the practical needs of the day otherwise they withered in the complex historical competition of ideas. This held as true for Catholicism in the medieval period as it did for Marxism in the twentieth century. 'Constructions', he wrote, 'which respond to the demands of a complex organic period of history always impose and prevail in the end, even though they may pass through several intermediary phases during which they manage to affirm themselves only in more or less bizarre and heterogeneous combinations'.[28]

These views of the relationship between class struggle and popular culture extended to a discussion of folklore and anthropological investigation. Gramsci rejected the contemporary antiquarian approach to folklore that represented it as a series of picturesque eccentricities. Instead he favoured studying folklore as a 'conception of the world and life'. These folkloric conceptions of the world were specific to a given time, place and social stratum, and were defined in opposition to official lettered conceptions of the world. Common sense developed as folklore's philosophy, peasant notions of natural law evolved as folklore's sense of law and justice. Folklore was also in a sense dependent on the culture of the dominant class because of that class's superior intellectual and material resources, to use Gramsci's metaphor, in the same way that artisans are dependent on artists. Folkloric conceptions of the world were therefore not systematic or fully elaborated – the common people were not able to develop the centralised political organisations necessary to achieve this – but many-sided, randomly accumulated, stratified, contradictory, 'a confused agglomerate of fragments of all the conceptions of the world and of life that have succeeded one another in history'.[29] The very heterogeneity of folklore created serious methodological problems because of its unstable and fluctuating meanings and cultural content. Therefore no firm conclusions were possible, but only probable conjectures.

Gramsci extended his discussion of folklore to popular religion, which was different from the religion of the ecclesiastical authorities. The religion of the people encompassed a popular morality, accepted codes of conduct, custom and behaviour which exercised a much stronger hold on the people than official religion, law and morality. Side by side with the static conservative relics of past life, folklore was innovative and progressive, determined by everyday conditions quite distinct from, and even oppositional to, the morality of the ruling class. Attempts by the Italian school system to root out folklore were therefore about overcoming conceptions of the world out of tune with that of the Italian State. Though these writings on folklore and popular religion are relatively piecemeal and sometimes obscured by the language employed, they have been tremendously influential and suggestive to later Marxist historians.[30]

▶ Lukács's *History and Class Consciousness*

Georg Lukács was born in Budapest in 1885, the son of one of the city's banking elite. Educated in Vienna and Heidelberg, he developed a romantic anti-capitalism under a variety of influences, including neo-Kantian **idealist** philosophers such as Rickert and Wendelbrand and the sociologist, Max Weber. Lukács did not adopt Marxism until he was radicalised by the First World War and the Russian Revolution. Georg Lukács's writings range from the philosophy of history to politics, aesthetics and literature. But his writings, like his life, underwent both evolutionary and abrupt changes. Some of Lukács's work is non-Marxist since he had already embarked on philosophical and literary studies before becoming a Marxist in the aftermath of the Russian Revolution. From an initially immature and ultra-left Marxism, his work in the mid-1920s – *History and Class Consciousness* (1923), *Lenin* (1925), and the recently discovered *Tailism and the Dialectic* (1925/6) – embodied a sophisticated Marxism sharply critical of intellectual developments associated with the rise of the Stalinist bureaucracy in Russia and the Communist International.[31] In 1930 he made his intellectual peace with Stalin. He, like so many others, was overwhelmed and bewildered by what must have seemed the grim logic of history.

Nevertheless, in the 1920s, Lukács produced work of the greatest significance for Marxist historians, although this work has often been underestimated.[32] Within a year of Lukács joining the Hungarian Communist Party, he and it were thrown into a revolutionary situation. Lukács had been the People's Commissar of Education and Culture in the ill-fated Soviet Hungary, which was crushed after a matter of months by the counter-revolutionary forces of Admiral Horthy. In exile in Vienna, Lukács's *History and Class Consciousness* was born out of his effort to come to terms with this defeat and the wider collapse of the European revolutionary possibilities. It also signalled the coming of age of Lukács's Marxism. His principal political conclusion, one that he reiterated in *Lenin* and *Tailism*, was that the revolutions were lost due to the immaturity and failings of the communist parties, and in some ways it anticipated Trotsky's case in *Lessons of October* (1924). Unsurprisingly, Lukács's assessments of international communism were drawn into the factional maelstrom to decide Lenin's successor. *History and Class Consciousness* appeared at a time of Zinoviev's secret alliance with Stalin and growing attacks on Trotsky. *History and Class Consciousness* came under fierce criticism within the pages of *Pravda*, from within the Hungarian Communist Party and even in Zinoviev's presidential address to the Fifth Congress of the Communist International. The substance of the criticisms centred on the relationship between working-class interests and consciousness, and the nature of Marxism as a science (the **dialectic**

of nature debate). Lukács's opponents combined a positivistic view of science, a mechanical view of working-class consciousness and an anti-intellectual malevolence, characteristics which were later unmistakably associated with Stalin's Comintern. In comparison, Lukács confronted what he saw to be the real difficulties, errors and problems of international communism in terms of historical materialism and Marx's philosophy of history. Shaped by an honest endeavour to grapple with the significance of momentous events, *History and Class Consciousness* has provided the Marxist tradition with a text of enduring relevance and sharp insight into the writing of history.

Georg Lukács's *History and Class Consciousness* assembled essays written between 1919 and 1922. It provided a robust response to external challenges to Marxist history and clarified certain elements of Marx's legacy at a time of disagreement within the socialist movement internationally. For much of their lives Marx and Engels were ignored by bourgeois academics but, by the first two decades of the twentieth century, with the work of Max Weber (1864–1920), Heinrich Rickert (1863–1936), Wilhelm Dilthey (1833–1911) and Georg Simmel (1858–1918), a number of important critiques of Marxism had developed. Lukács specifically addressed the issues that the emerging schools of professional historians and sociologists raised. He examined **Weberianism, empiricism**, academia itself and the overall development of bourgeois thought. In defence of Marx, he reasserted the importance of scientific method, of scientific truth, of the concepts of **totality** and dialectics; but at the same time he rejected an uncritical acceptance of Marx's work in favour of a consistent use of his scientific method. This stood in contrast to the Marxism of the Second and, after Stalin's grip upon it tightened, the Third International. Lukács returned to the writings of Marx and Hegel to reassert the dialectical method. Accordingly, several of the Russian leaders of the Comintern condemned Lukács's perspective.

▶ Reification and bourgeois history

'Reification and the consciousness of the proletariat', the most substantial of the essays in *History and Class Consciousness*, began with an analysis of commodity production under capitalism. With the spread of modern capitalism, for the first time in history, commodity production dominated all aspects of society. Here Lukács built on Marx's view that **capitalism** made a false god of the commodity that he had termed **commodity fetishism**. Whereas before society was constituted by relations between human beings or with nature, these social and natural relations were now turned into commodities; everything now had a price. Even human relations were commodified as the labour-power of the agricultural or urban wage-labourer was bought and sold on the market like any other commodity. Lukács termed this process **reification**, literally the transformation into a thing, meaning the fragmentation of social processes into a multitude of inauthentic and artificial things. The true social character of production remained disguised because individuals were confronted by a host of reified commodities on the market. Reification transformed the nature of phenomena: land became ground-rent, the machine became capital. The worker became a slave to capital and the wage system, his or her labour alienated. At the same time, this reification obscured the character of exploitation since the worker entered into a seemingly free and equal agreement with the employer who exchanged wages for the worker's labour power.

This reification and alienation of the social and natural world was highly significant because it helped to explain the character of bourgeois thought. Through his analysis of reification, Lukács sought to elucidate the contradictions of such thought. Initially he criticised the bourgeois idea that philosophy posed universal ahistorical problems. The connections made between, for example, the eighteenth-century German philosopher Immanuel Kant and the ancient Greek Plato ignored the way in which these ideas were bent to the differing needs of the societies of their day. This ahistorical method mystified the real connections that arose between capitalist and pre-capitalist thought because of the partial reification of those societies. Modern philosophy's great misconception was that *it* had created the modern world, ignoring the material contribution of capitalism. Lukács acknowledged that after a long battle of ideas bourgeois thought did supersede medieval thought. The dominant themes of these quarrels were: the continuity or separateness of all phenomena, the question of causation (whether mystical or transcendental or not), and the application of rational mathematical criteria to all phenomena. Modern rationalism claimed to understand the principles connecting all phenomena and had engendered technological advance with dramatic effects in production. Modern bourgeois thought culminated in the work of Hegel, who married dialectics with the historical resolution of the philosophical problems (two elements to which Marx was indebted). Where Marx parted company with Hegel was over what was the subject or driving force of history. For Marx this was human activity in the shape of the development of the forces of production and the class struggle. For Hegel it was the world spirit, the growing self-consciousness of humanity. Because of this idealism, Hegel (and modern philosophy with him) became 'lost in an endless labyrinth of conceptual mythology'. Hegel therefore groped towards the integration of philosophy and history but ultimately failed. History, for Hegel, had ended with the Prussian state which was the pinnacle of the development of the world spirit. Once this Hegelian highpoint was attained, according to Lukács, modern bourgeois philosophy shattered into pieces.

Marxism provided the only consistent scientific approach to history because bourgeois thought by its very nature was incapable of doing so. Unlike natural science, where new knowledge drove scientific progress, bourgeois social and historical inquiry produced 'an ideological weapon of the bourgeoisie' that aimed to demonstrate capitalism's 'eternal survival by eternal laws of nature and reason'.[33] Classical economics provided a good example of this ideological distortion of social and political thought into a justification of bourgeois rule. Its categories were indeed eternal and the operation of the market seen as the providential dexterity of the 'invisible hand' of God. This did not imply that history could not be written without dialectics or Marxism. Lukács acknowledged the factual accuracy of bourgeois historical accounts and their contribution to knowledge. Their deficiency lay in their inability to write of history as a comprehensible whole, or total history, because they lacked dialectics which was the very method by which history could be understood as a unified process. This might be seen as a defining insight into the relationship between Marxist and non-Marxist history. Lukács proposed that there was empirical common ground and some theoretical points of contact, but Marxist history was distinct from non-Marxist history because of its particular approach to history *as a whole*. The failure of Comte and Spencer (one might add Arnold Toynbee, Fernand Braudel and Francis Fukuyama) to provide a total history illustrated this for Lukács. Hence bourgeois history is characterised by two separate approaches: particular histories of descriptive accuracy, and the failed attempts at general accounts of the whole of human history. It might also be noted that bourgeois historians raised this flaw into a general historical approach with **historicism** and **empiricism**:

> Everything meaningful or purposive is banished from history. It then becomes impossible to advance beyond mere 'individuality' of the various epochs and their social and human representatives. History must then insist with Ranke that every age is 'equally close to God', i.e. has attained an equal degree of perfection and that – for quite different reasons – there is no such thing as historical development.[34]

The bourgeoisie was therefore incapable of a scientific understanding of history through its failure to overcome reification. Lukács used the example of Heinrich Rickert's view of history to illustrate this. Rickert, the German neo-Kantian philosopher, asserted that cultural disciplines such as history were not scientific in the same sense as chemistry and physics because history could only be free of the values of the historian in monographs written in a narrow, factual and narrative form. The philosophy of history was, on the other hand, subject to the influence of the historian's cultural values and therefore total history was impossible. For Lukács, this view led to the systematic inability to make connections, to provide historical explanation, or to advance historical understanding beyond the most elementary points. To avoid complete relativism, non-monographic history could be written according to shared normative cultural values, but Rickert neglected the question of how these consensual values were forged. The problem with such a view is that it ignored the extent to which the difference between the monograph and the total history was one of scope or method. All history involved philosophy of history, and any meaningfulness in history, required going beyond 'the facts'.

Rickert's problem was that he misunderstood total history. Lukács pointed out that it was not the mechanical aggregation of individual historical events, or a transcendent explanatory principle distinct from the events of history, or exclusively reliant on the philosophy of history. Total history could not be separated from historical reality. The historian or participant in events could not arrive at a real understanding of the historical process by direct immediate experience. For this, the historian had to break out of the immediacy of reified experience (or facticity). Thus bourgeois history constituted the 'prolongation of the state of immediacy': a static, atomised history of facts. According to Lukács: 'The very most that can be achieved in this way is to set up a formal typology of the manifestations of history and society using historical facts as illustrations.'[35]

Whereas bourgeois philosophy and writing of history was trapped in its own immediacy, Marxism, Lukács maintained, allowed the historian to go beyond the immediate through the process of **mediation**. Bourgeois history therefore was ensnared in either empiricism or attempts to understand change by the formal, rational, abstract examination of different atomised facts rather than processes as Lukács proposed. Lukács described how this could affect bourgeois historical methods:

> This may take the form of a 'naïve' sociology in search of 'laws' (of the Comte/ Spencer variety) in which the insolubility of the task is reflected in the absurdity of the results. Or else the methodological intractability may be a matter of critical awareness from the beginning (as with Max Weber) and, instead, an auxiliary science of history is brought into being. But in either case the upshot is the same: the problem of facticity is pushed back into history once again and the purely historical standpoint remains unable to transcend its immediacy regardless of whether this is desired or not.[36]

Bourgeois philosophy of history became abstract, formal and circular contemplation because it was separated from history itself. Bourgeois history was therefore unable to conceive of the present as a historical problem because it was tied to the immediate. The present, for Lukács, mediated the past and the future, so history was a practical question. This view should not surprise us given that the period in which Lukács lived was one of the most momentous in human history. Because of the reification and immediacy of bourgeois thought, bourgeois historians were not even capable of seeing the First World War and Russian Revolution in the context of the overall historical development, and their writing on contemporary events attained 'the pitiable or contemptible mental level of the worst kind of provincial journalism'. This only illustrated the open chasm between subjectivity and objectivity in bourgeois history and the sterile either/or solutions (or **dualism**) it proposed to this problem.

Lukács also addressed another crucial strand of bourgeois thought: the influence of Max Weber. By the 1920s Weber was emerging as one of the most important bourgeois sociologists on the writing of history. His conceptualisation of history centred on patterns of domination and has offered historians an alternative to Marxist social theory. A whole sub-discipline, historical sociology, has risen in Weber's image. It was within Lukács's framework of the general contradictions of bourgeois thought that he analysed Weber's view of capitalism. Lukács's discussion of reification turned to rationalisation and bureaucracy, which were the defining characteristics for Max Weber of the capitalist system. Unlike Weber, Lukács stressed the basis of this rationality as commodity capitalism. Commodification altered everything into a quantity, a money value, and therefore subjected it to a rational calculation. This happened within the factory via the ever-increasing division of labour and atomisation of the worker, which was most fully developed under the Taylorist system (the 'scientific management' of factory production through time and motion studies, etc.). Modern bureaucracies also underwent this self-same process. According to this logic, by the formal standardisation of the justice system and the civil service, the state took shape: 'Bureaucracy implies the adjustment of one's way of life, mode of work and hence of consciousness, to general socio-economic premise of the capitalist economy.'[37]

The lower echelons of the bureaucracy, for all their ethos of honour and responsibility, resembled the factory with the division of labour and the intensification of work, which Lukács described as 'a violation of man's humanity'. All aspects of life bent to this process of reification. But the formal rationality of the units of production or bureaucracy accompanied the irrationality of the overall market economy. Capitalism operated according to

> a law of mutually interacting 'coincidences' rather than one of truly rational organisation. Furthermore, such a law must not merely impose itself despite the wishes of individuals, it may *not even be fully and adequately knowable.* For complete knowledge of the whole would vouchsafe the knower a monopoly that would amount to the virtual abolition of the capitalist economy.[38]

Thus Lukács provided a powerful argument against the Weberian proposition that 'value-rationality' and bureaucracy provided the fundamental essence of the modern world, and suggested instead these were symptomatic of the deeper process of reification. According to Lukács, Weber's failure conformed to the general inability of bourgeois thought to understand the material and economic substratum (or base) to law, jurisprudence or philosophy. The bourgeois social sciences in general suffered from an increasing fragmentation and reliance on **formalism** corresponding to the process of reification. Consequently, bourgeois thought itself became a barrier to understanding the totality of historical development.

▶ The possibilities of Marxist history

Lukács then addressed the worker's intellectual standpoint and class consciousness in the final section of 'Reification and the consciousness of the proletariat'. He began this with a discussion of bourgeois historiography. For Lukács, the working class was both the object and the subject of history, capable of transforming society through a scientific understanding of the historical process. In order to do this it had to overcome the reification and alienation of bourgeois society, both consciously and practically.

From Lukács's perspective, history served very different purposes for the bourgeoisie and working class. In contrast to bourgeois thought, the working class was capable of overcoming the immediacy of its reified existence under capitalism, and indeed needed to do so in order to achieve its own emancipation. Thus the development of working-class consciousness was connected to the search for historical truths that overcame the structural weaknesses of bourgeois history. For the bourgeoisie, history was at an end with the victory of capitalism, a system that existed according to eternal laws of human nature. Although the bourgeoisie did not consider the present as part of history, for the working class historical knowledge began with the knowledge of the present, of itself and its own social position. From this standpoint, historical categories must be scientific: that is, they must be real categories which actually constitute historical development rather than merely describing it. The continuities, coherence and inner connections of the historical process were also 'structural components of the present'.

Having rejected empiricism, Marxist philosophy should not be used to formulate universal abstract ideas of total history. Instead the immanent social reality could only be mediated by seeing social reality as part of a totality caught up in the process of change. According to Lukács, mediation was not a subjective factor foisted on history from the outside, but a manifestation of its authentic objective structure. The working class was therefore capable of a higher plane of scientific objectivity than the bourgeoisie, but this was not guaranteed. Working-class ideas did not start from scratch but from bourgeois thought, and they too were subjected to reified social reality. Unlike the bourgeoisie, the working class was capable of escaping the illusions of the immediate, which allowed it to solve the theoretical difficulties insoluble from the bourgeois perspective.

To begin with, the worker could recognise him or herself as a commodity and grasp the way in which at work he or she was reduced to an instrument, subject to quantification and dehumanising rationalisation. In the same way, he or she could realise that social life in general was stunted and alienated by capitalist commodity production. The working class could not achieve this understanding either automatically, as individuals, or by abstract contemplation. Instead, the piecing together of the fragmented reality into a meaningful picture could only begin with a collective realisation of how the process of commodity production, and the reification stemming from it, exploited the worker, and that workers in general were the victims of exploitation. The development of class consciousness was therefore itself a practical collective struggle. This consciousness was not derived from the worker's individual or short-term interests. It could be hampered by interests and ideas such as craft pride. Instead, class consciousness represented the historical interests of the working class as a whole.

For Lukács, proletarian class consciousness combined theory and practice in a dialectical process termed praxis. This class consciousness was able to see beyond the reified world of things and dissolve things as different aspects of vital processes. From Heroclitus to Hegel, the dialecticians have viewed reality as fluid. Lukács therefore argued that modern bourgeois philosophy was mistaken in probing the static nature of 'being' instead of the transitional 'becoming'. History was essentially dialectical and therefore the 'developing realities of history constitute a higher reality than empirical facts'.[39] The consequence of the primacy of facts was to find oneself 'trapped in frozen forms of the various stages' of history.

The dialectic was itself not an unchanging method. The earliest dialecticians had attempted to fit everything into the triad of thesis, antithesis and synthesis. Lukács distinguished between this pedantic schematism and Marx's historically concrete dialectical method. Marx's starting point was real historical processes rather than abstract schemes. Lukács also observed that the bourgeois degeneration of Marxism, as with Bernstein (and as also happened with Stalinism), entailed an abandonment of the dialectic. The primacy of facts led to the view that 'every movement seems like a movement *impinging on* them, while every tendency to change to them appears to be a merely subjective principle (a wish, a value judgement, an ought)'.[40] All attempts to improve on Marx's method resulted in 'oversimplification, triviality and eclecticism'.[41]

In defending the dialectical notion of totality elaborated earlier by Marx and Hegel, Lukács reiterated that this did not imply a reductionism, a position taken by Popper and many other critics of Marxism. Again this problem of 'the parts and the whole' formed a crucial aspect of the defence of Marxism as a scientific method. Reductionism stemmed from envisaging the whole as being determined one or more of the parts: for Lukács the whole was greater than the sum of the parts:

We repeat: the category of totality does not reduce its various elements to an undifferentiated uniformity, to identity. The apparent independence and autonomy which they possess in the capitalist system of production is an illusion only in so far as they are involved in a dynamic dialectical relationship with one another and can be thought of as the dynamic dialectical aspects of an equally dynamic and dialectical whole.[42]

But when the truth of becoming is the future that is to be created but has not yet been born, when it is the new that resides in tendencies that (with our conscious aid) will be realised, then the question whether thought is a reflection [of reality] appears quite senseless. It is true that reality is the criterion for the correctness of thought, but reality is not, it becomes – and to become the participation of thought is needed.[43]

In contrast to those who argued the inevitability of socialism, such as Kautsky or Stalin, the question of the consciousness of the proletariat was the least automatic aspect of history. Objective economic processes did no more than create the working class; they did not make it class conscious. For Lukács, the achievement of class consciousness and the abolition of capitalism could only come about through the action of the working class itself.

Both empiricism and **postmodernism** share an explicit rejection of totality (or 'grand narrative' in postmodernist language) and Lukács therefore provided the Marxist tradition with a most robust critique of these positions. Both reflect the structural flaw of bourgeois thought which is incapable of viewing the whole picture because it needs to mystify the character of exploitation and the historical impermanence of all socio-economic formations. Thus history for both post-modernism and empiricism is decentred and fragmentary: a host of unique events and personalities. For Lukács, the task of Marxism, indeed its only intellectual advantage over bourgeois thought, was its 'ability to look beyond the divisive symptoms' to see the unity of 'the social system underlying it'.[44] Herein lay the crux of practical working-class consciousness as opposed to the veil of false consciousness that the bourgeoisie drew over the character of society. Lukács criticised the practical impotence those left theorists reduced 'to the "scientific" treatment of the symptoms of social change and as for practice they are themselves reduced to being buffeted about aimlessly and uncontrollably by the various elements of the process they hope to master'.[45] Just as scientific truth or error had practical implications, so too true or false political or historical theory had consequences in either holding up or enabling the actions of the oppressed in their struggles for change.

▶ Conclusion

Within the generation that followed Marx and Engels, in spite of distortions of the Second International and Stalin's inversion of Marxism, there were works of unrivalled importance in both the writing and philosophy of history. In each case the authors were able to produce this work beyond the debilitating influence of Stalinism. Their work enabled the continuity of a historical tradition faithful to, and renewing, Marx and Engels's fundamental principles. Because they were confronting questions of a world more modern than the one inhabited by Marx and Engels, subsequent Marxist historians have found them an indispensable reserve of insight both in terms of developing their own work and in criticism of non-Marxist historians. The post-Second World War generation of Marxist historians acknowledged their debt to Gramsci. Genovese's and Thompson's work on culture drew heavily on the Gramscian critique of bourgeois anthropology and his approach to paternalism. Lukács and Trotsky have not been so readily absorbed into the approach of Marxist historians. Both had insights into class consciousness that were complementary to Gramsci's and which built on those of Marx and Engels. It is unfortunate that many Marxist historians have neglected Lukács's views on science and his insights into the permanent faultlines of bourgeois history that are so tremendously helpful in the face of postmodernism.

5 'Rescuing the Poor Stockinger': History from Below

'The revolt is the only successful slave revolt in history, and the odds it had to overcome is evidence of the magnitude of the interests that were involved. The transformation of the slaves, trembling in their hundreds before a single white man, into a people able to organise themselves and defeat the most powerful European nations of their day, is one of the great epics of revolutionary struggle and achievement.'

C.L.R. James, *The Black Jacobins*, 1938[1]

'But since the Fathers of the City have thought good in one part of their show to call attention to an episode the London history, the murder of Wat Tyler, it may be worth while for the sake of practical moral to recall to our readers the story of which that murder was the climax; all the more as it has become a sort of nursery tale in which the figures of the wise and kingly youth, the sturdy loyal citizen, and the ruffian agitator have been made to stand out against the dark background of foolish and ignorant armed peasants, not knowing what they asked for.'

William Morris, 'The Lord Mayor's Show', *Justice*, November 1884[2]

Previously Marxist historians had been neither academics nor professional historians; they were revolutionaries with a range of interests which included history. After the Second World War, this was to change. In this period a generation of academic Marxists emerged and matured. Their research was, as a result, more systematically and exclusively oriented towards historical questions. The Hungarian Revolution of 1956 provoked the departure of several historians from the Communist Party who had thrived despite the generally stultifying influence of Stalinism. As a consequence, they attempted to shake off the mechanical materialism of Cominform orthodoxy. They squinted at Marx and history with rejuvenated eyes. The result, **history from below**, ennobled the resistance and non-conformity of bandits, peasants, artisans, industrial workers, poachers, religious millenarians and transportees. E.P. Thompson's *The Making of the English Working Class* (1963) acted as a manifesto for this perspective. But the groundwork had been prepared well before this in the Historians' Group of the Communist Party of Great Britain.

▶ Communist Party Historians' Group (1946–56)

The Communist Party Historians' Group (CPHG) was founded in 1946. In their different ways, A.L. Morton's *A People's History of England* (1938), Christopher Hill's *English Revolution, 1640* (1940) and Maurice Dobb's *Studies in the Development of Capitalism* (1946) set the tone for the approach of the group. The membership included such illustrious names as Christopher Hill, Eric Hobsbawm, John Saville, Victor Kiernan, Rodney Hilton and George Rudé. This roll-call might obscure the character of the group which did not just comprise stars. Its sizeable membership existed within the Communist Party which, whilst not a mass party, brought together intellectuals and workers in significant numbers in something – it might be argued – approaching Gramsci's notion of **organic intellectuals**.

Prior to the foundation of the Communist Party Historians' Group, there had already been an increase in historical work of the Party from the late 1930s. Alongside the popularity of A.L. Morton's *A People's History of England* published by the Left Book Club, the Party had recruited a number of talented history students, particularly at Cambridge. In 1940, Christopher Hill was the first of these to produce a major publication with the extended pamphlet on the English Civil War, *English Revolution, 1640*. As was to happen later in the 1960s, the depression decade radicalised significant numbers of young intellectuals. Eric Hobsbawm recounted the prevailing influence of great events upon their intellectual formation: 'Where would we, as intellectuals, have been, what would have become of us, but for the experiences of war, revolution and depression, fascism and anti-fascism, which surrounded us in our youth?'[3]

The group was formed at a conference to discuss the second edition of Morton's *People's History*. In organisational terms, it adopted a relatively formal structure with a chair, secretary, its own finances, and sections according to period of interest. The group, which was a section of the Party's National Cultural Committee, had a relatively heterodox composition of university and adult education lecturers, teachers (who had their own section) and Party members with an interest in history. Unlike other communist parties, historians were the most intellectually vibrant element of the British party. The group organised conferences on major historical issues, such as the famous debates over the **transition** from feudalism to **capitalism** and the **bourgeois revolution**. It also produced a four-volume series of collected documents in 1948–9 aimed at educational work among a labour movement and adult education readership. A certain chemistry was created by the fusion of these elements. As one participant recalled:

> Physical austerity, intellectual excitement, political passion and friendship are probably what the survivors of those years remember best – but also a sense of equality. Some of us knew more about some subject or period than others, but all of

us were equally explorers of largely unknown territory. Few of us hesitated to speak in discussion, even fewer to criticize, none to accept criticism.[4]

One of the great advantages of the group was that it offered Marxist historians a sense of perspective. They could assess the key trends of British historical writing and attempt to address them collectively. This was particularly beneficial given the general Cold War animosity to Marxism and conservative outlook of British historians at the time. Marxists surveyed the historiographical landscape to address questions of strategic importance. The life of the group coincided with the end of the old Whig interpretation of British history: that is, the view that British history followed a continuous enlightened trajectory through the battle of freedom and democracy against tyranny that stretched back to the Magna Carta. This had fallen from fashion due to a conservative critique mounted in the first instance by Sir Herbert Butterfield and Sir Lewis Namier (1888–1960).[5] Namier's investigation of politics at the time of George III outlined the gap between political rhetoric and practice. A detailed inspection of actions and espoused ideas revealed that hypocrisy was the norm and that formal political positions outlined in parliamentary speeches were no guide to the actions of politicians. The substance of politics was not high ideals but vested interest, faction forming and bargaining. For those who followed Namier's approach, these crude estimations of patronage and faction crowded principles and passions out of history. Such an approach was incompatible with the old Whig view of gradual British progress; continuity replaced the idea of progress in history. From the point of view of the Communist Party historians, the criticisms of the Whig view were valid but what was proposed in its place was not. Their critique of Namierism pointed out that it committed the vulgar materialist error of denying a role for political ideas in history. That resulted in a profoundly conservative and sceptical view of the potential for human progress.

The group identified a second main strand of British historical thought at the time: the Clapham school's reinterpretation of the Industrial Revolution.[6] First, Claphamites denied that there was such an event as the Industrial Revolution; instead, there was an 'accelerated evolution'. The very idea that revolutions of any kind transformed history was repugnant to these historians. Second, they maintained that the growth of industrial capitalism had a generally benign effect upon living standards. These positions constituted a historical defence, or (as the CPHG described it) apologetics, of capitalism. This school's boldest and most political expression came in the shape of T.S. Ashton and F.A. von Hayek's *Capitalism and the Historians* (1954). The historians' group played an important part in the **standard of living debate** that ensued. Hobsbawm noted with some satisfaction: 'A very small expenditure of research succeeded in dislodging the dominant academic orthodoxy which held that the material living standard of life of the British workers had improved in the first four decades of the nineteenth century.'[7]

A third crucial element of historical thinking was the Cold War empiricist attack on the Marxist view of history. According to the empiricists (Karl Popper, Michael Oakeshott and Sir Isaiah Berlin), theories of history were inherently totalitarian and closed, while explanations of the meaning of history implied inevitability and denied free will in history. The task of the historian was not to explain, predict or draw lessons for the present, but to show how the past was. J.P. Hartley's opening lines of his novel, *The Go-Between*, neatly expressed this view: 'The past is a foreign country: they do things differently there.' There were no overall patterns of historical development and progress since history was fragmentary and mean-ingless. The historians' group indicated the conservative political underpinnings of this approach and that the rejection of theory was in spite of itself a theoretical statement about the nature of history. The most able rebuttal of the resurgent British **empiricism** came from E.H. Carr's *What is History?* (1961). Carr, the historian of the USSR, was a non-Marxist but one clearly influenced by Marx. The historians' group was therefore able to combine its own agenda of developing Marxist historical writing with participation in contemporary historical debates, identifying allies and polemicising against the conservative trends of thought that typified the 1950s.

Writing 20 years later in a memorial volume for A.L. Morton, Eric Hobsbawm drew a balance sheet of the group's first decade. This was justifiably positive. The most obvious achievement was its contribution to the rise of social history, through history from below and what Hobsbawm called 'the social history of ideas' very much associated with Christopher Hill. The group also contributed to the modernisation of labour history and interpretations of the English revolution. These insights were disseminated through teaching, textbooks and the journal *Past and Present: A Journal of Scientific History*.[8] Hobsbawm's reminiscences also raised the two great paradoxes of the group: how did it remain so undogmatic despite the Stalinism of the communist parties of Europe, and why at the height of the group's powers should it collapse in 1956?

As has been noted before, outlining the differences between Stalinism and Marxism has been of inestimable importance to **classical Marxism**. The relationship between the two is complex when it comes to the question of many practising historians. Here, with the British Communist Party Historians' Group (and, for that matter, the French Communist Party historians of the French Revolution), it seems that the two are not incompatible. Few would deny that distinctions must be made between the brutal and cynical Russian leaders of the Communist International of the 1930s and the rank and file members who fought in good faith against fascism, marched against unemployment or unionised new industries. A similar distinction can be drawn between official history in the Soviet Union and the work of communist historians on the peripheries of the communist movement. Hobsbawm noted the specific conditions that allowed the historians' group very considerable latitude in writing Marxist history, even in Stalin's heyday. The first reason was that the study of Marx, Engels and Lenin (as well as Stalin) was encouraged. Second, genuine historical work was only impossible where it contradicted an existent Stalinist orthodoxy or in periods or subjects of political sensitivity such as the Russian Revolution or the Hitler–Stalin pact. The work of the historians' group benefited the Party in its battle of ideas. Its intellectual influence widened within the labour movement as its own historians were writing the history of the labouring people. Third, there was no official communist history of Britain which allowed considerable freedom of debate. There was no danger of writing a work that contradicted the authority of Stalin or one of his acolytes. Fourth, in the setting of Cold War anti-communism, the Historians' Group was open to fellow-travellers in the tradition of the Popular Front period of the late 1930s who had shared fields of interest. The greatest expression of this was the editorial board of *Past and Present*, whose membership expressly brought together Party members and non-Marxists. Hobsbawm explained how the academic climate encouraged this:

> Both we and the Party saw ourselves not as a sect of true believers, holding up the light amid the surrounding darkness, but ideally as leaders of a broad progressive movement such as we had experienced in the 1930s. We knew that the small group of Marxist academics was isolated. This very isolation enforced a certain unsectarianism on us, since many of our colleagues would have been only too ready to dismiss our work as dogmatic oversimplification and propagandistic jargon, had we not proved our competence as historians in ways they recognised and in language they could understand.[9]

Fifth, Hobsbawm noted a sympathy for history in the British Communist Party leadership which allowed a degree of protection and freedom for manoeuvre that might not otherwise have existed. Finally, an 'old-fashioned realism' held dogmatism at bay. The British Marxist historians, for example, had little time for the theory of absolute pauperisation (maintained by Jürgen Kuczynski and the French communists) which stated that workers were worse off in 1950 than 1850.

Having said this, there were serious exceptions to this freedom and an unconscious assimilation of some elements of Stalinism. In terms of method, a certain influence of Stalinism could be seen in attempts to frame arguments that conformed to received wisdom on questions such as absolutism and bourgeois revolution. Crucially, the historians' group could not seriously discuss the history of the Soviet Union and certain periods of the party's history were off limits, such as the third period and the Hitler–Stalin Pact. When it came to writing a history of the Communist Party of Great Britain, the Party leadership and the Historians' Group disagreed as the former wanted a history of 'the regimental variety, which maintained the spirit of the militants, especially in difficult times, by the memory of past sacrifices, heroism and glory'.[10] As a consequence, the twentieth century in general was a weak area amongst British Marxist historians and in effect broke the unity of past, present and future. These flaws were to be exposed in the events of 1956: Khrushchev's secret speech, the Polish riots and the Hungarian Revolution.

The year 1956 signalled the demise of the Communist Party Historians' Group: though it continued after that date, the real intellectual nucleus was shattered. As so often in Marxist historiography, the intimacy between the study of the past and contemporary events revealed itself. In February Nikita Khrushchev delivered a secret speech to the twentieth congress of the Communist Party of the Soviet Union that was to send the international communist movement into crisis. Khrushchev revealed and denounced the crimes of Stalin, a man who as ruler of the Soviet Union had been revered within the communist movement as an icon and source of infallible intellectual authority. These tremors only anticipated an even greater shock as Polish and Hungarian workers rose against their rulers. Only brutal suppression by Russian tanks halted the Hungarian Revolution, and events in Budapest exposed the truth behind the socialist mask of the Eastern European dictatorships. This was apparent to many on the left either in the Communist Party or sympathetic to it. Even *The Daily Worker*'s Budapest correspondent, Peter Fryer, who later went on to write important histories of black people in Britain and the British Empire, described this as a a real revolution from below.[11] It was his road to Damascus, and he was not alone. These events provoked a crisis in the British Communist Party. With their view that common people made history and their rejection of the strictures of official Soviet historical methods, this crisis was very keenly felt within the Communist Party Historians' Group. John Saville and Edward Thompson launched *The Reasoner* as a discussion forum through 'the smoke of Budapest' within the Party, which ultimately led to their departure. Soon they and many of the Historians' Group found themselves outside the Party (Hobsbawm remained), a move that effectively marked the birth of the New Left and eventually spawned the *New Left Review* and the *Socialist Register*.

This marked a fertile period in Marxist history. Freed from the constraints of Communist Party membership and suddenly aware of the need to rescue Marxism from Stalinist distortion, the work of these historians blossomed in a number of directions. *Past and Present*, now one of the pre-eminent journals of social history, began life in 1952, launched by members of the group but not restricting itself to contributions from Marxists alone. This allowed the British Marxists to engage with non-Marxist social historians (Hugh Trevor-Roper, G.R. Elton and Lawrence Stone were prominent early contributors) and the non-British Marxist historians (such as the French Marxist historians, Albert Soboul and Pierre Vilar, and the Eastern bloc historians, Porschnev, Polisensky and Klima). Thompson published his biography of William Morris in 1955 which attempted to rediscover the moral element of socialism stifled by King Street (the Communist Party headquarters). Hobsbawm also wrote *Primitive Rebels* (1959), a pioneering study of bandits, labour sects, millenarians, ritual and the labour movement which opened up new themes to Marxist social history.

▶ Christopher Hill

Christopher Hill (1912–) is one of the best known exponents of Marxist history. His work concentrates on seventeenth-century English history, the century of the English bourgeois revolution. His intellectual influences ranged from the Soviet historian, E.A. Kosminsky, to the Christian socialist historian, R.H. Tawney, and of course the members of the Communist Party Historians' Group who provided the 'greatest stimulus I have ever known'. His writings, which span seven decades, are associated with the development of history from below, or (as he put it) a 'worm's eye view' or 'upside-down' history. Much of his work rests on the exploitation of radical pamphlets and other literary sources that had previously been neglected or read in different ways. His most famous work, *The World Turned Upside Down* (1972), was based on these pamphlets which blossomed in a 20-year spell of unprecedented press liberty. When censorship returned in 1660 with the restoration of the monarchy, radical ideas were once again channelled into obscure and subterranean streams. John Morrill, a sharp critic of the Marxist account of the revolution, willingly acknowledged the originality of Christopher Hill's contribution with regard to: 'the interpenetration of religious, constitutional, social and scientific ideas; the social context of religious radicalism; the importance of "literary" sources as historical documents; the *vitality* of the English revolutionary decades'.[12]

▶ England's bourgeois revolution

For Hill, the English bourgeois revolution did not follow a course of Newtonian certainty. He rejected the unsatisfactory Tory, Whig or religious accounts. He proposed that the upheaval could be thought of as two revolutions: one bourgeois and one popular-democratic. The first established (finally, in 1688) a state apt for capitalist development, in which bourgeois property rights were enshrined, in which Parliament had decisively tamed the monarchy and the Church, and in which the Protestant ethic was triumphant and allowed the development of a far-flung commercial empire.

Christopher Hill was careful to clarify bourgeois revolution as it had been misunderstood and dismissed by non-Marxists. He was fond of quoting R.H. Tawney, who stated that of course the English Civil War was a bourgeois revolution but the trouble was that the bourgeoisie was on both sides. The revolution did not entail two distinct classes (the 'bourgeoisie' and the 'aristocracy') declaring themselves for the old order or capitalism and fighting it out; no revolution ever took this shape. There was a class dynamic to the revolution but it was much more complex than this. Previous misunderstanding partly stemmed from the fact that from the sixteenth century onwards capitalism arose on the land so that bourgeois revolution did not signal a primarily urban phenomenon: 'It is I fear necessary to emphasize the obvious point that in England early capitalism was strongest in the countryside, since many portentous refutations of Marxism are vitiated by confusion on this issue.'[13] Anyone familiar with Marx's *Capital* would be aware of this. The bourgeois revolution meant that 'the institutional restrictions on the development of capitalism had been removed'. This undertaking involved immense tasks not achieved elsewhere in Europe save the Netherlands. The Civil War resulted from the crisis of the Stuart monarchy. The revolutionary crisis could be delayed but the impediments to capitalist development were too great to be resolved by reform. The Stuarts and the interests of capitalist development, which was developing apace, were pushing in different directions over taxation, foreign policy, religion and absolutism. It was not necessary for parliamentary leaders consciously to foresee and plan the revolution. Neither did the mass of participants, particularly the radical and democratic forces of the revolution, intend its actual outcomes.

These tasks of bourgeois revolution were international in their scope: the conquest of Ireland and Scotland; a commercial policy aimed at the replacement of the Dutch as the major commercial power through the Navigation Acts and the Anglo–Dutch Wars; a strong navy as cornerstone of imperial expansion. They were also social: bourgeois property rights on the land were established with abolition of feudal tenures, the weakening of the copyhold tenants paving the way for further enclosure and clearance of the poor off the land. The power and wealth of the old regime was humbled with the taxation of the nobles to the point of ruin, the demolition of their fortresses and the expropriation of the Church, Crown, and Royalist landlords. These policies underlined the bourgeois character of the English Revolution. They could only be achieved as a result of a regime based on the army whose cost and unruliness meant that its life could not be permanent. Having crushed the popular-democratic aspect of the revolution, it had lost a possible alternative social base of support. So having irreversibly cleared the way for capitalist development, the army ultimately was forced to compromise with what was left of the old order in the shape of the restoration of the monarchy in 1660. Without an understanding of the seventeenth-century revolution, Christopher Hill argued that the British imperialist heyday, the institutions of British democracy and the British industrial prowess, were incomprehensible. Despite being criticised for lack of orthodoxy on this score by opponents of Marxism, the similarities between Marx's and Hill's conception of bourgeois revolution are striking. Writing in 1991, prompted by proclamations of the death of Marxism, Hill commented on the evolution of his views:

> So I have changed my vocabulary, but I don't think that I have shifted very far from my main 'Marxist' point about 17th century England. I still think that the events between 1640 and 1660 are aptly described as a revolution, since they led to vast changes in the history of England and of the world. England in the early 17th century was a third rate power. Governments of the old regime were both financially unable and politically unwilling, to support the expansion of English trade, in the Far East, the Mediterranean, or in America . . . It is absurd to say as some historians do, that this transformation could have happened without revolution. The new policy necessitated heavy taxation; before 1640 crown and parliament had failed to agree on reorganisation of finance because they could not agree on foreign policy. If parliament voted money for its sort of war, the king spent it on another. After 1660 parliament voted limitless supplies for the navy, none for a standing army, which might threaten a restoration of absolutism.[14]

▶ 'The revolt within the revolution'

The popular-democratic revolution was the radical undercurrent of mid-century, which sought to transcend the limits of bourgeois rule with far wider democratic and communal property rights for the poor. Hill's research has concentrated on this element: the Leveller radicals in the New Model Army, the religious sects of Diggers, Ranters, and Quakers. With traditional authority in flux, the revolution allowed a 'teeming freedom' in which ordinary people eloquently and dramatically found their own voice:

> For a short time, ordinary people were freer from the authority of church and social superiors than they had ever been before, or were for a long time to be again. By great fortune we have a pretty full record of what they discussed. They speculated about the end of the world and the coming millennium; about the justice of God in condemning the mass of mankind to eternal torment for a sin which (if anyone) Adam committed; some of them became sceptical about the existence of hell. They contemplated that God might intend to save everybody, that something of God might be within each of us. They founded new sects to express these new ideas. Some considered the possibility that there might be no Creator God, only nature. They attacked the monopolization of knowledge within the privileged professions, divinity, law, medicine. They criticized the existing educational structure, especially the universities, and proposed a vast expansion of educational opportunity. They discussed the relations of the sexes, and questioned parts of the protestant ethic.[15]

For Hill, the bourgeois and popular democratic aspects of the revolution signified that the outcome might have been different. His account of bourgeois revolution is far from deterministic. The different class elements fused together in varying combinations. Popular agitation in 1640 accelerated the war, regicide brought the radical phase to its apogee, restoration consolidated much of what had changed, and the Glorious Revolution of 1688 finally stabilised the state. Revolutions witness the unstable ebbs and flows of mass psychology, cycles of hope and despair mobilising or sapping the energies of the people. Hill's tremendous skill was to listen to the hubbub of the world of ideas and gauge the sensitive adjustments of popular consciousness. Great and minor poets, scientists, historians, dramatists, political pamphleteers and religious leaders were caught up in the emotional turmoil of their age. The adroit deployment of their words allowed his work to reverberate to sounds of the revolution. Who could better express its meaning than Gerrard Winstanley, who observed, 'the old world ... is running up like a parchment in the fire'?[16] In *The Intellectual Origins of the English Revolution* (1965), Christopher Hill showed how Sir Walter Raleigh, as political theorist and historian, and Sir Francis Bacon, as empiricist and scientist, and Sir Edward Coke, on the law, together set a critical and questioning tone during Stuart rule.[17]

His studies of the revolutionary decades drew on the array of religious congregational Puritan sects and strands, the Fifth Monarchists, the Diggers, the Ranters, the Muggletonians, the Quakers. He returned to these groups on many occasions. Previously ignored and still dismissed by conservative historians as 'cranks, screwballs and fanatics, the nutters and kooks', they were not for him a lunatic fringe but men and women attempting to grapple with the world through the religious idioms of their time.[18] Hill also charted the individual trajectories of such leaders as Gerrard Winstanley of the Digger communities who espoused a rural communism and free love, and James Nayler who, believing the millennium at hand, imitated Christ by riding into Bristol on a donkey in 1656. In *The Experience of Defeat*, he pointed out that none could escape the grim logic of defeat in which hopes died, horizons narrowed or temporal interventions were physically destroyed (as with the Digger communities) or sublimated to an inner spiritualism and pacifism (as with the Quakers). Nobody articulated this melancholy more poignantly than the poet, John Milton, whom Hill considered at length in *The Experience of Defeat* (1984) and *Milton and the English Revolution* (1977).

In *The Intellectual Consequences of the English Revolution* (1980), Hill examined the Restoration of the Stuart monarchy as a particular moment of intellectual reaction that even threatened scientific inquiry itself, which was equated with 'enthusiasm' and 'fanaticism'. The bishops, professions and Oxford and Cambridge were restored in the intellectual settlement of 1660. Science was safely channelled by the Royal Society, headed by Sir Isaac Newton. The great physicist's public 'abstract, empty, unfriendly mathematical universe' reflected the depersonalised market-based commercialism, despite the fact that in private he continued the millenarian project of attempting to calculate the Second Coming. In like fashion, John Locke's contractual view of government and the sanctity of property rights also articulated the spirit of the restoration and bourgeois order. The intellectual synthesis of Locke and Newton 'contributed to a shift in political thinking, from the past to the future, from the hereditary principle which had dominated in a relatively static agrarian society to the atomic individualism and contractualism more appropriate to a mobile and expansive economy'.[19]

Despite the radicals' decisive defeats, England's revolutionary past was relevant, according to Christopher Hill, because of the continuities of an authentically English tradition of radicalism. Ideas of Lollardy and the Peasants' Revolt, that had resurfaced during the Reformation, emerged once more in the Civil War and interregnum, and once again saw the light of day in the radicalism of the period after 1790. The 'World Turned Upside Down' exemplified this tenuous but real thread of continuity. This was the title of a broadside ballad of the Civil War, which was purportedly popular in eighteenth-century plebeian culture and was sung at the surrender of Cornwallis's British forces by American revolutionaries at Yorktown in 1781. The Shakers, the radical sect with its origins amongst the poor of Lancashire, adopted the phrase as they attempted to spread their message to the Americas. Tom Spence, the English Jacobin, wrote a pamphlet of the same name in 1805. The title had a further significance:

> Upside down is after all a relative concept. The assumption that it means the wrong way up is itself an expression of the view from the top ... We may be too con-ditioned by the way up the world has been for the last three hundred years to be fair to those in the seventeenth century who saw other possibilities. But we should try.[20]

The neglect of the losers and the historical emphasis on the victors of the seventeenth-century upheavals have ingrained into us the idea that the world is the right way up. Hill highlighted the strikingly modern elements of the thoughts of these radicals and asked whether it is not the world of the class system, the sanctification of private property and the straitlaced morality of Protestant ethic, that is the inverted, the irrational world. For Hill, the seventeenth century has much to teach us in our day. The democratic vision of representatives of the army Levellers who, in the Putney debates of 1649, believed that 'the poorest that lives hath as true a right to give a vote ... as the richest and greatest' took several centuries to achieve. For this English Marxist, no doubt told repeatedly how his creed was a foreign invention, writing at the very moment when Europe collapsed into the barbarities of the Second World War, the words of Gerrard Winstanley had a striking pertinence: 'Property ... divides the whole world into parties, and is the cause of all the wars and bloodshed and contention is everywhere. When the earth becomes a common treasury again, as it must, ... then this enmity will cease.'[21]

Looking back over the decades, Christopher Hill's work embodies a range of genres and analyses that is difficult to find in any other Marxist historian. With unconventional biographies of Cromwell, Bunyan and Milton, standard chronological textbooks, intriguing thematic investigations of *The Bible and the Seventeenth Century Revolution* (1993) and *The Anti-Christ in Seventeenth Century England* (1971) to his credit, it would be wrong to sort Hill into a particular category of history, even the 'history from below' to which he contributed so much. In particular, his dialogue with seventeenth-century literature and literary criticism is a model of the fruitful relationship that can be struck between disciplines when not corrupted by the aggrandisement of postmodernist literary specialists. For all Hill's formulation of bourgeois revolution and his ease in articulating the class character of events, movements and ideas, he does not neglect the need to take individuals and their ideas, intentions and hopes seriously. Indeed, he is able to present more convincing characters because he is aware of the social forces of the revolution. Individuals do not react to revolutions in uniform ways, but revolutions impinge inescapably on their lives. At the height of his influence in the 1960s and early 1970s, the seventeenth century was described (with some exaggeration) as his century. But from the late 1970s there has been an increasing questioning of Hill's and the Marxist interpretation. This revisionism has taken a variety of forms which Christopher Hill in his essays and later books has taken to task. The ferocity of the attack that Hill has on occasions been subjected to represents an unwitting tribute and a thinly veiled anti-Marxism.[22] The importance of the English revolution, the very term itself, let alone the notion of a bourgeois revolution, has been called into question. For the most ardent revisionists, the origins of the English Civil War resulted from misunderstandings and accident, and the consequences were minimal. Others would prefer to distinguish between two Christopher Hills, the early Marxist polemicist and the later scholarly Master of Balliol College. Yet in his essentials, Christopher Hill remained true and pretty consistent to his Marxism. Early on he worried about R.H. Tawney, thinking that he slipped at times into wooden Marxist jargon. Whereas he may, in all good faith, have sung the praises of Lysenko – Stalin's favourite distorter of science – in 1951, he split from the Communist Party in 1957. He, like E.P. Thompson, may have rejected the notion of **base and superstructure** as schematic but he could still demonstrate that 'Environment is more important than heredity in the evolution of ideas.'[23] In 1940, 1972 and 1991 alike, he could observe that we have much to learn from the revolution of the seventeenth century.

▶ E.P. Thompson

E.P. Thompson (1924–93) is the best known of the British Marxist historians. His most celebrated work, *The Making of the English Working Class* (1963), advanced a bold new thesis about the formation of the working class. He argued that between 1780 and 1832 the English labouring poor felt that they had shared interests, a common identity, and that these interests were antagonistic to the ruling class, which in turn became more cohesive largely as a result of the threat from below. This epoch witnessed the working class consciously form themselves into a class, and by the period's end they were the most significant aspect of British politics. *The Making of the English Working Class* was the most powerful expression of the gathering school of Marxist history, which took issue with the mechanistic traditions of official communist versions of history, looking ordinary people in the face as participants and makers of history. This celebrated passage in the preface to *The Making of the English Working Class* read like a call to arms of a new Marxist history:

> I am seeking to rescue the poor stockinger, the Luddite cropper, the 'obsolete' hand-loom weaver, the 'utopian' artisan, and even the deluded follower of Joanna Southcott, from the enormous condescension of posterity. Their crafts and traditions may have been dying. Their hostility to the new industrialism may have been backward-looking. Their communitarian ideas may have been fantasies. Their insurrectionary conspiracies may have been foolhardy. But they lived through these times of acute social disturbance, and we did not. Their aspirations were valid in terms of their own experience; and if they were casualties of history, they remain, condemned in their own lives, as casualties.[24]

'History from below' or 'from the bottom up' became one of the most important contributions to the development of history since the Second World War. Harvey Kaye described *The Making of the English Working Class* as the 'most influential work of social history ever written'.[25] Thompson wove together his sources and narrative, and with each turn of the page, new witnesses testified: the middle-class observers, romantic poets, the moralising church leaders and the working-class radicals themselves. The book evoked an authentic feel for the period and rang with the voice of the exploited. Thompson set new empirical standards for Marxist history but successfully avoided what he considered the anathema of academic empiricism. Many of his passages reflected his deep political passions and sympathies with the oppressed as well as a flowing literary style that revealed he had, like Marx, a love of poetry.

Thompson's volume entailed a particular and controversial vision of **class**. Like Lukács, the preface outlined the view that class was not an inert thing, a nominal category or an objective structure, but a real historical process of human relationships: 'The real relationship must be embodied in real people in a real context ... We cannot have love without lovers, nor deference without squires and labourers.'[26] He took issue with the dominant views of class of bourgeois sociologists and Soviet historians. At that time structural-functionalism dominated Western academic sociology and its views of class, according to which class derived from the social function of the individual. Western economic historians were preoccupied with narrow economic definitions of class and their statistical quantification. The Stalinist view of class also neglected the question of class consciousness as an aspect of class formation. When Soviet historians discussed class consciousness it was in purely objective and economic terms; workers arrived automatically at self-awareness. In sharp contrast, Marx, Engels, Trotsky, Lukács and Gramsci, as we have seen, all found ways of expressing the dialectical character of class by combining a common objective position in the process of production and exploitation, and the subjective or psychological self-awareness of common interests. Thompson found his own way of expressing this classical Marxist combination:

> The class experience is largely determined by the productive relations into which men are born – or enter involuntarily. Class-consciousness is the way in which these experiences are handled in cultural terms: embodied in traditions, value-systems, ideas, and institutional forms. If the experience appears as determined, class-consciousness does not.[27]

Intensified and more transparent exploitation set the scene for working-class formation. In the countryside, with enclosures and the loss of common rights, the tenant farmer, the Church and the landowner exploited and impoverished the rural labourer. In the domestic industries, the merchants became richer and their operations increased in scale, whilst the outworkers were reduced to wage dependency. In the new factories and the mines, the employers' wealth grew visibly as their workforce (which included large numbers of children) was subjected to the rigours of industrial production. 'All contributed to the transparency of the process of exploitation and to the social and cultural cohesion of the exploited.'[28]

Culture, for Thompson, was therefore a key constitutive element of the working class and this was reflected in the dazzling breadth of Thompson's study, which encompassed the influence of John Wesley and Robert Owen, Westminster and Luddism. Class consciousness entailed a cultural superstructure which lagged behind the objective situation and interests of class. In this sense, consciousness could emerge in many different forms and in changing degrees of fullness.

The Making of the English Working Class certainly attracted criticism. Some disputed his attitude towards Methodist revivalism, which he described as the 'chiliasm of despair', drawing its power from an era of revolutionary and counter-revolutionary energies. Others took issue with his account of Luddism, or his attitude to the standard of living debate: that is, the benign or catastrophic impact of the Industrial Revolution on the working population. Thompson was also taken to task for anticipating the creation of the working class which others saw as taking shape not amongst his outworkers and artisans but amongst the factory workers after 1832, or even later. As time has passed and the shape of social history has changed, Thompson's underestimation of women in class formation has been challenged, an error he subsequently confessed.[29]

Perhaps most importantly this book initiated an argument amongst the New Left over the direction of Marxism itself. Perry Anderson and Tom Nairn criticised the exaggeration of the role of the working class and its culture. They believed that the English working class was a passive force ill-prepared for revolutionary struggles because of the distance between this class and the English bourgeois revolution. In contrast, E.P. Thompson underlined the authentic revolutionary past of the English working class. Chapter 6 deals with these disagreements in greater depth.

▶ Eighteenth-century English culture

After writing *The Making of the English Working Class*, E.P. Thompson's attentions turned to the eighteenth century. The fruits of this research appeared in *Whigs and Hunters* (1975) and in a number of essays brought together in *Customs in Common* (1991). *Whigs and Hunters* examined the repressive Black Act of 1723 which extended the death penalty to the offences of the 'blacks', the face-blackened poachers of the forests. Thompson illuminated life in the Windsor and Hampshire forests: the nocturnal activities of the blacks, their anonymous threats to opponents, the claim and counter-claim of rights to the commons and forests, the battles between poachers and gamekeepers. He detailed the intervention of the law into these activities and its ultimate sanction: the sheer terrorism and theatricality of the hanging judge, the executioner and gallows. *Whigs and Hunters* opened new perspectives on the eighteenth century, demonstrating the way in which the Hanoverian Whigs used the law to terrorise the poor and to maintain the enormous flow of wealth into the hands of the rich oligarchs atop English society. Thompson challenged the complacent liberal view that the eighteenth century was a time of deference, consensus and the impartial exercise of law. But he also criticised Marxists for trivialising such episodes and dismissing the rule of law as just an ideological disguise and an instrument for the interests of the ruling class. It was that and more. Law was able to become the most important aspect of **hegemony** in the eighteenth century, displacing religious or royal authority, precisely because it was open to the ruled as well as the rulers, even if the courts were stacked in the favour of the latter. Nevertheless, the existence of the rule of law instead of arbitrary power imposed limits upon the activities and power of the ruling class and gave that class a measure of legitimacy which stabilised the rule of the men of property:

> The hegemony ... was expressed, above all, not in military force, not in the
> mystifications of a priesthood or of the press, not even in economic coercion, but in

the rituals of the study of the Justices of the Peace, in the quarter-sessions, in the pomp of the Assizes and in the theatre of Tyburn.[30]

Thompson also observed base and superstructure through the prism of the law. If law was part of the superstructure, as in the usual Marxist accounts, then it should be distinct from both production and the productive relations. Historical evidence suggested otherwise. Neither in formal rules and procedures of jurisprudence nor as an ideology was the law aloof from the world of daily toil, or 'the base' according to the troubled metaphor. The legal codification of property and use rights delineated the very productive relations themselves and as such percolated throughout every level of society: 'Productive relations themselves are, in part, only meaningful in terms of their definitions at law: the serf, the free labourer; the cottager with rights, the inhabitant without; the unfree proletarian, the picket conscious of his rights; the landless labourer who may sue his employer for assault.'[31]

In *Customs in Common*, Thompson's general thesis about the eighteenth century proposed an increasing cultural estrangement between the poor and their rulers, between **plebs** and **patricians**, which articulated itself through a robust plebeian culture of defensive customs. These essays revealed vivid episodes, customs and experiences: food riots in which grain was seized and sold at a fair price within the framework of a **moral economy**, the ritualised public shaming or rough music used to enforce accepted norms of behaviour, and wives sold as a plebeian form of divorce. 'The moral economy of the crowd' and 'Time, work-discipline and industrial capitalism' were written in the 1960s and had been influential in challenging the narrowness of economic history and the institutional fetishes of labour history. *Customs in Common* was able to do this because it engaged in a sustained dialogue with folklore and anthropology. Some of his sources had been preserved by the nineteenth-century antiquarians and folklorists who had recovered individual local practices. But the folklorist approach failed to recognise the broad implications of their discoveries. For Thompson, custom was a general **mentality** and ambience, and had a pivotal significance for eighteenth-century social history. Many customs had rational communal functions. They were at times retained by popular pressure and at others they were methods of protest. The plebeian culture of custom was fluid, contradictory and not consensual; it clashed with the innovations of the market culture or mentality. Traditional or customary rights were often invented or asserted anew in the face of waning paternalistic protection and menacing economic change (enclosure, work discipline, or free-market food prices). Here Thompson developed his distinctive synthesis of cultural history and class struggle analysis through which this work was able to reconsider the accepted view of the eighteenth century as an era of social stability and order.

Thompson embraced the language and approach of the **Annales** school to cultural history, with the influence of anthropology and the concept of mentality apparent in his work. He explicitly rejected the approach to culture that sees historical individuals and communities as being prisoners of their own language and cultural traditions. In this respect, he explicitly challenged the trend towards postmodernism in social history:

> In these studies I hope that plebeian culture becomes a more concrete and usable concept, no longer situated in the thin air of 'meanings, attitudes and values', but located within a particular equilibrium of social relations, a working environment of exploitation and resistance to exploitation, of relations of power which are masked by rituals of paternalism and deference. In this way (I hope) 'popular culture' is situated in its proper material abode.[32]

▶ Thompson's wider impact

Thompson's most direct influence can be seen on his students, particularly those he attracted during his time at the Centre for the Study of Social History at the University of Warwick (1965–70). These endeavours bore fruit in *Albion's Fatal Tree: Crime and Society in Eighteenth Century England* (1975) with Thompson, Douglas Hay, Cal Winslow, John Rule and Peter Linebaugh as contributors. In the year of Thompson's death, an edited collection dedicated to him included essays from P. Searby, J.M. Neeson, Alec Morley, Victor Bailey, Sheila Rowbotham, Leon Fink, Barbara Winslow and Robert Malcolmson, together with the *Albion's Fatal Tree* contributors; all (with the exception of Sheila Rowbotham) were at one time his students. Several of his students went on to write on themes they had broached under Thompson's tutelage. Such works as John Rule's *Labouring Classes* (1986) and *Albion's People* (1996) and Peter Linebaugh's *The London Hanged* (1985) have commanded the highest respect within social history. *The London Hanged* continued examinations of eighteenth-century crime as an aspect of class relations. With mastery of neglected judicial records of London hangings in the west of the city, Linebaugh constructed the case that Tyburn Tree was 'the central event in the urban contention between classes, and indeed [was] meant to be so'.[33] Developing capitalist relations and crime shaped one another in Europe's most advanced centre of commercial and financial capitalism: 'First ... the forms of exploitation pertaining to capitalist relations caused or modified the forms of criminal activity, and, second, the converse was true, namely, that the forms of crime caused major changes in capitalism.'[34]

Thompson's personal impact went well beyond his graduate students at Warwick. In the USA, a few significant historians followed Thompson's lead. Herbert Gutman's *The Black Family in Slavery and Freedom 1750–1925* (1976) shared Thompson's attitude to class, the importance he accorded to 'experience' and his attention to culture. His introduction paralleled the famous stockinger passage of Thompson.

This is a book about ordinary black men, women and children mostly before the general emancipation but after that time, too – a study of enslaved Afro-Americans, their children and grandchildren, how they adapted to enslavement by developing distinctive domestic arrangements and kin networks that nurtured a new Afro-American culture, and how these, in turn, formed the social basis of developing Afro-American communities, which prepared the slaves to deal with legal freedom. This book is also about poor Americans, nonwhites who spent a good proportion of their American experience enslaved. It is therefore concerned with a special aspect of American labor history: those men and women who labored first in bondage and then mostly as half-free rural workers ... Only bits and pieces of their individual histories survive, fragmentary clues about who these ... people were and what they believed. Our concern is with what sustained and nurtured their beliefs and behavior. Nothing more.[35]

Eugene Genovese also adopted a series of like-minded positions to Thompson. His attitude to class is very similar, as is his utilisation of hegemony and paternalism, which Thompson developed from Gramsci:

The idea of 'hegemony', which since Gramsci has become central to Western Marxism, implies class antagonisms; but it also implies, for a given historical epoch, the ability of a particular class to contain those antagonisms on a terrain in which its legitimacy is not dangerously questioned.[36]

Genovese also concurred with Thompson on the obsolescence of base and superstructure:

Thus, the fashionable relegation of law to the rank of a superstructural and derivative phenomenon obscures the degree of autonomy it creates for itself. In modern societies, at least, the theoretical and moral foundations of the legal order and the actual, specific history of its ideas and institutions influence, step by step, the wider social order and system of class rule, for no class in the modern Western world could rule for long without some ability to present itself as the guardian of the interests and sentiments of those being ruled.[37]

This marriage of Thompson and Gramsci continues in the work of Genovese, who used the Gramscian notion of the split consciousness of the oppressed. In Genovese's case, this meant the acceptance of the condition of subjection as well as a hostile resistance to it in black slave America:

The everyday instances in which 'docile' slaves suddenly rebelled and 'kind' masters suddenly behaved like wild beasts had their origins, apart from the frequent instabilities in the participating personalities, in this dialectic. Master and slave had both 'agreed' on the paternalistic basis of their relationship, the one from reasons of self-aggrandisement and the other from lack of an alternative. But they understood very different things by their apparently common assent.[38]

In the late 1970s, several Indian historians enthusiastically embraced E.P. Thompson's approach to social history. As well as the fame of *The Making of the English Working Class*, this influence stemmed from various elements of Thompson's account of eighteenth-century England that were particularly suggestive for Indian comparison. First, the moral economy of the crowd, which revealed how riots took place within the framework of a broad customary morality, promised a general intellectual framework for the disjointed, geographically scattered and seemingly irrational episodes of peasant and labour protests in India before independence. Second, 'class struggle without class' opened the possibility of understanding conflict in a society in which the working class had not achieved 'maturity' and where ties of religion, caste and kinship remained pervasive. The scholars who adopted Thompsonian assumptions launched a journal, *Subaltern Studies*, in 1981 (subaltern classes – meaning of inferior rank – is Gramsci's term for the oppressed social groups in his *Prison Notebooks*). Because of their concern with explaining anti-imperial resistance, the Subaltern scholars found a resonance amongst Latin American and African scholars and provided one element within **post-colonial studies**. Subaltern scholars in India imported a Thompson that suited their requirements, leaving out certain crucial features of Thompson's own approach. Like Thompson they emphasised the cultural dimension but, unlike him, did this at the expense of the state and the economy. Central to the explanation in Dipesh Chakrabarty's *Rethinking Working Class History: Bengal 1890–1940* (1989) of the immature character of the Indian working class was the persistent trace of peasant culture on the urban working class: 'a precapitalist, inegalitarian culture marked by strong primordial loyalties of community, language, religion, caste and kinship'.[39] Chakrabarty equated capitalism with its cultural manifestations of eighteenth-century England, and not with its productive relations. Consequently, the Indian working class bore the imprint of precapitalist *culture* as they had not come into contact with the capitalist culture of Locke and Smith, together with their ideas, such as equality before the law, natural rights and individualism.

In addition, Subaltern historians explained the legacy of peasant culture in terms of orientalism. This notion is appropriated from Edward Said's *Orientalism* (1985) which proposed that the West's representations of the East, namely colonial discourse, trapped and subjugated the Middle East and Asia in a self-reproducing language of victimisation and backwardness.[40] Through Said, this preoccupation with popular culture evolved into an emphasis on language, on discourse and on text. From a Thompsonian starting point, *Subaltern Studies* drifted towards postmodernism with its growing concern with colonial discourse.[41] This further reinforced the interpretation of Indian peasants and workers as fragmentary, highly differentiated and culturally exceptional. From this perspective, the key question became the nuance and plural character of identity and the local subversion of colonial discourse. In spite of its beginnings, *Subaltern Studies'* prioritisation of texts shifted the gravitational centre of research towards the Indian educated elite: that is, a return to the preoccupations of nationalist social history before the advent of the Subaltern approach. One critic described this full circle turned in the historiography:

> As Subaltern scholars attempted to assert and claim difference, they have tended to re-affirm the assumptions about the culturally specific, unique and exceptional character of Indian society. As a result, they have sometimes been led to restore some of the fondest shibboleths of colonial ideologues – for instance, about the propensity of the working classes to violence, their susceptibility to rumour, the paternalism of the expatriate capitalist and the filial deference to their employees or the centrality of religion to their political consciousness.[42]

▶ Conclusion

History from below widened the scope of history to the hidden realms of the defeated and oppressed in history. The British Marxist historians have collectively made a telling contribution to Western Marxism and to the writing of social history in general. They engaged with other major schools of history, such as the empiricists, the conservative economic historians, the Annales school and later with postmodernism. The overwhelming focus on Thompson in academia can often obscure the breadth of this achievement. Having said that, Thompson stood out as the most influential of these historians for a number of reasons. His conceptual innovations – the moral economy of the crowd, the new light of experience on labour history, class struggle without class, the importance of custom – were all highly suggestive to other scholars. The boldness of Thompson's reformulation of class and historical materialism also made him the subject of criticism in particular from the **structuralist** Marxists who are discussed in the next chapter. Though history from below opened up new avenues of historical inquiry, past a certain point there was the danger exhibited by some of its practitioners that its vision remained narrowly fixated on the bottom of society and thus drifted away from Marx's holistic and dynamic approach to history. This in part explains the sense of loss of momentum and stalemate amongst some Marxist historians in the past couple of decades.

6 Marxism, Structuralism and Humanism

'Marxism, as a theoretical and political practice, gains nothing from its association with historical writing and historical research. The study of history is not only scientifically but also politically valueless. The object of history, the past, no matter how it is conceived, cannot affect present conditions. Historical events do not exist and can have no material effectivity in the present. The conditions of existence of present social relations necessarily exist in and are constantly reproduced in the present.'

B. Hindess and P. Hirst, *Pre-Capitalist Modes of Production* (1975)[1]

'Economists explain how production takes place ... but what they do not explain is how these relations themselves are produced, that is the historical movement which gave them birth, M. Proudhon, taking these relations for principles, categories, abstract thoughts, has merely to put into order these thoughts, which are to be found alphabetically arranged at the end of every treatise on political economy. The economist's material is the active, energetic life of man; M. Proudhon's material is the dogmas of economists. But the moment we cease to pursue the historical movement of production relations, of which the categories are but the theoretical expression, the moment we want to see in these categories no more than ideas, spontaneous thoughts, independent of real relations, we are forced to attribute the origins of these thoughts to the movement of pure reason.'

K. Marx, *The Poverty of Philosophy* (1847)

If, for Marxist history, the 1950s and 1960s might be seen as a heroic age of discovery, the 1970s brought more uncertainty and less coherence to the project. Partly, Marxist history had become victim of its own success. Large numbers of academics were drawn under its influence and the tight spirit of comradeship and a common past in the CPHG no longer ensured the cohesion that it formerly did. Events of the late 1960s had radicalised a generation of students who enthusiastically took up **history from below** but also transcended it. Naturally enough, areas of inquiry widened and history from below helped to spawn new types of history: women's history, gay history and the history of sexuality, cultural history and historical sociology. In some cases Marxists were at the forefront of these new histories as with Sheila Rowbotham's *Hidden from History* (1973), Tim Mason's work on women in Nazi Germany and Marian Ramelson's *Petticoat Rebellion* (1967). In others these developments emerged via a sharp rupture with Marxism: for instance, Michel Foucault's *History of Sexuality* (1976). Some of these areas potentially reinforced Marxism but some discarded it, searching for alternative attitudes towards knowledge, social totalities and power. These fragmentary forces grew ever stronger as the character of the New Left – increasingly constituted in the late 1960s by specific social movements (the women's liberation movement, the gay liberation movement, the black movement and the student movement) – had intellectual consequences. So even before the ideological climate changed in the mid- to late 1970s with the growing confidence of the New Right, Marxist history was facing a serious external challenge.

▶ Structuralism and Marxist history

In these circumstances, deeply rooted divisions within British Marxism took on a more overt and bitter character. After 1956, with the emergence of the New Left, it had became apparent that substantive internal disagreements existed. These tensions were revealed within the editorial board of the *New Left Review*, which E.P. Thompson left in 1962. The disagreement marked a divergence in their approaches to history. Broadly speaking, there were two positions – history from below and **structuralist** Marxism – which over time parted company. These frictions took two forms. First, there was theory. Here, **Althusserians** formulated a critique of the **'humanism'** of history from below, provoking the counter-thrust that Althusserianism's neglect of human agency and disdain for history were a rationalisation of Stalinism. Althusser himself famously described history as a process without a subject and said that people were merely the 'bearers' of structures, namely unconscious agents of forces beyond their will. The Althusserian approach to history culminated in Hindess and Hirst's *Pre-Capitalist Modes of Production* (1975). Second, disagreements took place in the field of British history. On this terrain, Thompson engaged in a polemic against Perry Anderson and Tom Nairn's structural interpretation. Anderson and Nairn argued that the crisis of British capitalism and the political weakness of the British working class stemmed from the incompleteness of the bourgeois revolution. These faultlines among the historians of the New Left persisted for two decades, finally erupting in 1978 with the publication of *The Poverty of Theory* (1978).

From the 1950s, a variety of structuralisms had spread throughout the social sciences. Ferdinand de Saussure's influence in linguistics, Levi-Strauss in anthropology and Talcott Parsons (1902–79) in sociology reflected this growing belief that particular ascertainable forces shaped or structured human society and behaviour. As Marx combined structure and **agency** (or, as he was apt to put it, freedom and necessity), there was scope to extract a one-sided interpretation stressing structure over agency. Althusser's method was to select diligently those elements of Marx that could be read in a structuralist manner, to discard those large parts of Marx that celebrated human agency and to invent conclusions through listening to 'his silences'. In this manner, Althusser proposed that Marx underwent an 'epistemological break', a rite of passage between the young humanist Marx and the mature structuralist one. Only a highly selective reading of Marx and the repudiation of Engels allowed this distinction. In Althusser's version of Marxism, men did not make history, they were not the dramatists of their own emancipation, they were not the active subject of history: instead, they were simply extras, the unconscious 'bearers of structures' in 'a process without a subject'. Althusser opposed economic determinism (and, for that matter, **base and superstructure**), offering a model of a **mode of production** as composed of different, relatively autonomous, levels or instances, such as politics, economics, ideology and so on. Adapting Engels, the autonomy of these levels was conditioned by the economic only 'in the last instance' (if at all, as he stated that that moment in actuality never arrived). Althusser's notion of ideology relied almost exclusively on false consciousness and state ideological domination. The implications were an ahistorical condition in which the state chloroformed the working class or other oppressed classes through false consciousness. This static top-down view of the realm of ideas was of little use to historians concerned with explaining the complex ways in which consciousness changed through processes of collaboration and resistance. As a consequence, Gramsci and Lukács have provided much more fertile ground on which to understand the consciousness of the oppressed or ideas more generally.

In the early 1970s, Althusser was at the height of his international influence with numerous acolytes plying a similar trade. Nicos Poulantzas, the Greek Althusserian, employed such an approach in *Political Power and Social Classes* (1973). His theorisings led him to the highly contentious conclusion that absolutism combined a feudal economic level with a capitalist political state level. Hindess and Hirst's *Pre-Capitalist Modes of Production* was the most ambitious and radical exposition of British Althusserianism. Its subject was the historical modes of production that Marx outlined in his various writings: primitive communism, the ancient mode of production, the **Asiatic mode of production** and feudalism. In line with the philosophical approach of Althusser, the authors tackled modes of production from a purely abstract and theoretical perspective, with the aim of clarifying these by discussing various concepts in Marx's theory. The aim was to prove the internal coherence of Marx's categories or, in the case of the Asiatic mode of production, to prove that the internal inconsistencies rendered this a flawed concept. According to the Althusserians, this idealist method constituted a science, a scientific means of producing knowledge. They explicitly rejected historical proof, namely testing these modes of production against historical experience or the historical facts. This, they claimed, reduced Marxist theory to **empiricist** historical method. They went further, arguing that the procedures that historians – Marxist ones included – normally adopted were useless and misconceived. Because historians relied on 'given' facts they were necessarily empiricists and they laboured under the illusion that they could retrieve the object of their study. Instead, facts were not given but produced: they were representations of the past: 'And yet, by definition, all that is past does not exist. To be accurate the object of history is whatever is *represented* as having hitherto existed. The essence of this representation is preserved records and documents ... The real object is accessible *through* its representations.'[2]

History was futile. All that was left was the intricate theoretical procedures that Althusser pioneered to elaborate and validate modes of production. Given that *Pre-Capitalist Modes of Production* had done this, even the Althusserian new science of history seemed at a dead end. These positions incurred the wrath of Thompson and the debate around the future of Marxist history polarised around these questions. There is much here that **poststructuralists** inherited from their structuralist forebears. For example, Hindess and Hirst could say:

> Far from working on the *past*, the ostensible object of history, historical knowledge works on a body of *texts*. These texts are a product of historical knowledge. The writing of history is the production of texts which interpret these texts. The limitations of history are widely recognised, not least by sceptical historians. History is a potentially infinite text, constantly doubling back on itself, constantly being re-written.[3]

In contrast to the abstract and ahistorical Althusserian theorists, others sought to practise history from a structuralist perspective. What distinguished them from those who adopted the history from below perspective was that they placed much greater emphasis upon the structural dimensions of historical change. Where Christopher Hill underlined the efforts of millenarians, Perry Anderson focused on evolving state structures. In these works there was much greater explicit attention paid to Marxist concepts such as modes of production, absolutism and **exploitation**. Indeed, the extreme incompatibilities of the abstract anti-history of the theorists with history from below is not so certain when it comes to this second group of structuralists. Even defining this second group is difficult.

Indeed, within this second category the broadest definition of structuralism might include such a wide spectrum of historians as G. De Ste Croix, Guy Bois, Geoff Eley and David Blackbourn, Arno J. Mayer, Perry Anderson, Peter Kreidte, Hans Medick, Chris Wickham and even some of the writings of Eric Hobsbawm and Rodney Hilton. All of these authors place much greater emphasis on long-term structural development and would reject parts of the Thompsonian approach to class, science or base–superstructure.

One of the key concerns of these historians is to tackle the question of the long-run development of particular societies or modes of production. Geoffrey De Ste Croix sought to conceptualise and explain the dynamics of the ancient Greek and Roman society – the ancient mode of production – which was based on slavery. Within these structural constraints, the class struggle takes distinctive forms and these societies have their own pattern of development and collapse. Guy Bois and Rodney Hilton similarly examined European feudalism, or what Marx would have called its 'laws of motion'. Both were concerned with the long-run pattern of origins, development and crisis of the feudal system. But these concerns were not necessarily incompatible with examining the struggles of the oppressed as Hilton's brilliant work on peasant revolts demonstrated. Geoff Eley and David Blackbourn examined the complexity of modern Germany's structural development in *The Peculiarities of German History* (1984).[4]

The relationship between the aristocracy and the bourgeoisie in Britain and Europe from the seventeenth century to the present has been a recurrent controversy and interest for historians of a long-run or structuralist persuasion. In 1964, Perry Anderson's 'Origins of the present crisis', written for the *New Left Review*, established the bold thesis that because of the immature development of British capitalism at the time of the English Civil War, the **bourgeois revolution** was incomplete. This article spurred a series of others by himself and Tom Nairn, and the Nairn–Anderson thesis was born. The 'supine' bourgeoisie deferred to the aristocracy and the easily 'subordinated' working class had no memory of the experiences of bourgeois revolution. The particular repercussions were the intellectual poverty of English ideology with its empiricism and traditionalism, the non-revolutionary character of the British working class, the dominance of the City of London over manufacturing industry and the antiquated character of the constitution. In short, the flawed British pattern of development explained its twentieth-century decline. This structuralist interpretation gained wide currency on the emerging New Left and was extended by others, such as Barrington Moore Jr and Arno J. Mayer, to Europe.

▶ Thompson's critique of structuralism

Edward Thompson's 'Peculiarities of the English', a polemic against the Nairn–Anderson thesis, appeared in *Socialist Register* in 1965. He criticised the schematic view of the English Civil War as an inadequate bourgeois revolution. In Thompson's view, Anderson failed to appreciate the crucial agrarian aspect of capitalist development from the fifteenth century. The bourgeoisie were not subordinated to a feudal aristocracy, for in many parts of the realm the great landowners had become big capitalists. Tension between manufacturers and aristocrats in the eighteenth century and early nineteenth century was not an antagonism between aristocrat and bourgeois but between big and petty capital, in particular against those with the greatest access to royal and parliamentary patronage: according to the parlance of the day, the 'Old Corruption'. Anderson's errors stemmed from his use of the French Revolution as the prototypical bourgeois revolution to which other revolutions should conform. Consequently, according to Thompson, Anderson and Nairn adopted an overly schematic view of British development, paid scant regard to historical research and exhibited ignorance of the real historical process. Anderson and Nairn also underestimated and neglected the vitality and self-confidence of bourgeois thought in England and Scotland, which, for example, in the shape of Adam Smith, had made an unrivalled contribution to bourgeois intellectual development. Thompson deployed Walter Bagehot's distinction in *British Constitution* (1867) between the decorative (the aristocratic style of the elite, the monarchy, judiciary, House of Lords, etc.) and the efficient aspects of the British state, a feature Anderson and Nairn overlooked. 'Peculiarities of the English' was a plea against the fashion for structuralism. But it also called for a renewal of Marxism by highlighting the recurring themes facing Marxist theory: the inadequacy of base and super-structure, the thorny question of **class**, the relationship between theory and evidence. In his next tirade against structuralism, he expended even more energy in addressing these questions.

In *The Poverty of Theory* (1978), Thompson seized the lapels of the premier structuralist philosopher, Louis Althusser. According to Thompson, the French communist's approach was tantamount to a denial of history, and as such constituted a fundamental rupture with the method of Marx. Instead of Marx's historical materialism, Althusser sought 'theoretical practice', which entailed formal and abstract contemplation. Many Marxists had criticised this approach in its former incarnations. The title consciously echoed Marx's demolition of Proudhon's idealism. E.P. Thompson aimed a stinging invective against the circular character of Althusser's philosophical abstractions, which were 'a break *from* disciplined self-knowledge and a leap into the self-degeneration of 'knowledge' according to its own theoretical procedures: that is, a leap out of knowledge and into theology'.[5] *The Poverty of Theory* also set out Thompson's own theoretical position and his view of historical method. Whilst this took the form of a critique, it did range widely from the weaknesses of Western Marxism to the character of historical knowledge. It was the fullest theoretical elaboration of the British Marxists, and whilst it plainly did not speak for all of them, it did provide a landmark in historical theory. Partly, it returned to the themes – the character of class, human agency, rejection of base and superstructure – that were first elaborated in *The Making of the English Working Class*.

Thompson believed that Althusser was poisoning both history and Marxism, the two sources that intellectually nourished him. This accounted for his unconcealed bad temper. For Thompson, Althusser's attack on **socialist humanism** was the intellectual counterpart to the Soviet invasions and repression in 1956 and 1968. It was no less than 'an intellectual police action'. *The Poverty of Theory* marked an important stage in Thompson's understanding of Marxism. Whereas before he had conceived of Marxism as a single tradition, now there were distinct Marxisms, different traditions. Having undergone a process of separation, what Thompson called bifurcation, on the one side stood **Stalinism** and Althusser, on another socialist humanism.

However, according to Thompson, in a sense, Marx did 'license' Althusser's reading because of an obsession with political economy. For many years Marx toiled obsessively on *Capital*. His method in *Capital*, and especially *Grundrisse* (the post-humously published notebooks he used as a preliminary to *Capital*), started from the concepts of bourgeois political economy and sought to destroy them through their own logic. But this logic trapped Marx within its own rigid procedures. Thompson described this as Marx's 'Grundrisse face', a static idealist critique rather than historical materialism. It was this side of Marx that Althusser sought to generalise into grand theory.

Thompson also traced Marx's original sin in Althusser's discussion of base and superstructure. The base and superstructure metaphor posited that the ideological, political and state forms (the superstructure) were derived from the economic foundations (the base) of a society. The base and superstructure implied a static, unchanging, inhuman historical structure. Thompson denounced the use of metaphors of this inert kind because they suggested that history was a structure, not a process, and denied human agency. In other words, it entailed a rejection of the dialectical method. This is certainly the case with Althusser's elaboration of the base and superstructure model, which ultimately entailed a rejection of it. Thompson cruelly mocked Althusser's mechanical construction in a series of diagrams to demonstrate the absurdity of the structuralist's scheme, which the English Marxist dubbed 'an orrery of errors': literally, a crank-operated mechanical model of the universe. 'I am sorry to disappoint those practitioners who suppose that all that it is necessary to know about history can be constructed from a conceptual meccano set.'[6]

Thompson criticised Althusser for mistaking a metaphor (an aid to explanation) for a category (a real element of the historical process). Yet Thompson committed the same mistake when rejecting the base–superstructure. On a number of occasions, Engels pointed out the limitations of the metaphor: the superstructure could be relatively autonomous, the base might assert itself only 'ultimately' or 'in the last instance', the economic underpinnings of history were clearest over the broadest comparison and the longest run. In prose style, as well as historical explanation, metaphors allowed to run free defeat their original purpose. Thompson denied the crucial but necessarily limited value of the base–superstructure metaphor, and this denial has become widespread amongst Marxist historians such as Robert Brenner. This led Thompson to claim that base and superstructure was inadequate for explaining the transition from feudalism to **capitalism**, precisely the kind of question for which it should be most applicable. Given the intricacies of debate on the transition, this casual aside does not do justice to the application of the base and superstructure metaphor to this question.

In opposition to Althusser, Thompson clarified the Marxist theory of historical knowledge (**epistemology**). Althusser, like postmodernists after him, denied the possibility of real historical knowledge. The empirical endeavours of the historian to recover evidence in order to reconstruct the past was in itself, Althusser told us, empiricism. From the elementary error of confusing empirical mode of investigation (Marx repeatedly stressed this mode) and empiricism, Althusser dismissed the procedures of the history discipline: 'His comments display throughout no acquaintance with, nor understanding of, historical procedures: that is, procedures which make of 'history' a *discipline* and not a babble of alternating ideological assertions: procedures which provide for their own relevant discourse of the proof'.[7] Without this engagement with the empirical evidence, the production of knowledge itself is impossible. In its place, Althusser offered the theory of a theory with no test of proof and thus Thompson designated it as a theology, an idealism, an ahistorical theoreticism.

Thompson also demonstrated the common ground between Althusser and the empiricist Cold War opponent of Marxism, Karl Popper. Whilst for Althusser history should be abandoned for theory, for Popper only the discovery of discrete facts was possible and any attempt to shape these into patterns of causation or concepts was purely ideological. For both Popper and Althusser, the sources of history were ideological, open to arbitrary manipulation and fitted into an already existing theory. This challenged the very 'epistemological credentials' of history or, in other words, the theory of knowledge upon which history as a discipline is based. If facts and the sources from which they are derived are ideological then there could be no means of validating or falsifying any historical proposition. There could be no 'court of appeal' within the historical discipline, no 'discourse of proof'. This amounted to nothing other than ignorance of the character of historical research and sources. In the first instance, many of the sources that historians use are unintended historical raw material produced with no eye to posterity. Even with sources that were written for posterity, it is the most elementary aspect of the historians' craft to analyse these intentions critically. Challenging Popper's empiricist condemnation of attempts to draw together separate facts and events in wider historical explanations, Thompson pointed out that Popper's idea of a discrete fact independent of theoretical context is unintelligible. A feudal tenure was more than a Latin inscription on paper: its meaning had to be understood in the context of society. The Marxist historian also disputed Popper's view that generic terms (such as feudalism) were historians' fictions (**nominalism**), using the example of the need to have an idea and understanding of the army in order to understand the soldier. These historical concepts, to which Popper objected so much, were necessary to make history intelligible and were therefore not merely fanciful inventions. Tested and refined in historical research and debate, these categories and concepts were integral to the arduous struggle for historical knowledge. Theories, concepts and hypotheses interact dialectically with the objectively determining (though not singular) properties of evidence in order to advance historical knowledge. Thus knowledge for Thompson derived from the interaction of two dialogues between social being and consciousness (giving experience), and theoretically organised evidence and the determinate character of its object.

At the same time, Thompson rejected the claim that history or **historical materialism** was a science. Again Thompson was recoiling from the pseudo-scientific boastfulness of Althusser and Stalin. Althusser's philosophy, his system of thought within thought, was supposedly 'scientific' because it elaborated its own procedures of truth despite the fact that this was done with no empirical control: that is, without reference to the material world. Stalin's world-view claimed to be scientific because it disclosed the inevitable processes of the historical mechanism. Thompson reasoned that history was neither an experimental science that produced laws (such as physics) nor a system of pure logic (such as philosophy). History's logic was distinctive because it necessarily involved a fluid process engaging constantly with new contexts and new evidences. Thus the unambiguous static categories on which philosophy was premised was a historical impossibility. As for science, history could not have recourse to the laboratory and neither can it have positive and universal proof, but simply the contingent confirmation, modification or falsification of a certain hypothesis within historically limited parameters. For Thompson, each and every attempt to define history as a science had been unhelpful. Here Thompson broke ranks with the classical Marxist tradition, understandably given the bombastic scientific claims of his opponents. He offered an alternative to the scientific rhetoric of Marx borrowed from the science of his day. Laws of motions should be understood as 'logic of process' and the analogy of mechanical determinism refined to a more open determinism that set limits and brought pressures to bear. These refinements, according to Thompson, entailed a rejection of Marxism's claim to scientific truth. However, his reasoning for this was based on flawed grounds. He offered as the sole positive justification the inability to recreate laboratory conditions, therefore equating science with experimental science. This assumption would deem various natural sciences, including certain branches of physics, unscientific.

Thompson's critique of Althusserianism extended to its academicism. According to Thompson, structuralism displayed several features of bourgeois academia. Young scholars sought to make a name for themselves by espousing intellectually fashionable theories impenetrable to the layperson. For these academics, Thompson argued, the arcane language was itself a virtue as it was academically 'reputable' and it underlined their own theoretical prowess. This elitism was incongruous with the spirit of history from below.

Thompson portrayed Althusser cloistered in his study in the prestigious *École Normale Supérieure*, attended by deferential research assistants and students, capable only of artificial abstract speculation and disdainful of knowledge formulated outside academic procedures. His masonic vocabulary of correspondence and non-correspondence, articulation, tortion, overdetermination, dislocation, relative autonomy and discrete levels was an academic gloss which posed as a more sophisticated alternative to the 'economism' he deplored. Yet this evasive flexibility in its essentials remained a structuralism incapable of handling such indispensable categories and concepts as experience, history, culture, process and agency. Althusser's language created a self-sufficient community of scholars – an 'elitist intellectual couche', an 'Oxbridge lumpen-intelligensia' – who resembled the schoolmen in the theology departments of the Middle Ages. 'They torture us', Thompson complained:

> on the rack of their interminable formulations until we are brought to the limits of endurance. We may not answer in any other language: only this one is rigorous and reputable. Above our heads, in the high academies, the inquisitors dispute; they fiercely disagree, but they recognise each other's complexity and repute.[8]

The insularity of their approach created its own momentum of disputes, heresies, neo-Althusserians, post-Althusserians, linguistic and **semiotic** structuralist variants. This played up to the academic fetish of novelty and hair-splitting which gathered pace because of the absence of empirical controls to curb their pretensions.

Their elitism also severed these 'theoretical practitioners' from the world of political engagement, of **class struggle**. This constituted a fundamental contrast with previous generations of Marxists. It allowed the 'aspirant academic' to revel in 'harmless revolutionary psycho-drama' and ascend his or her career path, particularly as Althusser shared so much intellectually with the bourgeois academic milieu he found himself in (structuralism, epistemology, etc.). Academia denied the insights afforded by active engagement in the historical process itself.

Thompson pointed out that, for all their structural analysis, the Althusserians seemed blissfully unaware of the institutional and social dynamics of academia. Thompson's generation of Marxist historians was the first which found a place in the universities. He identified the pull of the bourgeois ideas within the faculties where Marxist historians encountered both hostile polemic and those who were open to a dialogue. Either way, academia could exert a gravitational attraction against classic Marxism.

This has subsequently been exhibited by the drift of journals and individual academics away from Marxism. *Past and Present* has long ceased to embrace Marxist historians in the way that it used to and *History Workshop Journal* has more recently shuffled part way along the postmodernist track, of which more will be said in the next chapter.

Heated debate followed the publication of *The Poverty of Theory*. The allusion to Marx's *Poverty of Philosophy* that mauled the anarchist Pierre-Joseph Proudhon (1809–65) with the aim of discrediting his ideas and ending anarchist influence of the embryonic workers' movements of Europe was a statement of intent. In defence of structuralism, Richard Johnson, from the Centre of Contemporary Cultural Studies at Birmingham University, took the opening shot in an exchange of articles in *History Workshop Journal*, anticipating *The Poverty of Theory* by a few weeks. Johnson's article consisted of a critical discussion of the historical work of Thompson and Eugene Genovese (the American Marxist historian of black slavery whose approach was very close to that of Thompson). Johnson described the division between structuralist Marxism and the culturalism of Thompson and Genovese. Despite opening with the claim that these strands of thought were potentially complementary, his sympathies clearly lay with structuralism as 'The most powerful criticisms of the Thompson–Genovese positions derive from a structuralist marxism.' Culturalism, according to Johnson, encompassed three errors: a stress on culture and 'experience', the displacement of the mode of production as the Marxist 'master category' by class (defined in cultural terms) and the rejection out-of-hand of theory in favour of an empiricist approach: 'We may say, then, that there is a necessarily anti-theoretical tendency in culturalism, a tendency to prefer "experience" to "theory"'.[9]

Johnson identified three elements of Thompson and Genovese's work that revealed their anti-theoretical culturalism: the absence of abstraction, their **reductionism** of the economic to the cultural, and their inadequate notion of determination. Johnson took exception to the way in which Thompson maintained that evidence shaped the historian's view, that the historian should listen to the evidence and that history provided a discourse of proof through evidence. This, for Johnson, was too close to traditional empiricist and **historicist** history with its disregard for theory. Thompson and Genovese's tenuous relationship with theory took the shape of a largely unacknowledged debt to Marx, Dobb and Gramsci. They also attempted to conceptualise American slavery and eighteenth-century plebeian culture in terms of **hegemony** and paternalism. In defence of abstraction proper, Johnson proposed a theory of knowledge in which an account of the Peterloo massacre and the theoretical discussion of modes of production were equivalent representations of reality (entirely blurring Marx's crucial distinction between 'abstract' and 'concrete' elements of his method). A discussion of *Capital* followed, which was heavily influenced by Louis Althusser and Étienne Balibar's *Reading*

Capital (1970). Johnson argued that *Capital* demonstrated Marx's use of sustained abstraction:

> Now, according to the Althusserian reading of *Capital*, it is a work of theory. It is not the history of a particular social formation, nor even, despite its reliance on English illustrations, a history of English capital. It is concerned rather to develop the categories that may be used in such a concrete analysis. This is true as far as it goes. It is true that *Capital* is not a history book. But it would be still more accurate to say that there are *different discourses present in* Capital, *distinguished mainly by their degrees of abstractness*.[10]

To claim that *Capital* is exclusively a work of theory and not history, concerned with elaborating abstract categories, is highly contentious if at that time a fashionable interpretation. *Capital* was a centrepiece of Marx's intellectual labour and combined an analysis of the historical development of capitalism (mainly in England), criticism of contemporary political economy and the working out of the dynamics of a capitalist system. *Capital* was far from an ahistorical abstraction as it incorporated *both* the abstract and the concrete, history and economic theory. In this sense, it was – centring on the capitalist system – both a work of theory and a work of history: namely, history in the widest sense of careful explanation of the past, analysis of the present and the use of theoretical insights to predict the future.

Johnson also proposed that Thompson and Genovese reduced the economic to the cultural. Crucially, he claimed that the two socialist humanists, in their desire to avoid the 'economism', had no concept of the economic context, in particular the mode of production within which class struggles took place. Class was a lived relationship reduced to the political and cultural level, neglecting the economic dimension of exploitation in class relations. Thus in E.P. Thompson's chapter on exploitation in *The Making*, he was concerned to reject other approaches to class and to present evidence of the 'experience' of intensified exploitation through allowing the victims of the Industrial Revolution to speak through the sources. Because of Thompson's denial of theory, he was unable to go beyond mere description to explanation proper. What Johnson was in effect proposing was the employment of abstraction to elicit a general explanatory model of social change, incorporating a number of different elements of modes of production. Thus, for Johnson, Thompson had no adequate notion of causation and his writing failed to provide the reader with an explanatory framework.

The scene was set for a number of responses in *History Workshop*. The journal also organised a public debate between Johnson and Thompson at St Paul's Church on 1 December 1979. Johnson initiated the discussion by appealing against the polemical mode 'mischievously' employed by Thompson in *The Poverty of Theory*. Outlining the chronology of the rise of culturalism and structuralism, he again maintained that he espoused a middle way that saw a complementarity between the best elements of culturalism and structuralism. But again he argued that the culturalist emphasis on experience led to a rejection of theory.

E.P. Thompson opened with a rejection of the label 'culturalist', which he described as a spurious category which lumped him together with people such as Raymond Williams, with whom he had sharp disagreements. Thompson rejected Williams's notion of cultural history with the counter-proposal of class struggle history. Thompson defended himself on each of the grounds of criticism alleged by the Althusserians. Thompson acknowledged the importance of both the mode of production and cultural elements, 'I argued, explicitly, that we could not grasp the one pole without the concept of the "mode of production" nor the other pole without the concept of "ideology".'[11]

He pointed out that Johnson's chronology was also flawed because it side-stepped the question of **Stalinism** as 'structuralism has enabled vast areas of guilty silence to be kept as to Stalinist practice'. Thompson's polemic resulted from a decade of charges against him of empiricism, historicism, moralism and theoretical vacuity. Instead he had adopted a position in regard to culture that was materialist and contextual in both his history and theory rather than abstract, ahistorical, transcendental.

▶ Evaluations I: base and superstructure

The contribution of the British Marxist historians is undeniable as they transformed the face of social history. The overwhelmingly positive appraisal has to be tempered by a more thorough evaluation of three problem areas: the question of the base and superstructure, history or Marxism as science and the question of class. Harvey Kaye has argued that a new model of Marxism pioneered by Thompson and Hill has emerged based on history from below which rejects base and superstructure, privileging instead the class relations and class struggle in historical change. This new version of Marxist history rejects 'productive force determinism', which Stephen Rigby perceived to be Marx and Engels's central flaw. Robert Brenner, the American Marxist, exemplified such an approach with his class-struggle centred explanation of the transition from feudalism to capitalism. According to Brenner, the different national paths to capitalism resulted primarily from the different outcomes of great struggles between the peasant and the lord in the late Middle Ages and early modern periods.

The base and superstructure was a metaphor employed by Marx on a couple of occasions to demonstrate the distinction between the economic or productive base of society and the ideological and institutional superstructure. It is most famously elaborated in the *Preface to a Critique of Political Economy*. The infrequency of its use in Marx contrasts sharply with the transformation of the metaphor into a universal formula by Second International and Stalinist thinkers. It was privileged over other of Marx's metaphors such as the 'four moments' of the historical process in *The German Ideology* and the 'general illumination' in *Grundrisse*. Elsewhere Marx employed other non-metaphorical distinctions: social being and social conscious-ness, the ideal and the material, which may, in many cases, be interchangeable with the base and superstructure. Nevertheless, base and superstructure has become Marxism's Battle of Verdun: a conflict of great endurance, an attrition of strategic and symbolic importance.

From the 1950s, Hill and Thompson rejected Marx's formulation of the base and superstructure.[12] Thompson objected to the inorganic and static character of the base–superstructure metaphor. Understandably, they sought to distance them-selves from the wooden language and sterile determinism of their Stalinist pasts. Nevertheless this did not entail a formal rejection of Marxism: far from doing that, they sought to rejuvenate Marxism. Dispensing with base–superstructure, Thompson preferred the 'general illumination' metaphor from *Grundrisse*:

> In all forms of society it is a determinate production and its relations which assign every other production and its relations their rank and influence. It is a general illumination in which all other colours are plunged and which modifies their specific tonalities. It is a special ether which defines the specific gravity of everything found in it.[13]

R.S. Neale, another Marxist historian, has stressed the 'four moments' metaphor in the *German Ideology*.[14] Thompson suggested that an organic metaphor would be better and that even this would not express the irreducibly human characteristic of consciousness. Thompson objected to the arbitrary dividing line between the base and the superstructure. The law in eighteenth-century England did not 'politely restrict' itself to superstructure: it insinuated itself into 'every bloody level'.[15] Also the moral order of a mode of production was equally intrinsic to its basic character as its economic order. Yet, for Marx, base and superstructure was not just a metaphor, with which his followers might discover unfortunate connotations, but an abstraction that captured a necessary distinction that was fundamental to materialism itself. Thompson fell into the trap of attributing to Marx the errors of his critics and vulgarisers. Marx's method was historical; it was concerned with process, how things actually changed. Abstraction was drawn from this process and then reapplied to it. Marx's intention was not to construct, in the style of Weberian social science, a universal model or 'ideal type'. Marx did not suggest that in the real flow of history the elements of the base and the superstructure could be easily lined up here and there. He did not spend time on carefully categorising what was in the superstructure and what was in the base. The dialectical method suggested instead the 'unity and interpenetration of opposites'. The base-and-superstructure concept was a metaphorical distinction that was useful in certain circumstances. Rereading the actual passages in which Marx used the distinction there is a strong case for saying that, despite its misappropriations, this has been a highly insightful and suggestive tool for research. Furthermore, Prinz has suggested that the error of counterposing class struggle to base and superstructure in Marx stemmed in part from the absence of any mention of class struggle in the preface to *A Contribution to the Critique of Political Economy* (1859), which avoided the reference because of the Prussian censors.[16]

That vulgar Marxists should use base and superstructure in a static, universal and inorganic way does not invalidate the distinction itself. It was against this misuse that Thompson reacted. But the passages that Thompson favoured from *Grundrisse* and *German Ideology* articulated what were fundamentally the analogous propositions. Also despite Thompson's objections on this note, a building metaphor, such as base and superstructure, is not an inorganic and static metaphor. Consider the Norman church that has been many times renovated, rebuilt, extended by conscious human toil, constructed on a former Saxon settlement, constantly at odds with the elements or with the hazards of warfare, fire or flood; or the monuments of now lost civilisations, like the massive stone heads of the now desolate Easter Island, which lie in ruins. These can provide rather effective metaphors for particular modes of production, their development and crises. Eric Hobsbawm pointed out that base and superstructure allowed us to assess progress and direction in human history, and our growing conscious control over nature:

> the model of levels, of which those of the social relations of production are primary, and the existence of internal contradictions within systems, of which class conflict is merely a special case. The hierarchy of levels is necessary to explain why history has a *direction*. It is the growing emancipation of man from nature and his growing capacity to control it and make history as a whole ... A hierarchy of levels not arising from a base of the social relations of production would not have this characteristic.[17]

Victor Kiernan warned of revising Marxism out of existence and, though troubled by base and superstructure, he sensibly proposed: 'The proper safeguard may be to judge every human activity as having some of its roots in the soil of social production, but experiencing its influences directly or indirectly, at one or more remove, each of these imparting to it a quality peculiarly it own.'[18]

David Blackbourn, the Marxist historian of nineteenth-century Germany, warned of overreaction to the vulgar base and superstructure position in his field:

> In fact perhaps only vulgar Marxists and vulgar anti-Marxists cling to the view that 'superstructure' should be a perfect reflection of 'base' ... The problem now, however, is that arguments of this kind run the risk of becoming frozen and

hardened by habitual repetition. The relationships among the economic, social and political spheres threaten to become rigidly dissociated as they had been rigidly associated in the base/superstructure mode. As a result, the impact of dynamic economic change on both civil society on the one hand and public and political life on the other has been undervalued, yielding an unnecessarily attenuated picture of bourgeois society in nineteenth-century Germany.[19]

Without base and superstructure, its more sophisticated defenders argued, Marxism was robbed of its ability to explain the questions of the larger historical scope: the rise and fall of civilisations, the **transitions** between different socio-economic systems, and the paradoxical but real progress in human history. As Engels noted, the economic asserted itself most definitely over the long run and in the broader comparative frame. The focus of history from below on the particular struggles obviated the clearest necessity for base and superstructure. Hobsbawm, whose principal work has been the century-by-century histories of the rise of European capitalism, was more sensitive to the need for the base and superstructure metaphor.

For the humanist Marxists, the programmatic rejection of base and super-structure did not imply a practical rejection of materialism. Indeed, both Hill and Thompson were sensitive to the economic context of ideas, individuals and events. Hill's century of bourgeois revolution was explicitly tied to the rise of capitalism. For Thompson, the **plebeian** world of the eighteenth century was threatened by the encroachment of capitalist market relations. At the most basic level, they implicitly retain something similar to base–superstructure in the non-reductionist sense that Engels patiently elaborated in his late letters on historical materialism. This contradiction between the explicit theoretical abandonment of base and superstructure and the practical attachment to it, allowed their work to continue within the very best tradition of Marxist history. It did, however, lead to very considerable problems for the transmission of Marxism as a historical theory and practice to a wider and younger audience. This is also true of their lack of clarity about the experience of Stalinism (neither really demonstrated a convincing understanding of this), and this infected their Marxism with theoretical uncertainties and hesitations. Where Hill largely steered clear of theoretical pronouncements *per se*, Thompson engaged in a dialogue with culturalist historians. Both had a tendency to reject longer-run structural history for the concentration on the particular. Thompson incorrectly distinguished between a left-wing **Annales** concerned with culture and anthropology and a right-wing Annales concerned with the long-run. Robert Darnton is no closer to Marxism than Fernand Braudel; Marxist historians have had a fruitful dialogue with both. Thus Thompson's very effective lambasting of Althusser's structuralism, the Anderson–Nairn thesis, and Hindess and Hirst's *Pre-Capitalist Modes of Production* hit the mark, but his rejection of the entirety of Marxist structuralist history implied a dismissal of some excellent Marxist work, such as Perry Anderson's *The Lineages of the Absolutist State*, Chris Wickham's work and Geoffrey de Ste Croix's *Class Struggles in the Ancient Greek World*.

▶ Evaluations II: science

On science, Thompson firmly rejected history as science in favour of a more poetic moral Marxism, taking William Morris and William Blake as inspiration. Thompson listed the members of the rogues' gallery who had posed as scientists. Lysenko, Toynbee, Malthus, Bentham, Comte, Spencer, the Webbs and Althusser all claimed scientific grounds for their views, but in each case these were closed intellectual systems that locked 'the prison-gates to knowledge'. This rejection was also born of a hostility to the moribund language of social science history and the spurious claims made from the 1960s for quantitative history. Thompson reserved particular (and to some extent justified) bile for quantification, which led to an overcompensation in his work. At times he was a 'skilled quantifier though he pretends seriously otherwise'; at other times he defied logic to avoid statistical assessments. As one reader of *The Making of the English Working Class* observed:

> It comes as something of a shock to realise, at the end of 900 pages, that one has never learnt such an elementary fact as the approximate size of the English working class, or its proportion within the population as a whole, at any date in the history of its 'making'.[20]

To be fair, Thompson was taking issue with the structuralisms of Stalinism and bourgeois social science. The intellectual climate today (with the prevalence of **postmodernism**) is a very different one in which reason itself is questioned as being outmoded. In such circumstances, a defence of the seemingly elementary features that Marxism and history share with science are worth spelling out. The loss of nerve with science was not confined to Thompson. The **Frankfurt school** theorists, Adorno and Horkheimer, in their *Dialectic of the Enlightenment* (1944) pessimistically argued that science and progress had been enlisted to make war and organise the death camps. As such the belief in scientific values and progress was, for them, intimately connected to the barbarism of the twentieth century and should be rejected. The Frankfurt school had abandoned all hope of socialist revolution and the potential of the working class to emancipate humanity from the shackles of capitalism. This pessimism reflected events: the obvious betrayal of the ideals of the revolution in Stalin's Russia, Hitler's victory in 1933 (and thus the Frankfurt school's exile from Germany), and the horrors of the Second World War and the Holocaust. Adorno and Horkheimer could write, for instance:

> In the most general sense of progressive thought, the Enlightenment has always aimed at liberating men from their fear and establishing their sovereignty. Yet the

fully enlightened earth radiates disaster triumphant. The program of the Enlightenment was the disenchantment of the world; the dissolution of myths and the substitution of knowledge for fancy ... What men learn from nature is how to use it in order wholly to dominate it and other men. That is the only aim.[21]

Thompson was right that the Althusserian notion of science as a set of autonomous self-validating procedures was alien to establishing historical knowledge. The danger with drawing on the moral strengths and anti-capitalist romanticism of Blake or Morris, as Thompson did, was that there was also a backward-looking element to romanticism which rejected the notion of progress and science in their entirety. On the other hand, it was also true (as Christopher Hill recognised in an article in 1948) that the historian's adoption of scientific posturing has often led to 'works [that] are written only too obviously without any view to being read'.[22] Hill indicated that this was certainly not what Karl Marx drew from science. Instead Marx incorporated the words of Dante, Shakespeare and Goethe, utilised metaphor after the fashion of the romantic poetry that his youthful self had dabbled in and punctuated his writings with epigram, witticism and imagination. Thus, *Capital* blended the rigorous documentary research of the government reports and Blue Books, and careful political economy, with the gothic imagery of the capitalist exploitation as the vampire drinking the blood of his victims. Following his lead, Hill called then for Marxist history to combine the scientific approach to knowledge with poetic insight into the human condition and the art of storytelling. In the work of the best Marxist historians (for example, Hill himself and Thompson certainly), this practical synthesis of knowledge and the poetic are in evidence. Science and art are not mutually exclusive but connected in historical writing. C.L.R. James made a very similar point in his introduction to *The Black Jacobins* (1938):

> The analysis is the science and the demonstration the art which is history. The violent conflicts of our age enable our practised vision to see into the very bones of previous revolutions more easily than heretofore. Yet for that very reason it is impossible to recollect the historical emotions in that tranquillity which a great English writer, too narrowly, associated with poetry alone.[23]

Hobsbawm more recently defended Marxist history as a science. He asserted that the natural sciences such as history combined scholarship with political or moral partisanship and engagement and that this had always been part and parcel of the progressive advance of knowledge. Such commitment has been a positive spur to new inquiry (for example, with the scientist searching for the cure for a terrible disease). Likewise in history, Marxist commitment has opened up new fields of historical study or posed different questions in old fields of investigation. Perry Anderson, in his reflections upon Thompson's work *Arguments within English*

Marxism (1980), went further and contended that the English historian mistook his own crude appreciation of the procedures of physics or chemistry for the attributes of science in general and was ill-acquainted with current philosophy of science. Thompson failed to see past Popper's historicist fog to acknowledge the importance of the idea of **falsification**: that falsification rather than verification was the key to *scientific* advance. Failing to appreciate this, Thompson believed that history's reliance on falsification rendered it unscientific. Neither was Thompson seemingly aware of Imre Lakatos's revised notion of falsification, which said that scientific theories could even survive specific falsification but stood or fell on the overall development of the research programmes that they engendered:

> What Thompson thus takes to be the exceptional condition of history is, in fact, the normal status of all science. Provisionality, selectivity and falsifiability are constitutive of the nature of the scientific enterprise as such. Even the lack of experimental controls is not confined to historiography: astronomy permits no laboratory tests either.[24]

▶ Evaluations III: class

Another controversial element of Thompson's view has been his attitude to class. First, he emphasised time and again working-class agency in its own class formation. Second, he prioritised the way in which the experience of class was culturally 'handled'. Third, Thompson viewed class as a relational process for which static definitions would not suffice. Class was forged in class struggle through specific patterns of events:

> Class formations ... arise at the intersection of determination and self-activity: the working class 'made itself as much as it was made'. We cannot put 'class' here and 'class consciousness' there, as two separate entities, the one sequential upon the other, since both must be taken together – the experience of determination, and the 'handling' of this in conscious ways. Nor can we deduce from class a static 'section' (since it is a *becoming* over time), nor as a function of a mode of production, since class formations and class consciousness (while subject to determinate pressures) eventuate in an open-ended process of relationship – of struggle with other classes – over time.[25]

From a classical Marxist standpoint, Thompson correctly criticised bourgeois economic and sociological notions of class but, apart from scant references to Marx, he did not elaborate the theoretical tradition within which such an approach stands. This led some to overestimate the theoretical originality of *The Making of the English Working Class*. Thompson sought to go beyond the base–superstructure approach which he saw as static. Instead he talked in *The Making of the English Working Class* of the importance of 'cultural superstructure'. He asserted that this was neither idealist nor voluntarist. Whilst Thompson heavily underscored the subjective side of class formation (the **class-for-itself** in Marx's terminology), he never abandoned the objective or material element in class formation (the **class-in-itself**). This over-emphasis was a response to an environment that ignored the former. Marx used a similar over-emphasis in his materialist rejection of idealism, yet many of those who followed Thompson rejected or ignored his warnings about neglecting the objective side of class.

There was also a periodisation implicit to all Thompson's writings on English society: the period of the making of the working class (1790–1832), before its making and after. This view shaped his assessment of class in the eighteenth century. As Peter Linebaugh noted, his proposition for a plebeian world of contesting customs was a world that was centred on the villages of rural England. It omitted London, and the seaborne and soldiering proletariat. It neglected the labour process and conflicts over exploitation. The continuities of eighteenth-century wage labourers and the nineteenth-century working class were deflected into cultural disjunctures, although even here there may be more continuities than Thompson implied.[26]

As a consequence, some of Thompson's followers have focused on elements of his account (culture, identity and experience) and uprooted them from their grounding in Marxist theory and in the material process of production and exploitation. Gareth Stedman Jones saw Thompson's cultural preoccupation as a staging post to the **linguistic turn** and Jones described his own approach as the attempt to emancipate Thompson from materialism. As an alternative to Thompson's cultural slant on class, Geoffrey De Ste Croix, the Marxist historian of ancient Greece, who also had to confront class struggle before the existence of the modern language of class, preferred a more classical Marxist definition of class:

> *Class* (essentially a relationship) is a collective social expression of the fact of exploitation, the way in which exploitation is embodied in a social structure. By *exploitation* I mean the appropriation of part of the product of the labour of others. .... *A class* (a particular class) is a group of persons in a community identified by their position in the whole system of social production, defined above all according to their relationship (primarily in terms of the degree of ownership or control) to the conditions of production (that is to say, the means and labour of production) and to other classes.[27]

▶ Conclusion

Given Stalinism's malign influence on Marxism, defence of the classical Marxist propositions of base and superstructure, science and class had to go beyond the doctrinaire. Classical Marxism, if it is to survive, has to identify its differences with Stalinism and its relevance to the unfolding character of history and historical debate. It is the test of time that underlines the value of the propositions of base and superstructure, science and class. This is the very battleground over which the postmodernists call social history in general into question. Unfortunately and unbeknown to them, some of Thompson and Hill's programmatic statements, though not necessarily their historical practice, have perhaps made the footing less sure. In the light of social history's entanglement with postmodernism, the utility of these propositions became all the more apparent.

Hill's and Thompson's reaction to Stalinism was healthy and understandable. Tasting the bitter residue of Stalinism in the words science, base and superstructure, they spat them out whole. Men once again made history. Their emphasis on humanism, human agency, was an important corrective to the determinism of Stalinism. However, some have maintained that Thompson overcompensated and opened the door to a rejection of materialism. This was certainly not Thompson's intention and he explicitly stated as much on a number of occasions. Some, including Bryan D. Palmer and Raphael Samuel, have suggested that Thompson abandoned Marxism altogether towards the end of his life.[28] It should be stressed that in his late writings on culture he leant heavily on Gramsci, not on a rejection of classical Marxism. Thus Thompson, even in 'culturalist' mode, was careful to state that popular culture inhabited a 'material abode'.[29]

The notion of the materiality of culture potentially blurred the distinction between the ideal and the material. Both Marx and Gramsci, for example, had adopted such formulations as they embraced the dialectical unity of the material and the ideal. For Gramsci, ideology stabilised class society forming a social cement between the fissures of class and other social divisions. For Marx, ideas became a material force when they gripped the masses. With a selective reading of any of these, it was also a short step from the materiality of culture to the materiality of language or ideas in general. This was the route that Gareth Stedman Jones and other postmodernists followed.

7 Marxism and Postmodernism in History

'Once upon a time a valiant fellow had the idea that men were drowned in water only because they possessed the *idea of gravity*. If they were to knock this notion out of their heads, say by stating it to be a superstition, a religious concept, they would be sublimely proof against any danger from water. His whole life long he fought against the illusion of gravity, of whose harmful results all statistic brought him new and manifold evidence. This valiant fellow was the type of the new revolutionary philosophers in Germany.'

K. Marx and F. Engels, *The Germany Ideology* (1846)[1]

Postmodernism provoked talk of crisis in history in the 1990s, particularly in labour and social history. Most major history journals hosted debates about the merits of postmodernism.[2] For instance, in 1993 a special supplement of the *International Review of Social History* asked whether labour history was in its death throes, and Arthur Marwick and Hayden White locked horns in the *Journal of Contemporary History*.[3] Patrick Joyce, Britain's most noted postmodernist historian, even announced the end of social history in the journal of the same name.[4] Postmodernism had been a late arrival to history as it had become widespread in other disciplines in the 1970s. The challenge emanated from multiple sources. Philosophers of history, notably Hayden White and Richard Rorty, subjected historians to the methods of literary criticism. Poststructuralist literary scholars, such as Roland Barthes (1915–80) and Jacques Derrida (1930–), took issue with historians' purported complacent and naïve realism. Writing histories of madness, sexuality and punishment as socially constructed **discourses**, Michel Foucault (1926–84) has been highly influential upon postmodernist historians. Through these diverse lineages, a new breed of social historian emerged concerned with discourse, symbols, language, identity and the literary and narrative character of historical writing. **Class**, the social interpretations of political events, rational and scientific analysis have passed from favour. Significantly these postmodernist revisionists singled out the influence of Marxism on social history for particular criticism.

► What is postmodernism?

Postmodernism embodies a variety of intellectual trends and there is no firm consensus on its meaning. It is an elusive term and postmodernists, with characteristic admiration for the relativity of all knowledge, see this 'decentredness' as a great virtue. Postmodernism can describe the present epoch ('new times'), particular ironic and nostalgic styles of art and architecture, history and politics; in fact almost any aspect of the humanities and culture. Postmodernism denotes an epochal change, being **modernism**'s and modernity's successor. Groping towards a definition one key postmodernist, Jean-François Lyotard, has described it as 'an incredulity towards metanarratives'; namely, a rejection of overarching attempts to interpret and shape the world, be that the belief in science or Marxism or modernist art.[5] Postmodernism signals the end of the modernist period of art and culture with the dawning of a new epoch, postmodernity. Perry Anderson charted the original use of the term to the Latin American poet, Frederico de Onís, in the mid-1930s.[6] If definition is a difficult task, identifying the central themes of postmodernism is more straightforward. The dominant concerns of postmodernism consist of irony, relativism and scepticism. Because postmodernism is such an umbrella term it subsumes within it other terms (**poststructuralism**, the **linguistic turn** and **postmarxism**) that are connected to the present debate in history.

In the first instance, the term poststructuralism was adopted. Poststructuralism is often the preferred term because at least it clarifies its intellectual lineage from Fernand de Saussure's (1857–1913) linguistics to the poststructural linguistics of Michel Foucault and Jacques Derrida. Alternatively, some historians have employed Richard Rorty's term, the 'linguistic turn', because it specifies language as the primary concern. This is how the British postmodernist historian James Vernon rather guardedly described the linguistic turn:

> [A] *critical* engagement with a range of very different influences – from the work of Barthes to Baudrillard, through Derridean deconstruction, Foucauldian analysis, Lacanian psychoanalysis and the French feminisms of Kristeva, Cixous and Irigaray (subsequently conflated under the largely unhelpful categories of post-modernism and post-structuralism) – the 'linguistic turn' has created new cultural histories in all shapes and sizes.[7]

A third label sometimes adopted in this debate is postmarxism. Stuart Sim defined postmarxism as, 'a series of hostile and/or revisionary responses to classical Marxism from the poststructuralist/postmodernist/feminist direction, by figures who at one time in their lives would have considered themselves as Marxists, or whose thought processes had been significantly shaped by the classical Marxist tradition'.[8] Some postmarxists, as with Jacques Derrida's *Specters of Marx* (1994), have advocated a plural Marxism with the incorporation of poststructuralism, postcolonialism and feminism.[9]

That many of the most prominent postmodernists are former Marxists is no accident. Jean-François Lyotard was in the group *Socialisme ou Barbarie*, Julia Kristeva was a Maoist, Jean Baudrillard was one of Althusser's fellow travellers and Michel Foucault and Jacques Derrida were briefly in the French Communist Party. Several past generations of Marxist intellectuals, enthused by dramatic events and the turning tides of ideological fashion, eventually renounced Marxism when those initial conditions abated. One might note that the celebrated contributors to *The God That Failed* (1950) had all abandoned, by the onset of the Cold War, the Marxism that they had adopted in the 1920s or 1930s.[10] What happened to the 1930s generation in the 1950s occurred with 1960s generation, or at least to a significant part of it, in Thatcher and Reagan's 1980s. Furthermore academia, with its emphasis on novelty and intellectual fashion, is relatively inhospitable to stable intellectual traditions, doubly so for revolutionary ones such as Marxism. Disillusionment with 'actually existing socialism' in China or Eastern Europe was also a key ingredient in the making of postmodernism. The collapse of the Stalinist dictatorships in 1989 confirmed the trend despite the fact that the New Left was founded upon a more or less thoroughgoing critique of Stalinism. Geoff Eley and Keith Nield, editors of the journal *Social History*, objected that

> The vanished – or vanquished – utility or plausibility of marxism is apparently connected in the minds of Joyce and others with the implosion of the Soviet Union, and the irreversible 'failure' of the experiments begun in 1917. But for those of us educated in the New Left and the anti-Stalinist radicalisms after 1956, this reductive reading of marxism makes absolutely no sense.[11]

Those Marxist historians with more ambivalent attitudes ultimately could not escape the need for an explanation of their present. Postmodernists invoke the events of 1989 to indicate why in these 'postmodern times' social history is no longer appropriate. Time and again, postmodernist critics of Marxist history simply reduce Marxism to **Stalinism** both as a social system, now defunct, and as a mechanistic, economically determinist view of history.

The next step, to reduce social history to Marxism, further compounds this error. At times postmodernists even treat social history and Marxism as synonymous. Orlando Figes, a historian of the Russian Revolution, even elides them into 'Marxism/social history'. The danger with such an approach is that those historians attempting to distance themselves from their Marxist past (or to demonstrate their hostility to Marxism) hasten to reject social history through guilt by association. The refutation of this reductionist error lies in a simple observation. It was not Marx but the French restoration historians – or arguably Ibn Khaldun (1332–1406) and Giambattista Vico (1668–1774) – who pioneered social history.[12] Social history has furthermore always had a majority of non-Marxist adherents. Consider, for example, great names of social history past and present: Marc Bloch, R.H. Tawney, the Hammonds, Hugh Trevor-Roper, Keith Thomas. None was a Marxist. Social history cannot therefore be put in the dock as an accomplice to Marxism as postmodernists might wish.

▶ The postmodernist gauntlet

Postmodernism's objections to history may be grouped into four areas: its conceptual agenda; its theory of knowledge and attitude to science (**epistemology**); its methods; and the writing of history. The conceptual agenda of representations, symbols, memories, texts, language, identity and discourse has been noted earlier in this book.

The actual impact of the linguistic turn is difficult to assess. Many simply evade the issue of how influential it has been altogether. Whereas Patrick Joyce has repeatedly decried the widespread resistance to postmodernism amongst historians (especially British ones), Geoffrey Elton saw it lurking throughout the discipline. In some fields, from the French Revolution to nineteenth-century Britain, the questions of language, myth, symbol, identity and the literary quality of history were setting the agenda in the 1990s.[13] Certain journals, such as *Past and Present* and the *Russian Review*, seem to devote themselves increasingly to these concerns. New journals, such as *Rethinking History* and *History and Memory*, have even been founded to accommodate the increasing postmodernist output. The difficulty in assessing the impact of postmodernism stems from the fact that these issues are not the exclusive preserve of postmodernists; there is considerable overlap with the **Annales history of mentalities** and with anthropological approaches (especially those influenced by Clifford Geertz). There are also important distinctions to be made between those who conceive of language as primary and determining and those who have a much more nuanced understanding of language and culture. So whilst the agenda and elements of postmodernism are extremely widespread, historians have not yet been convinced of the most radical philosophical positions of postmodernists such as White and Rorty. By the end of the twentieth century, the historians advocating such positions were still a small but vociferous voice. In areas such as economic history, it has made very much less progress than others. What can be said with certainty is that the general influence of postmodernism has both reflected and accelerated history's fragmentation as a subject. Broadly speaking, with this linguistic turn, language and symbolism have replaced social and economic forces and '**history from below**' at the centre of historians' investigations. There is an accompanying flight from holistic or total history.

History has become more concerned with continuity rather than change. Uncertainty has become the general climate in which history is now practised, casting a shadow over total history and the idea that history can be scientific.

The postmodern method

In the late 1960s, Jacques Derrida, the French literary critic and philosopher, broke ground beyond the structuralisms prevalent at the time. In 1967, Derrida's three texts (*Of Grammatology*, *Speech and Phenomena*, and *Writing and Difference*) shattered the structuralist mould. Accepting some of **Saussure's** assumptions, Derrida transcended the Swiss linguist's rigid link between **signifier** and **signified** and postulated that **signification** – the act of creating meanings – was open to infinite possibilities; *post*structuralism had arrived. Far from discourse being determined, it was open to 'play' or difference within it. Because of the flexibility of meaning, the external world and language were decoupled and language assumed a new eminence. Derrida famously articulated the transcendental quality of language in daring invective: 'There is nothing outside the text' and 'Everything is discourse.' Such a view required a new methodology called **deconstruction**, a particular brand of discourse analysis. Suspending the traditional concern for authorial intent or historical context, the deconstructionist unravelled texts revealing their linguistically-constructed and multiple meanings. Deconstructionists sought to probe a text through its internal inconsistencies and clues to meaning. As part of this deconstructionist method, Derrida rejected the **'binary oppositions'** (such as light and dark, nature and nurture, male and female) of conventional wisdom, proposing in their place a more decentred, less certain world of difference. Derrida premised the entire deconstructionist method on the assumption that intentions and meanings were not real but word-like. As a consequence, Derrida contributed to postmodernism by developing **textualism**: namely, privileging the study of texts as the paramount research procedure and treating all historical phenomena as though they were texts ('the text analogy'). The emphasis on texts also implied an emphasis on the written word over speech.

With the discursive cat out of the structuralist bag, Michel Foucault also explored the use of discourse analysis in his writings of the 1960s and 1970s. Others, such as Kristeva, Irigaray and Lacan, have combined discourse analysis with psychology and feminism in suggestive and influential ways.

Coining a new phrase to encapsulate these new approaches, Raphael Samuel identified 'reading the signs' as a broad front emerging in the 1970s, within which postmodernism, the linguistic turn and poststructuralism were a part. Whilst much of this new research brought fresh perspectives on the past, Samuel warned of the implications for the overall direction of history.[14] He indicated that methodologies such as **semiotics**, cultural anthropology and **hermeneutics** displaced history into the **synchronic** study of the subjective realm of 'signs'. Samuel's article had its origins in disagreements on the editorial board of the *History Workshop Journal*, which included the postmodernist Cambridge historian Gareth Stedman Jones.

To translate postmodern methods into historical research was not immediate or unproblematic, but those practising historians who did, such as Patrick Joyce, Gareth Stedman Jones and James Vernon, posed the keenest threat to history. This group, being a step closer to the heart of the discipline, has had the most obvious effect on history and has provoked the debates witnessed in the 1990s. In a famous essay, 'Rethinking Chartism', Gareth Stedman Jones applied discourse analysis to the Chartist movement of 1830s and 1840s Britain. He observed that the movement's rhetoric centred not on the working class and socialism but on the vaguer notion of 'the people'. It was therefore unable to move beyond populism to express the demands of the working class. He concluded that Chartism was not a predecessor to the labour movement and failed because of the limitations of its populist discourse. Revealingly, he noted that the political climate had a direct bearing on his desire to abandon the established procedures of social history that had borrowed so much from Marxism, and coincidentally on the centrality of the working class as agent of socialist transformation:

> In the new historical epoch which we appear to have entered, in which a whole set of conventional beliefs about working-class politics have been put into doubt – both nationally and internationally – a critical scrutiny of some of the intellectual premises upon which these beliefs have been based can only be a gain ... It may not be possible for a historian to ask what sort of substantive reality 'the working class' as such might have possessed outside the particular historical idiom in which it has been ascribed meaning.[15]

Jones had been part of the New Left and a structuralist Marxist, but the intellectual climate was now less favourable to Marxism. Jones challenged some of the key categories, taken to be axiomatic not only of Marxism but also of social history as a whole, such as class, experience and consciousness. Too often, Jones claimed, historians took the category of class as given. This was an error because whilst class may have been a key political discourse in Britain since the 1830s, it was not in France and America where the discourse of citizenship prevailed, or Germany where a greater residue of the medieval ideology of social orders remained. It was only in mid- to late nineteenth-century Europe that the socialist and trade union movements generalised the terminology of class. Class was consequently, for Jones, a discourse:

> The title, *Languages of Class*, stresses this point: firstly, that the term 'class' is a word embedded in language and should be analysed in its linguistic context; and

secondly, that because there are *different* languages of class, one should not proceed upon the assumption that 'class' as an elementary counter of official social description, 'class' as an effect of theoretical discourse about distribution or production relations, 'class' as the summary of a cluster of culturally signifying practices or 'class' as a species of political or ideological self-definition, all share a single reference point in an anterior social reality.[16]

The term 'class' is to be placed in its linguistic context, placing a word in the context of words (namely, decontextualising it from history). Unlike his early work, Jones treated class as 'a discursive rather than an ontological reality, the central effort being to explain language of class from the nature of politics rather than the character of politics from the nature of class'.[17]

Alongside deconstruction and textualism, the discursive nature of class (or 'the language of class') approach has been a major methodological theme of postmodernist history. It is this last question that has posed the most recurrent question to social history. Patrick Joyce's *Visions of the People* (1991) examined popular art and theatre, local dialect, the broadside ballad and popular political language, estimating that the cultural identity of nineteenth-century industrial workers needed 'to look beyond class'.[18] Like Jones, Joyce discovered a more widespread populist language or 'visions of the people'. Following this, James Vernon attempted to write a 'new political history' of the nineteenth century from these methods. His *Politics and the People* (1993) reinterpreted the century, conceiving of the contested 'meaning of the constitution' as the century's most vital conflict.[19]

Also in line with these themes, in a very different context, Orlando Figes and Boris Kolonitskii devoted a chapter to 'the language of class' in their *Interpreting the Russian Revolution: The Language and Symbolism of 1917* (1999). Examining the language of texts such as workers' resolutions, the authors identified the frequent use of a language of citizenship and human rights in the aftermath of the February Revolution. As 1917 progressed, a narrower, more exclusive language of class increasingly displaced the inclusive notion of the citizen. By the summer–autumn, workers' resolutions increasingly equated democracy and 'the people' in opposition to an anti-democratic bourgeois enemy. The political divide was not based on different class experiences but different nuances of the word 'democracy'. 'Here was the crucial political divide', argued Figes and Kolonitskii, 'between the common people and the privileged class: each spoke a different language of democracy'.[20] Towards October 1917, Western liberal notions of democracy were eclipsed. Because of the narrowing concepts of class, the Bolsheviks, who most persistently articulated class rhetoric, grew in popularity. The Bolshevik language of class appealed both *exclusively* to the workers and *inclusively* to peasants and soldiers. This flexibility of their language of class was, for the authors, the key to their success.

Likewise, the language of class has been deployed in the study of Nazi Germany. Thomas Childers's examination of electoral propaganda sought to establish the social language of politics and attributed Nazi success to their synthetic rhetoric of the people's community.[21] Again in discursive and revisionist mode, Alf Lüdtke surmised that the German Labour Front was popular amongst the German working class because 'The Nazi language of labor expressed meanings attached by ordinary workers to work that the Marxist language of class did not.' Commenting on the effect of postmodernism on the history of the Third Reich, Peter Baldwin noted that, for several historians, 'ritual, drama, rhetoric and symbolism have become causal forces themselves'.[22]

The language of class has spawned a considerable body of research and constitutes a sizeable part of the postmodern historical *oeuvre*. Yet neither Jones nor Sewell initiated the examination of the language of class; instead, it was Asa Briggs, the social historian, who did so in his study of the early nineteenth-century emergence of class. Just as the language of class was not an invention of postmodernism, neither did it inevitably lead to postmodern conclusions:

> The word 'class' has figured so prominently in subsequent development of the socialist – and of other social – vocabularies that a study of the origins and early use of the term in Britain is not simply an academic exercise in semantics. There was no dearth of social conflicts in pre-industrial society, but they were not conceived of at the time in straight class terms. The change in nomenclature in the late eighteenth and early nineteenth centuries reflected a basic change not only in men's ways of viewing society but in society itself. It is with the relationship between words and movements – in an English context – that this essay is concerned.[23]

▶ Postmodern knowledge

The most contentious and troublesome aspect of postmodernism for historians is its view of knowledge (epistemology), and in particular its view of knowledge of the past. Just as White spearheaded the growing attention to narrative, Foucault raised the profile of discourse in history. Borrowing heavily from the German philosopher of power and knowledge relations – **Friedrich Nietzsche** – Foucault rejected liberal or Marxist views of social change and instead opted for a more random, differentiated pattern of development characterised by forms of domination and the **will to power**. As a horrified witness to the growth of industrial capitalism, socialism and democracy, Nietzsche rejected the nineteenth-century faith in science, reason and progress and dismissed the prevalent notions of knowledge based on reason. Following Nietzsche's irrationalism, Foucault displaced human **agency** from social history and emphasised socially-constructed practices that were essentially exercises in power and knowledge. His lexicon revealed this denial of agency as he wrote of practices or modes of behaviour rather than actions or deeds. These practices, in particular discourse, moulded individuals and their actions. Describing his aims in *The History of Sexuality* (1976), he outlined the role of discourse and power-knowledge thus:

> The object ... is to define the regime of power-knowledge-pleasure that sustains the discourse on human sexuality in our parts of the world ... My main concern will be to locate the forms of power, the channels it takes, the discourses it permeates in order to reach the most tenuous and individual modes of behavior, the paths that give it access to the rare or scarcely perceivable forms of desire, how it penetrates and controls everyday pleasure.[24]

With human agency thus refuted, the individual was no more than an effect of power. Foucault himself did not escape this logic, and he announced that in the conventional sense as an intentional source of writing, the author was dead (**'death of the author'**). This had the important and startling implication that: 'I am well aware that I have never written anything other than fictions.'[25] Discourse equated knowledge and language, on the one hand, with power and social discipline on the other. So women and men did not make history; instead, an 'apparatus' of power and knowledge animated them and discursive and non-discursive social practices shaped them (note that Foucault, unlike Derrida, admitted the non-discursive). Foucault's notion of power-knowledge illustrated a number of common and defining features of postmodernism. He rejected unitary explanations of the exercise of power but maintained that knowledge was a fragmented multiplicity, locally practised, undetermined and an expression of its relationship with power. Foucault in this way provided the premises of poststructuralist epistemology: scepticism, the decentred, local or discontinuous character of knowledge, relativism and irrationalism.

Foucault concluded that historical analysis should not attempt to discover intentions, or have any truck with notions such as progress, liberation or reason as these were nothing more than ciphers for particular forms of domination (this has dramatic implications for history). Thus, in *Discipline and Punish: The Birth of the Prison* (1975), he described the 'great confinement' of the nineteenth century – an apparatus of knowledge and power – when prisons, schools, factories, mental hospitals and workhouses supervised and disciplined people. Foucault contrasted this with declining forms of domination that had relied on the violence and ritual of the public execution. Sexuality, likewise, was not a basic human need as Freud proposed, but conformed to a socially constructed discourse, 'a technology of the self'. Despite Foucault's denial of human agency, he also maintained that discourses of knowledge and power engendered resistance, such as resistance to norms of sexual behaviour. His critique of modernity as a form of domination again mirrored a Nietzschean vision of history as successive modes of domination.

Foucault has been invoked as an intellectual influence in women's history, the history of gender, the body and sexuality. His influence can be seen in a range of work: for instance, Dorinda Outram's *The Body and the French Revolution* (1989), which looked at the changing discourses and representations of the body as a key feature of the revolutionary period, and Joan W. Scott's critique of E.P. Thompson.[26] The poststructuralist influence has been such that some women historians have articulated feminist epistemologies that reject objectivist epistemologies as an agent of male domination.[27] Poststructuralist epistemology has also been strongly influential among postcolonial scholars, including the Subaltern Studies group discussed previously.

The consequences, if Foucault were right, would shake social history in particular to its very epistemological foundations. If knowledge were just a product of power relationships, the assumptions about the reality of the material world would be flawed. Patrick Joyce noted this 'anti-foundationalism' of postmodernism thus:

> However, it is history behind the epistemology that matters just as much, the history of power and of the regimes of knowledge that have produced ways of knowing the world ... The 'foundations' that have been attacked are many ... Two that have been critical in the foundation of social history are the 'the material' and 'the social', and with them the cognate idea of class.[28]

Such postmodernists as Tony Bennett, Frank Ankersmit and Hayden White have developed this idea further and redefined the relationship between history (the activity of historians) and the past. These theorists radically separate the two, saying in effect that the past may have been real but that history cannot embody this reality. Various processes (the assembly and storing of evidence, the public and academic historical institutions, and research and writing) sever the past and history. Though documents may convey traces of the past, those traces are never sufficient to write a historical account which therefore relies on a context and an interpretation (or, in other words, a **totality**). This interpretative context can be nothing other than a social discourse, a framework of power-knowledge. History is, according to White, as much invented as found. The denial of the context leads in turn to a concentration on the representational rather than the real or the form rather than the content. To use White's phrase, 'the content of the form' is concerned with the formal characteristics of history, and principally its narrative quality.

Postmodernist historians (or more properly theorists of history) have questioned the nature of history itself. They have objected to the 'objectivist', 'certainist' or 'naïve realist' views of historians to their own practices. Their concerns mark a radical departure from the debate about the nature of the discipline that E.H. Carr's *What is History?* launched in 1961. In *Rethinking History* (1991), Keith Jenkins baldly outlined this new stance.

History is a discourse, a language game; within it 'truth' and similar expressions are devices to open, regulate and shut down interpretations. Truth acts as a censor – it draws the line ... Truth prevents disorder, and it is this fear of disorder (of the disorderly) or, to put this positively, it is the fear of freedom (for the unfree) that connects it functionally to material interests.[29]

In his *On What is History* (1995) Jenkins claimed to supersede Carr's outdated work, proposing that modernist epistemologies of Carr (and, for that matter, Geoffrey Elton) should be replaced by the postmodernist ones of Hayden White and Richard Rorty. In similar fashion, Alun Munslow's *Deconstructing History* (1997) advocated a deconstructionist history in the place of the reconstructionist attempt of the empiricist historian to bring the past back to life or the constructionist goal of a social theory-orientated history of Annales, Marxist or historical sociological hue. Beverley Southgate also brought out a primer on the nature of history which sought to encompass the postmodern developments in the understanding of history.[30]

▶ Writing postmodern history

Although somewhat removed from history proper, Hayden White, the American historiographer, has been one of the most radical of the postmodernists and has made the writing of history his particular focus. In his *Metahistory* (1973), he subjected several historians and philosophers of history to formalist procedures of literary criticism. Thus he approached Ranke, Marx, Nietzsche, Michelet, Burchardt and Croce as a literary expert would analyse Thomas Hardy or Jane Austen. This was because, for White, 'historical work ... manifestly is: a verbal structure in the form of narrative prose discourse'.[31] He therefore underlined the narrative qualities of history, proposing a more self-conscious **narrativism** that abandoned attempts to reconstruct past reality in a scientific manner. His conclusion that history can be nothing more than fiction or poetry was radical and obviously difficult for many historians to accept. Historians, according to White, chose – whether consciously or not – to write in a particular literary genre (or **mode of emplotment** as he calls it), be that romance, satire, comedy or tragedy. As such concerns gained ground, emphasis on the narrative and increasing uncertainty about past realities have become widespread. Alex Callinicos has stated that White was 'undoutedly the decisive influence on contemporary discussion of history as narrative'.[32] As Lawrence Stone, the British social historian, announced, the narrative has made a return in history with the waning of social science approaches to history. Consciously blurring the distinction between historical imagination and fiction, Natalie Zemon Davis's renowned *Return of Martin Guerre* (1983) recounted a story at the margins of history about a woman who accepted an impostor as her long-lost husband. This has coincided at times with efforts to reach a wider commercial audience through the reassertion of the literary and narrative virtues of writing over a dry and pseudo-scientific style. In his introduction to *Citizens* (1989), a narrativist treatment of the French Revolution, Simon Schama paid his dues to Hayden White. His concerns for story-line, intrigue and literary embellishment (for example, 'the bones under the buttercups') were also prominently displayed in his BBC documentary series, 'The History of Britain' (2000). Orlando Figes, a historian of the Russian Revolution, has also adopted various elements of narrativism. The very title, *People's Tragedy* (1996), suggested the conscious choice of the tragic literary genre or mode of emplotment and his use of a select number of participants to narrate events (a narrativist technique called **polyphony**) also signalled the influence of the linguistic turn on this work.[33]

▶ Marxism and postmodernism

With a perverse irony, given postmodern hostility to it, the classical Marxist tradition is ideally positioned to rebuff the philosophical challenge that postmodernism poses to history. From its inception, Marxism brought together various elements needed to mount an effective defence of history.

▶ The Marxist critique of idealism

Given that postmodernism is a particular form of idealism, and that Marx's intellectual genesis rested on a critique of Hegel's idealist philosophy of history, Marx himself can lay heavy blows upon postmodernism from beyond the grave. Consider as examples Marx's discussion of the young Hegelians in *The German Ideology* or Proudhon in *The Poverty of Philosophy*. In the former, he attacked the idealist position, demonstrating that ideas do not have a existence independent from real living human beings:

> Morality, religion, metaphysics, all the rest of ideology and their corresponding forms of consciousness, thus no longer retain the semblance of independence. They have no history, no development; but men, developing their material production and their material intercourse, alter, along with this their real existence, their thinking and the products of their thinking. Life is not determined by consciousness, but consciousness by life.[34]

In his critique of the French anarchist, Marx accused Proudhon of drowning the real world in the language and logical abstraction:

> Instead of the ordinary individual with his ordinary manner of speaking and thinking we have nothing but this ordinary manner itself – without the individual

... Thus the metaphysicians who, in making these abstractions, think that they are making analyses, and who, the more they detach themselves from things, imagine themselves to be getting nearer to the point of penetrating the core – these metaphysicians in turn are right in saying that things here below are embroideries of which only logical categories can constitute the canvas ... If all that exists, all that lives on land, and under water, can be reduced by abstraction to a logical category – if the whole real world can be drowned thus in a world of abstraction, in the world of logical categories – who need be astonished?[35]

The Marxist critique of idealism also rejected the separation of theory and practice. Whereas today too many academics specialise in theory or history, Marx was acutely aware of the intimate relationship between evidence and theory in understanding history. The controversy over Richard Evans's *In Defence of History* (1997) revealed, at its extremes, a mutually incomprehensible dialogue conducted between postmodern theorists and practising historians. Explicitly rejecting an engagement with the philosophical underpinnings of the postmodernist historians, Evans himself took the practitioner's perspective. What sought to be a robust defence of history turned out to be an undertheorised appeal for consensus. This was a cardinal mistake as it abandoned the opportunity to uncover the intellectual lineage of postmodernism and its flawed premises. Nietzsche's irrationalism, Saussure's linguistics, Foucault's discourse analysis and Derrida's textualism are vulnerable foundations; yet the postmodernist reveres them and the uninitiated practising historian treats them with trepidation. Patrick Joyce's assertion that postmodern history is anti-foundationalist is true in the sense that it rejects the foundations of social history or Marxism, but untrue if taken to mean that postmodernism does not have any fixed theoretical premises or foundations.

▶ Marxism and language

Whilst it may be argued with some justification that many traditional historians may have neglected language, this is not true of Marxism. Marxist categories of ideology, hegemony, superstructure and consciousness are all concerned with the relationship between language and history. Also, Marx and Engels wrote a number of suggestive passages on language in, for instance, *The Transition of Ape to Man* and *The Germany Ideology*. And as we have already noted, Marx anticipated the question of revolutionary symbolism and language in his *Eighteenth Brumaire* long before Sewell, Jones or Hunt. More importantly, a number of Marxists (Volosinov, Vygotsky, Gramsci and Bakhtin) went beyond these isolated comments to develop a Marxist tradition of linguistics in opposition to the dominant Saussurian approach so influential in postmodernism.[36] Perhaps the best example – Volosinov's *Marxism and the Philosophy of Language* (1929) – rejected Saussurian linguistic determinism with some sophistication. Volosinov's book was originally published in 1929 but only appeared in English in 1973. Unfortunately for him, from 1929 to 1950 Nikolai Marr's linguistics had found favour in Stalin's court. Stalin banned Volosinov's work and the author disappeared in 1934 during the purges. The dictator himself claimed to be an authority on linguistics, but his *Marxism and Linguistics* (1950) amounted to little more than a naïve realism that posited a crude, automatic and unproblematic correspondence between words and objects. In diametric opposition to latter-day postmodernists, Volosinov viewed language primarily as a form of social interaction, as dialogues that could not be separated from the temporal-spatial and socio-economic context in which individuals speak or write. This stood in stark contrast to Ferdinand de Saussure, who judged language not to be a process of social interaction but primarily an independent self-referential system of signs. Aware of the emerging linguistic debates, Volosinov observed that:

> A vehement struggle is going on over 'the word' and its place in the system [i.e., of philosophy], a struggle for which analogy can be found only in the medieval debates involving realism, nominalism and conceptualism. And indeed, the traditions of those philosophical trends of the Middle Ages have, to some degree, begun to be revived in the realism of the phenomenologists and the conceptualism of the neo-Kantians.[37]

Thus, for Volosinov, Saussure was a neo-Kantian incapable of grasping the relation between the subject and object, (the **thing-in-itself**). He went on to tackle directly Saussure's structural linguistics (what Volosinov called abstract objectivism). In so doing he attacked what was to become a central characteristic of poststructural linguistics too:

> The idea of the conventionality, the arbitrariness, of language is a typical one for rationalism as a whole; and no less typical is the comparison of language to the system of mathematical signs. What interests the mathematically minded rationalists is not the relationship of the sign to the actual reality it reflects or to the individual who is its originator, but the relationship of sign to sign within a closed system already accepted and authorized. In other words, they are interested only in the inner logic of the system of signs itself, taken, as in algebra, completely independently of the meanings that give the signs their content.[38]

The difference between Saussure and the poststructuralist position was that where the former saw logic, poststructuralists found none. Like Saussure, Volosinov believed that language was integral to social life, requiring serious analysis, and that a naïve one-to-one correspondence between words and reality would not do. For Volosinov, this was because language was the medium through which human social interaction took place. Unlike Saussurian structuralism, language was not self-contained but was always made for an audience (listener or reader). Even inner speech was like a dialogue made with others in mind. Volosinov also stressed that because language was social in nature, that because it could not be separated from its users and its context, language depended on context for meaning. For instance, Volosinov highlighted the way meaning could be altered by the variation of accent. This was what he called multi-accentality. So for Volosinov, language was not a system in itself because it took place in the shared territory of time and place, and in a context of broader aggregate conditions, social relations, and therefore class. He pointed out the importance of ideology in language and the way in which language was 'an arena of the class struggle'. The **class-struggle** dimension of language was demonstrated in word selection, in the different accents given to words, and in contextual interpretations of words. So, in sharp contrast to Saussure, for Volosinov language is incredibly sensitive to social reality (including class struggle) which it 'reflects and refracts'.

The salient question for Volosinov, around which all linguistics hinged, was the 'actual mode of existence of linguistic phenomena': that is, the social context of language. Volosinov would have applauded C.L.R. James's analysis of cricket in the West Indies in which he identified the way that the joy of the game mingled with the context of racism and imperialism. Unlike Derrida's denial of context, James tellingly asked, 'What do they of cricket know who only cricket know?'[39] Meaning, understanding, the generation of language, and verbal interaction, Volosinov asserted, all depend upon this mode of existence of language: its place in the social world. And for Volosinov the 'fundamental idea' of his work was 'the productive role and social nature of the **utterance**'.[40] Volosinov therefore linked language as a process and a system (or Saussure's **diachrony** and synchrony) because of the creative force of utterance ('parole') within the language system ('langue'). Dave McNally highlighted Volosinov's superiority over poststructural linguistics:

> Volosinov's theory of language is thus above all historical; as such it is a powerful corrective to the static and ahistorical notions prevalent within the new idealism. It is striking that idealist treatments of language, even when they appear to be stressing the historicity of discourses – as Foucault is famous for doing – are profoundly ahistorical. History appears for them as a series of discursive *differences*, a disconnected succession of linguistic paradigms, not a dynamic process generated by the interactions and conflicts among people in concrete social relations.[41]

▶ Marxism and knowledge

Marx proposed a particular epistemology or approach to knowledge. Marxists have firmly rejected **relativism**. Whilst pointing to the importance of interpretative difference, they have formulated the grounds for, and limits of, scientific objective truth. Marx indicated the dialectical connection between subjective thought and activity, and the objective outcomes of intellectual and practical inquiry, in the *Theses on Feuerbach* (1845):

> The question whether objective truth can be attributed to human thinking is not a question of theory but is a practical question. Man must prove the truth, i.e. the reality and power, the this-worldliness of his thinking in practice. The dispute over the reality or non-reality of thinking which isolated itself from practice is a purely scholastic question.[42]

Marx had already underlined the unity of theory and practice as basis of historical knowledge in *Contribution to the Critique of Hegel's Philosophy of Law* (1843): 'the criticism of the speculative philosophy ... cannot end with itself, but in the tasks for which there is only one solution: [**praxis**]'.[43] Philosophy of knowledge, moreover, should not undermine the claims of historical knowledge but rather examine the ways in which human society conceals and disorganises historical truth:

> It is therefore the task of history, now the truth is no longer in the beyond, to establish the truth of the here and now. The first task of philosophy, which is in the service of history, once the holy form of human self-alienation has been discovered, is to discover self-alienation in its unholy forms. The criticism of heaven is thus transformed into the criticism of earth, the criticism of religion into the criticism of law, and the criticism of theology into the criticism of politics.[44]

By contrast, the epistemology of most practising historians, implicit though it may be, is solely concerned with the status of evidence and interpretation. Marx and Engels referred to this epistemology in *The German Ideology* as 'a collection of dead facts as with the empiricists ... or an imagined activity of imagined subjects as with the idealists'.[45] Both philosopher and historian, Marx's **materialism** and empirical mode of investigation (not to be confused with **empiricism**) recommends him to history's defence. Evans and others shy away from the conclusion that history can be scientific and as a result weaken arguments against postmodernism. Hesitation about history as a science stems from a number of sources: Nietzsche; the **Frankfurt School**'s erroneous equation of the **Enlightenment**, rationalism and science with the Holocaust and the horrors of the Second World War; the dissatisfaction with empiricist or **positivist** approaches to history; the institutional division between the sciences and the humanities; and the quirk of the English language in which science and knowledge are not synonymous, as in other languages.

For whatever reason, the idea that history is not a science is extremely prevalent. If we are to decide whether history is to be considered a science, then we must initially ask what science is. Usually, partial aspects of the natural sciences are mistakenly taken as general attributes of science. Thus, for example, science is equated with experimental methodology, yet there are a number of sciences that do not rely on experiment. The comparison between history and physics or chemistry is much less meaningful than an analogy with sciences concerned with the temporal dimension, such as paleontology, astronomy, climatology, ecology and evolutionary biology. Provided we understand science as the search for knowledge of reality through agreed procedures which result in an expanding body of knowledge that brings us to a closer approximation to reality, then history can surely qualify as a science. Though historical truths may be provisional, they are expanding as more research is undertaken, and the line between what is undisputed and disputed within the realm of reason (postmodern diversions aside) has over the long run advanced. History, like any other science, makes discoveries and has interpretative controversies, but it also makes genuine progress. It is ironic that postmodernists reject science as objectivist when twentieth-century science too has been the site of analogous disputes over relativism and subjectivism.[46]

Scepticism is another aspect of the scientific mode of investigation that is also a core concept of postmodernism. Emphatic on this point, Marx's favourite motto was, 'You must have your doubts about everything.'[47] Science and Marxism, at their best, do not propose naïve views of realism but subject their premises and findings to sceptical scrutiny. This scepticism is a necessary accompaniment to an advancing frontier of knowledge. Postmodernists, in contrast, elevate scepticism beyond this mediating function to doubt the very possibility of historical knowledge. Scepticism is thus transformed from facilitating the growth of knowledge to undermining the very foundations of knowledge in a journey from reason to irrationalism.

Neither does the partisanship in history, as some claim, invalidate the claim to scientific status. Scientists themselves have always been personally motivated and committed to intellectual, political or moral causes. This partisanship and personal conviction has been a tremendous spur to innovation. Stephen Jay Gould noted that the startling palaeontological achievements of Leonardo da Vinci came about because he sought to confirm the erroneous theory that the planet and the body operated in the same way.[48] Eric Hobsbawm observed that those from opposite ends of the political and religious spectrum, Mendels (a Catholic priest), Galton (an elitist) and Haldane (a communist), all had a hand in the development of modern genetics.[49] Subjectivity and partisanship exist in science just as much as they do in history; what prevents the collapse into relativism is the ability provisionally to prove research findings independently through agreed procedures (hence archives and footnotes). One has only to consider the vast amount of previously hidden history that Marxist historians have uncovered about workers, slaves and rebels to understand the genuine breakthroughs that partisans make in history. The scientific model also provides tests for falsification, suppression of evidence and mystification in history that do not exist in other epistemologies of history. These set boundaries of legitimate partisanship; boundaries crossed by Stalin in history and Lysenko in biology.

Finally, because of the previous points, Marxism has already provided some of the most consistent and trenchant rebuttals of postmodernism's encroachment into history. Neville Kirk, Bryan Palmer, Alex Callinicos, John Saville, Eric Hobsbawm and Perry Anderson (amongst others) have all attacked the anti-Marxist critique of history developed by postmodernism. The younger Raphael Samuel was a Marxist. Some Marxist non-historians have criticised postmodernism, although the following discussion will concentrate on the work of historians.

▶ The Marxist critique of postmodernism

Neville Kirk, a British Marxist labour historian trained by Thompson at Warwick University, has mounted a sustained critique of Gareth Stedman Jones and Patrick Joyce's postmodernist sortie into nineteenth-century British labour history.[50] Whilst differing in some respects, Jones and Joyce had strong affinities in their central preoccupation with the language of class and their advocacy of the post-structuralism. Kirk's first point was that the term postmodernism itself is based upon a nominal and contentious division of intellectual history into modernist and postmodernist epochs. Despite its elusiveness, he observed that three themes recur within postmodernist historical analyses: discourse, decentredness and deconstruction. These concepts purportedly allow a greater relativity, complexity and openness in history than social determinisms of social history and Marxism. Kirk formulated an explicitly Marxist defence of social history. At the outset he objected to Joyce's description of Marxist historians as 'dinosaurs' and his failure to acknowledge the anti-reductionist approach of many Marxist historians following in the footsteps of Raymond Williams, E.P. Thompson and so on. Being scrupulously fair, Kirk noted that Patrick Joyce and Gareth Stedman Jones did not lapse into the more extreme postmodernist positions as they saw people not only as bearers but also as agents of language. But he admonished the two postmodernists for their failure to explain the way these agents were able to modify their languages of class and for the neglect of the relationship between social and economic transformation and language change. Kirk then broached the postmodern concern with the decentredness of **identity** – particularly the question of gender, race, ethnicity – as against the unitary Marxist notion of class. He drew up a preliminary list of Marxist studies which have examined the diversity of oppression and its relationship to exploitation. Kirk admitted that there were positive and stimulating elements to Joyce and Jones's work that could take social history forward: they challenged the error that language was an entirely passive reflection of a given social reality; and, by examining the language of workers, they also proposed an alternative to the (Althusserian) notion of ideology and false consciousness in which workers were simply seen as passive recipients of ruling class ideas. Kirk then asked whether Joyce and Jones exchanged linguistic determinism for the social one that they decry. Kirk uncovered an ambiguity and discrepancy between theoretical statements and historical practice of both these historians. James Cronin also noted this inconsistency within Jones's work on Chartism, at times arguing that language is non-referential but then referring it to the political.[51] Both at various times object to the rejection of 'the social' yet at other times make statements about the purely discursive nature of social phenomena, such as class: 'In his opposition to economism, and in his 'non-referential' usage of language, Stedman Jones effectively ignores (or denies?) the 'social' and inflates the autonomy enjoyed by political language and ideas within Chartism. *The* Chartist reality becomes, in fact, a discursive reality.'[52]

Following this observation, Kirk criticised Jones and Joyce for their linguistic **formalism** and the consequent failure to explore the possibility that there may have been class renderings or nuances of populist rhetoric. Kirk also warned that the consequence of the linguistic turn was that it threatened a return to writing British history almost exclusively from the perspective of high politics and of consensual gradualist change:

> In sum, the considerable gains registered during the post-1950s radical phase in social history are in danger of being lost in the current linguistic return to, or restoration of 'traditional values': to the importance of ideas and political concepts at their 'natural' Cambridge home; and to the central importance of narrative and description at pragmatic, 'no nonsense' Manchester.[53]

Whereas Neville Kirk has concentrated on those who have taken the linguistic turn in the field of nineteenth-century British history, Bryan Palmer very much widened the field of criticism. Despite being curtly dismissed by Joyce and Richard Evans, Bryan Palmer's *Descent into Discourse: The Reification of Language and the Writing of Social History* (1990) outlined perhaps the most thorough Marxist account of the influence of postmodernism/poststructuralism in the history discipline.[54] Palmer did not object to the use of discourse and language in historical analysis *per se* but insisted that there was a point past which it overshadowed the project of social history. In perhaps more generous spirit than some other Marxists, he could say: 'For before critical theory reaches the point of the reification of language, it contains insights and guides capable of opening new doors of understanding to historians committed to a materialism that recognizes the need for a rigorous reading of documents and texts/contexts.'[55]

Unfortunately, Palmer found that this transgression occurred all too frequently and social history itself was very much on the defensive with a growing poststructuralist bandwagon of social historians, often left-wing ones, jumping aboard.

Palmer ably demonstrated that within the Marxist tradition there were both historians (notably Thompson, Hill and C.L.R. James) and theorists (Marx, Trotsky and the Bakhtin circle) who were sensitive to the questions of language and discourse. He also noted the slippery slope from a hostility to economism to a rejection of materialism; that several poststructuralists such as Rancière and Jones, employed E.P. Thompson's critique of base and superstructure and economism in their rejection of materialism is a salient indication of this. This poststructuralist rejection of materialism entailed, Palmer observed, social historians abandoning an array of Marxist-inspired and still fruitful concepts, such as class struggle, accumulation, capital, labour, exploitation, class formation and **revolution**. For him, the declining credibility of this conceptual agenda has severely impoverished social history as a whole. A further price paid for poststructuralism was the drift from thorough archival research to the prioritising and rereading of certain landmark texts. With considerable range, Palmer's work plotted the development of poststructuralism: the displacement of social with political interpretations (of the French Revolution and American working-class republicanism), refutations of materialist notions of class (Jacques Rancière, Gareth Stedman Jones and William Reddy) and feminist discourse analysis (Julia Kristeva, Luce Irigaray and Joan Wallach Scott). Palmer's principal conclusion was that the linguistic turn amounted to a descent into discourse because the connections with material reality were lost, 'language is reified, texts are decontextualised, and politics and understanding textualised'.[56]

Alex Callinicos, the Marxist political philosopher, has opened up a number of fronts against postmodernism, engaging postmodernist philosophers, literary critics and historians in rigorous critique. In *Against Postmodernism* (1989), tackling it as a broad philosophical and cultural trend, he located its resonance in the particular features of the 1980s and 1990s. In social and cultural terms, postmodernism's pervasive hold over the imagination of that generation of former radicals was in part connected to the affluence and consumerism of the new middle class. This expanding social group occupied professional, managerial and semi-managerial positions in the expanding bureaucracies of the public institutions and private corporations. Unlike the old middle class, which saved its additional income, the new middle class channelled its growing affluence into consumption. Coupled with this socio-economic location, postmodernism expressed their political pessimism and despair: the 'experience of defeat' of the 1968 generation, the sceptical souring of their revolutionary dreams and their retreat into ironic disdain for projects of social transformation:

> The political odyssey of the 1968 generation is, in my view, crucial to the widespread acceptance of the idea of a postmodern epoch in the 1980s. This was the decade when those radicalised in the 1960s and early 1970s began to enter middle age.

Usually they did so with all hope of socialist revolution gone ... This conjuncture – the prosperity of the western new middle class combined with the political disillusionment of many of its most articulate members – provides the context to the proliferating talk of postmodernism.[57]

Though this did not explain the particular form that postmodernism had taken in history, or its origins in the late 1960s, it does describe the fertile conditions for its growth across academia and the media. It also accounted for the continuities between the cultural despair and reactionary anti-democratic anti-Enlightenment angst of Nietzsche and latter-day postmodernists who celebrate their affiliations with the late nineteenth-century German philosopher.[58] This reaction against any idea of progress, against the Enlightenment and science, is a principal deficiency of the postmodernist case. They move from the uncontroversial statement – which Marxists have long subscribed to – that knowledge is socially constructed to the idea that the workings of the natural world themselves are a social construction, rather like Marx's 'valiant fellow' quoted at this chapter's opening. Science, rather than capitalism's distortion of its priorities, was therefore a form of oppression *per se* and postmodernists rejected existing epistemologies and science as imperialist, sexist, and racist. As Ellen Meiskens Wood observed:

> postmodernists – either deliberately or out of simple confusion and intellectual sloppiness – have a habit of conflating the forms of knowledge with its objects: it is as if they are saying not only that, for instance, the science of physics is a historical construct, which has varied over time and in different social contexts, but that the laws of nature themselves are 'socially constructed' and historically variable.[59]

Whereas *Against Postmodernism* was concerned with the rise of postmodernism in philosophy and social and cultural theory, Callinicos's *Theories and Narratives* confronted postmodernism in the philosophy of history. A sizeable proportion of the text dealt with the American conservative State Department official Francis Fukuyama's proposal that neo-liberal capitalism had triumphed and history was at an end. This dovetailed with the postmodernist assertion that Marxism was relevant no more and that a novel epoch had been reached in which the old conflicts and certainties no longer applied. Callinicos saw in American hegemony and the neo-liberal agenda not a benign force which could overcome fundamental human conflicts, but the cause of conflicts to come.

Callinicos then took issue with Hayden White's narrativism whereby White postulated that historical writing was nothing other than a series of narrative choices rather than the reconstruction of a lost historical reality. Historians cannot recover the past but only representations of the past – texts – from which they weave a meaningful tale from an unknowable and meaningless past. Callinicos indicated the problem with this:

> If the historian's evidence is a wall, then what's on the other side of the wall ceases to be an issue; it becomes besides the point to ask what referents [i.e., connection to past reality] her own discourse has, when she uses this evidence to reconstruct the past. Once the referents of historical writing have been occluded, the boundary separating it from fiction is inevitably blurred.[60]

As White believed that historians chose between romance, tragedy, comedy and satire in their story-telling – which was nothing other than a fiction – he therefore reduced historical writing to its formal characteristics, ignoring the truthfulness or otherwise of its content. For White, the history of the Holocaust was a series of linguistic representations. This implied an epistemological relativism of different representations. None could make a claim to be a true representation of past reality and therefore none could make a greater claim to represent the truth of past reality than any other. As White maintained at a conference that discussed the representations of the Holocaust: 'There is an inexpugnable relativity in every representation of historical phenomena. The relativity of the representation is a function of language used to describe and thereby constitute past events as possible objects of explanation and understanding.'[61] Callinicos used White's discussion of the Holocaust to illustrate the bankruptcy of such an approach. At the time, the Holocaust was beset by controversies of denial (Holocaust revisionism), representation (the danger of aestheticising and trivialisation) and explanation (with the danger of relativisation provoking the *Historikerstreit* controversy in Germany).[62] Within this context, Hayden White's denial of a knowable past led him to a 'hopeless muddle' in which he could not find a way of refuting the coterie of Nazi apologists who currently deny the Holocaust. His scepticism and relativism confronted 'disciplinising history' (i.e., historians whose goal it is to understand past realities) and led him to celebrate effectiveness of the sublime, the intuitive and the mystical in history. He cited Nietzsche, Schiller, Heidegger, Hitler, Mussolini, Zionism and various national myths as examples. Whilst stating that White was not a fascist, Callinicos indicated that narrativism attracted White towards historical views that are more story-like in their qualities. Lacking a realist truth–fiction criterion by which to judge these, he could not reject the absurd, falsified and mythologising aspects of these irrationalist views of history. Given the appalling consequence of this position, Hayden White did attempt to distance himself from Nazi apologetics in, it must be said, a highly convoluted manner. As Callinicos demonstrated, these qualifications were inconsistent with his overall position. Thus the flawed narrativist epistemology and contorted logic of postmodernism have contributed to the current confusion over fascism which has alarmingly coincided with the rise of the fascist right in Europe.

In a similarly confused manner, Jacques Derrida applied his technique of 'deep misreading', which searches for any possible reading at the margins of a text, to Paul de Man and Martin Heidegger, resulting in the obscuring of their fascist or collaborationist ideas and practices.[63] Having refused the 'binary opposition' of resistance and collaboration, Derrida was drawn towards the moral and political apologetics of relativism, in effect asking who was he to judge Paul de Man's wartime anti-semitism? Likewise Jean-François Lyotard, a prominent French postmodernist, stated that evidence or appeal to the reality of the past could not refute the Holocaust revisionism of Robert Faurrison.[64] In such a context, the result, Callinicos contended, was not only an epistemological dead-end but also an ethical and political one. Tim Mason, the British Marxist historian of the Third Reich, enunciated a much more satisfactory ethical approach with the epigram: 'If historians do have a public responsibility, if hating is part of their method and warning part of their task, it is necessary that they should hate precisely.'[65]

▶ Conclusions: totalities, opposites and praxis

The defence of history against the supposedly sulphuric advance of theory is not new and not one that Marxists would entirely sympathise with. Traditional empiricist historians have long argued that theory distorted historical research because it generated prior assumptions into which facts are uncomfortably coerced. Geoffrey Elton's *Practice of History* (1967) typified the conservative approach which attempted to hold the portcullis firmly shut in the face of an onslaught of Marxists, sociologists and anthropologists; and in 1991, in *Return to Essentials*, his theorising foes were leftist allies: postmodernists and Marxists.[66]

Callinicos defended the mainstays of the classical Marxist tradition that post-modernists object to most fiercely. He pointed out that totality was not only a concept but a social reality, and **capitalism** was (and has been for several hundred years) a global system, 'into which all the human activities on the planet, in all their richness and variety, are integrated; indeed, they are all subordinated to the logic of competitive accumulation governing the system'.[67]

In contrast to postmodernists, for Marxists, totality is a crucial part of their (dialectical) method. White designated the contextualisation of a fragment of the past in a historical totality or bigger picture as the process of invention. Joyce underlined the dismissal of totality: 'There the whole emphasis is against understandings of society as a system of totality, and upon self-constitution, randomness and the reflexivity of subjects.'[68]

Postmodernists simplistically equate the totality or total history and totalitarianism. This dangerous conflation condemns not just Marxists but also the Annales and historical sociologists. It sidesteps the obvious point that the assertions of a generalised condition of randomness, broken knowledge and indeterminancy are themselves totalising claims. As Raphael Samuel remarked of Foucault: 'Foucault refuses the Marxist notion of ideology and distances himself from the idea of general theory. Yet his cast of mind is a totalising one, and Foucault's genius that of finding common trends in seemingly disparate discourses.'[69] There are many traditions that emphasise the importance of totality, from the French Annales historian Fernand Braudel's conviction that historians should write 'total history' to the German nineteenth-century philosopher Hegel who believed 'the truth is the whole'. In the dialectical method of Marx following Hegel, the category of totality was connected to 'becoming' (i.e., the conviction that history was not a total system but also a process). Whereas postmodernists possess an unacknowledged static (or synchronic) totality, Marxism makes explicit the coupling of system and process (or the diachronic and the synchronic).

The undiluted practitioners' perspective gives a mirror image reflection of the postmodernist case. With a certain amount of (justifiable) schematism, the practitioners' and the postmodernist approaches to history can be catalogued as shown in the diagram. As this diagram demonstrates, postmodernism is empiricism cast back to front on to the camera obscura. It expresses the same theoretical incapacity of dealing with complex dynamic contradictory worlds. Stephen Jay Gould criticised similar false dichotomies in science: 'or our desire to parse complex and continuous reality into division by two (smart and stupid, black and white)'.[70] Some, such as Derrida, denied that these dilemmas (or binary oppositions) exist in their work but this is merely to wish the problem away.

Empiricism/practitioner	Postmodernism/theorist
Induction not **deduction**	Deduction not induction
Practice not theory	Theory not practice
Objective not subjective	Subjective not objective
Past not present	Present not past
History as science not fiction or art	History as fiction or art not science
Impartial search for the truth	Search for power-knowledge
Reconstruction of past reality	Deconstruction of texts
Interpretative disagreements resolvable by new evidence	Interpretative disagreements irresolvable and therefore simply moral or aesthetic or political choices

Lukács also noted the inherent tendency, replicating the **dualisms** of Descartes or Kant, to such dichotomy in bourgeois thought. The source of this failing, according to Lukács, was the refusal of Kant to admit knowledge of the 'thing-in-itself': namely, to find a method of connecting the subjective perception to the objective material world (poststructuralists refuse at the outset the knowledge of the 'thing-in-itself'). All this returns us to the dialectical method outlined in the first chapter. What we witness in all of these examples is the inability on both sides of the theorist–practitioner divide to understand the 'unity and interpenetration of opposites' locked together in an ever-changing process. Marxism seeks therefore to understand the historical process by the combination of theory and practice, as a dialogue between the past and the present. Recognising the falsities of these dichotomies, poststructuralists turn their backs on 'binary oppositions', proposing a fluid and differentiated, ultimately unascertainable, world of meanings. The poststructuralist rejection of determinism and of causation in practice turns into an abdication of the historian's responsibility to explain the past. This is entirely consistent with Nietzsche's irrationalist legacy.

One of the strengths of Marxist history, and an obvious weakness of post-modernism, is praxis: the unity of theory and practice. For Marxist historians this has a dual meaning: first, the attempt to overcome the divide between the practising historian and the theorist, often individually and at least collectively; second, the combination of historical writing and practical interventions into the political world. Reflecting the particular *zeitgeist* of the 1980s and 1990s, postmodernism has been on the retreat with the changing intellectual climate of the late 1990s. Unsurprisingly, postmodernists have had little to contribute to the growing intellectual and political critique of global capitalism and its international institutions (multi-nationals, the World Bank, the International Monetary Fund and the World Trade Organisation). This all smacks too much of totality. Given the postmodernists' insistence that they alone are reflecting the contemporary intellectual conjuncture, several commentators have noted the uncomfortable truth that class inequalities of wealth and power have been widening and that the reach of capitalism as a truly global system has been extended considerably into areas of the world, into aspects of human life and into the domain of the natural environment in these purported postmodern times. These features seem closer to Marx's analysis of capitalism made in the *Communist Manifesto* and *Capital* than the rejection of the very idea of social totality that postmodernists propose. Eley and Nield bluntly observed the indisputable fact that, 'Capitalism continues to make people poor.'[71] Several Marxist critics of postmodernism have noted how it supposes not only the defeat of emancipatory politics, but also the victory and accommodation to consumer capitalism.

Discussions of discourse and the attention to texts can provide certain insights, but these are greater if the context and the author are not rejected in advance.

Indeed the Marxist notions of **ideology** and class struggle as a battle of ideas provides an alternative model which is carefully attentive to meaning and which rejects the reading of texts at face value alone. Displacing history into the playful currents of texts and discourse, poststructuralism entailed a denial of human agency, especially revolutionary agency. This perpetuated the errors inherited from Saussure. Where Saussure proposed a rigid formal codified idealism, poststructuralists offer an idealism of indeterminacy and contingency. Neither genuinely allowed for purposive human activity. In contrast, the great insights of history from below were in part derived from the experience of the Communist Party historians who had themselves been embroiled in class struggles. Debating the 'end of labour history', John Saville made the point that Marxist history was often written by those who were also immersed in political organisations and campaigns, allowing insights into the historical process with which they themselves were wrestling. In response to Stephen Fielding, who dismissed the labour history approach that focused on working-class activists, Saville poignantly observed:

> One must assume from these remarks that Fielding himself has never understood how the various organisations and institutions of what is commonly called the labour movement were actually created ... It must of course be further presumed that Fielding is innocent of how politics, in the broad sense, are conducted, and that he himself has never been outside his own cloisters to engage in any campaign against authority, since such engagements would have taught him certain elementary things about how change, on whatever level, can be brought about, or not brought about, as is so often the case.[72]

Conclusion

'This is how one pictures the angel of history. His face is turned toward the past. Where we perceive a chain of events, he sees one single catastrophe which keeps piling wreckage upon wreckage and hurls it in front of his feet. The angel would like to stay, awaken the dead, and make whole what has been smashed. But a storm is blowing in from Paradise; it has got caught in his wings with such a violence that the angel can no longer close them. The storm irresistibly propels him into the future to which his back is turned, while the pile of debris before him grows skyward. This storm is what we call progress.'

Walter Benjamin, *Theses on the Philosophy of History*

'Last words are for men who have not said enough.'

Marx's dying words, 14 March 1883

'From the end of the 1970s,' declared Gareth Stedman Jones, 'the marxist approach to history, which had flourished in Britain and elsewhere for two decades entered a period of abrupt and terminal decline'.[1] There is a large measure of exaggeration and a suspicion of wishful thinking in Gareth Stedman Jones' assessment. Nevertheless, there is also an element of truth. Marxist history did enter an impasse in the late 1970s. Jones explains that this resulted from the challenge of alternative political and historical projects, such as feminism and environmentalism, and the inability of Marxism to theoretically renew its **epistemology** through Althusser. We might also point to the debilitating effects of the **structuralist–humanist** schism. This debate was never really resolved but passed over in silence as historians got on with writing history. **History from below** seemed to have exhausted its new possibilities. Structuralism spawned poststructuralism. Although more than mere symptoms of Marxist history's impasse, these factors alone cannot explain it. It should be obvious that the 1930s and the 1960s played the pivotal role in the opening-out of an audience for Marxist history. Unearthing the paving stones and erecting barricades in Vienna, Barcelona and Cable Street did for the 1930s generation what those of Watts, Prague, Grosvenor Square and the Sorbonne did for the generation of the 1960s. Like the 1950s, the late 1970s and since have been a period where the intellectual climate seemed closed off to Marxism. The latter were the decades of conservative ascendancy of Reagan and Thatcher when the bastions of working-class industrial strength suffered defeat, and we can add to that the disorientation of many Marxists over the collapse of the Stalinist monolith in 1989–91.

Looking back over a century and a half of Marxist historical writing, there are some striking continuities. Marxism remains a dangerous spectre that haunts the establishment views of history. In each generation, Marxism has provoked hostile reactions and bitter attacks. Although the language has changed, the questions of the philosophy of history addressed by Marx in the 1840s remain pertinent today. Idealist forms of history writing live on in modified form. The young Hegelians are not flattered by comparisons with James Vernon or Hayden White but several of their core propositions are obviously similar. Marx was also sensitive to the twists and turns of intellectual fashion, which transformed erstwhile collaborators and sympathisers into hostile critics. It is no accident that some of Marxist history's most trenchant opponents were once found in its ranks: François Furet, Gareth Stedman Jones, Michel Foucault. If **postmarxism** means anything, it does describe the intellectual odyssey of several academics. Postmarxism articulates their desire to sever their connection with Marxism, which they see as determinist, crude and reductionist, but it is also a rupture with their own past. Furthermore, as the intellectual clarity of several Marxists in the debate over **postmodernism** has demonstrated, Marxist historians did not really lose the argument, and these new approaches have more than a touch of the emperor's new clothes about them.

There are also discontinuities, however. Marxist history now exists within academic institutions that are themselves integral to capitalist society. The student protest movement and the new left of the 1960s developed critiques of the universities. Protests about curriculum content or access for the underprivileged, teach-ins and campus activism radically challenged the universities. It exposed the way in which the universities embodied a contradiction between their ties to the state and corporate capitalism and the essential function of academic and intellectual freedom. The balance sheet of academic Marxism is mixed. It did little to transform the institutional character of universities. It might be argued that Marxist historians may have reshaped academic debate but it was also true that academia reshaped Marxist history. In an essay on the rules of academia, Howard Zinn described how academic conventions (of disciplinary specialism, disinterested scholarship, the deference to experts, etc.) were in many ways antithetical to the development of radical history in addressing the vital issues of the day. The pessimistic case could be made that history from below participated in the academic fragmentation that has had the effect of ghettoising Marxist historians into ever-decreasing social and labour history circles. It is quite right that Marxist historians have defended social history against certain aspects of **poststructuralism**, but there is also a crying need for a broadened vision. Where, for example, are the Marxist economic historians or the Marxist historians of science today?

Marxist historians have also had to deal with what used to be called by many 'actually existing socialism'. This has undoubtedly been the greatest block to the development of a coherent Marxist tradition and the greatest single cause of paralysis on the part of Marxist historians. Many Marxist historians have simply shied away from rigorously applying Marxist analysis to the character of these states. The old habit of the Communist Party Historians' Group died hard; 1917 and all that was taboo unless, as with Hill in 1940, it was recorded as a simple paean to Lenin. History had its revenge. Connected to this is the deep political pessimism on the part of some Marxist historians. They have abandoned the conviction that the possibility of working-class self-emancipation exists. Eric Hobsbawm's political essay 'The forward march of labour halted?' (1978) articulated such a pessimism about the prospects of social democracy based on class. One highly revealing aspect of his *Age of Extremes* (1994), which in many ways is an excellent volume, is the virtual absence of the working class as an agent of historical change. History from below, it would seem, is all well and good as long as it is in the past. Partly this is because some of the great working-class upheavals have been directed against Stalinist rulers, as in Hungary in 1956 or Poland in 1980–1. As for the character of these states, Hobsbawm leaves us no clearer. They are not totalitarian. He refers to them as 'socialist'. He does not really address the fundamental questions required of a materialist account. As the Eastern European joke went, 'Capitalism is the exploitation of man by man, under communism it's the other way around.' The British Marxists' failure to tackle this problem allows such foes of Marxism as Gertrude Himmelfarb to judge the entire project guilty by association:

> It is thirty years since most of the members of the Group left the party. Yet there is no scholarly study of Marxism or Communism by the historians who were personally, actively committed to those ideologies. Nor has there been any serious reevaluation by them of the histories inspired by those doctrines – or, indeed, of the philosophy of history that posits an ultimate relationship between 'praxis' and theory, politics and history. This omission is all the more conspicuous in the light of developments in France, where eminent historians have confronted, seriously and candidly, both the experiences in the Communist Party and the implications for Marxist history.[2]

Yet within the Marxist tradition real attempts, beginning with Trotsky, to analyse these countries do exist and their elaboration would seem to be indispensable for the future of Marxism, in whatever form. It is not the place here to discuss the merits of state capitalist, degenerated workers' state, or bureaucratic collectivist interpretations of **Stalinism** as a historical phenomenon; but historians should be more aware than most of the ironies, complexity and deceiving appearance of history, and less willing to take on trust the idea that these societies were socialist because their official ideologies claimed to be so.

All this aside, the essential propositions of Marx's conception of history and his historical writings continue to provide insights for historians. For those historians who seek a systematic structural explanation of historical development or a total history approach, Marx will remain a yardstick against which they measure themselves. Also, Marxist history can provide a critical counterpoint to the major theoretical influences on historians today, such as postmodernism, neo-**Weberianism** and **empiricism**. Whether or not a new generation of Marxist historians emerges is another matter. That depends in no small part on how Marxists respond to the political events of the past decade and how they respond to the challenges set by the current impasse in Marxist historical writing.

The synonymy of E.P. Thompson and Marxist history has proved to be a mixed blessing. It is necessary to praise but also to bury Thompson. All too often the rest have been ignored, not only other (by implication lesser) third-generation historians but also the pioneers of Marxist historical writing and theory. Thompson has been accorded an eminence, superseding all that went before. Some, like Harvey Kaye, have systematised Thompson's approach into the authoritative new Marxist or 'Thompsonian' method of history. Notwithstanding Thompson's brilliance, the preoccupation with him exaggerates his originality, risks making a virtue out of his flaws and foibles and obscures the work of such earlier Marxist historians as Engels, Gramsci, Lukács and Trotsky, thinkers indispensable to the renewal and defence of a Marxist tradition. His death elicited a flood of tributes and scholarly discussion that has continued for the best part of a decade. Many found the temptation too great and wrote obituaries to Marxism.

There is also the danger, for all the obvious malaise amongst Marxist history, of ignoring a continuing vitality of several Marxist historians. Here it might be worth mentioning, amongst a host of other examples that might be cited, Robin Blackburn's recent two-volume history of European slavery and Chris Harman's *People's History of the World* (1999). Peter Linebaugh and Markus Rediker's *The Many Headed Hydra* (2000) addressed transatlantic revolutionary traditions in the seventeenth and eighteenth centuries in innovative and refreshing ways. Perhaps more interestingly, it spoke to a new generation of anti-capitalist radicals, describing a system that was already exhibiting globalising tendencies and provoking international opposition. As they wrote: 'The globalising powers have a long reach and endless patience. Yet the planetary wanderers do not forget, and they are ever ready from Africa to the Caribbean to Seattle to resist slavery and restore the commons.'[3]

Whilst many looked to postmodernism to supersede Marxism, there are also signs that postmodernism is a passing fashion. Partly this is internal, through exhaustion and a number of damaging episodes, such as the revelations about Paul de Man's wartime activities or the publication of a spoof article written in post-structuralist jargon in the journal, *Social Text*.[4] Partly it is external as an intellectual challenge has come from various quarters such as new historicism in literary studies, or Marxist historians and social theorists. Partly it is because postmodernism, like the coterminous social phenomenon of the yuppie, was a product of its time. The fall of the Berlin Wall created a moment of capitalist triumphalism. The claims of Francis Fukuyama that history had ended were enthusiastically endorsed by postmodernists. Yet the descent into war in parts of Europe, the Balkans and parts of the former Soviet Union that had known peace since 1945 has severely dented that confidence. The marketeers' promises of rapid and painless economic transition have also evaporated.

As for the future of Marxist history, it would be dangerous to speculate. Marxism has never flourished by the persuasiveness of its case alone, but always by the turn of historical events. As Dorothy Thompson observed: 'I found teaching Chartism quite different to kids who had actually been at a big demonstration – they suddenly got the sense of how something captures a crowd. Unless that happens, you don't really – it's like you never felt what it's like being a parent until you have a baby.'[5] Even if there does seem at the moment to be a growing generalised critique of global capitalism, this does not necessarily or automatically reflect itself in a growth of Marxism. Indeed the spokespersons of this mood – Noam Chomsky, Susan George, Naomi Klein, Walter Mosley, Pierre Bourdieu, the Zapatistas – are not Marxists. But the protest against military interventions in the Balkans and the Middle East, against the World Trade Organisation at Seattle, and against Haider in Vienna alongside this changing intellectual atmosphere, at least opens the possibility of a revival of Marxist history and its popularisation amongst a new generation within whose ranks will be students and teachers of history.

This changing *zeitgeist* has taken its toll on postmodernism. Now a number of voices call for theoretical renewal through social theorists who pose as an alternative to postmodernism: Anthony Giddens, Michel de Certeau, Jürgen Habermas and Pierre Bourdieu.[6] The virtue of these thinkers is that they overcome the debilitating decentring of social world and the uncoupling of system and process. Significantly these are features that they share with Marx. Indeed it seems almost inconceivable with the emergence of a new critique of global capitalism that its profoundest critic, Karl Marx, should not contribute to this process.

The space for a radical history that sees, in Walter Benjamin's words, that its 'task is to brush history against the grain' continues to exist, and is perhaps even growing.

Glossary

Agency The subject of the historical process. Human agency signifies that human beings make their own history.

Alienation The estrangement of humans from their own productive nature with the consequence that social relations of production and the products of our labour seem alien, like things beyond our control that dominate our lives.

Althusserianism The **structuralist** Marxism of Louis Althusser (1918–90) and his followers.

Annales A school of French social historians initially grouped around the journal *Annales* including such historians as Lucien Febvre, Marc Bloch and Fernand Braudel. An **Annaliste** is a member of the Annales school.

Asiatic mode of production A mode of production within Marx and Engels's writings which is based on exploitation of the peasantry through the taxation of a centralised bureaucracy. It was supposedly widespread amongst Asian civilisations, and characterised by the lack of private property (agricultural production was based on communal villages), the absence of **class struggle** and social stagnation.

Base and superstructure The metaphor used to describe the relationship between production (base) and politics, ideas and the state (superstructure). Thus the productive base of society is seen as fundamental and shapes, or to some extent determines, the superstructure.

Binary oppositions See **dualism**.

Bourgeois revolution The series of revolutions that marked the **transition** from feudalism to capitalism. These revolutions brought about political changes that cleared the way for capitalist development. According to vulgar accounts of bourgeois revolution, this simply entails the **class struggle** between the bourgeoisie and the aristocracy. The English Civil War (1640–9) and the French Revolution (1789–1815) are two important examples of bourgeois revolution.

Brenner debate   The debate that began in the 1970s over the transition from feudalism to capitalism in Europe occasioned by the work of the American Marxist, Robert Brenner. He argued that key to the transition was the particular outcome of class struggles between the lords and peasants. His account has been accused of privileging **class struggle** over other factors such as the development of the **forces of production**, trade and the merchants, etc.

Capitalism   A phase of economic development (or **mode of production**) characterised by the competitive accumulation of capital and the exploitation of wage-labour.

Class   Classes emerge from the social relations of production and exploitation. A **class-in-itself** is the objective common position in the process of production. A **class-for-itself** is a class in the fuller sense in that it is conscious of itself and its own goals.

Class consciousness   The development of an awareness of the existence of class and one's own class interests.

Class struggle   The conflict between different social classes.

Classical Marxism   A term used to denote the Marxist tradition defined in such a way as to maintain a consistency of principles and ideas across the generations. Classical Marxism rejects thinkers and trends such as **Stalinism**, **vulgar Marxism** and **postmarxism**.

Commodity fetishism   The way in which capitalism and the market turn all aspects of life into commodities and then turns these commodities into the goals or fetishes of human endeavour.

Common sense   A Gramscian term denoting popular belief: that is disordered, largely inherited from the past, embodied in local dialects and sayings and constituted in part by popular religion. It is distinct from **good sense**: that is, the element of popular consciousness that is dynamic, rational and critical, or instinctively class conscious.

Conceptualism   The view that (social and historical) categories (like class, for instance) are not 'real' but classificatory concepts in the mind. See **nominalism** and **essentialism**.

Contradictory consciousness (or split consciousness)   A Gramscian term denoting the manner in which the contradictory effects of (1) ruling class ideology, and (2) experience of class society create contradictory views held by workers.

Death of the author The poststructuralist notion that the understanding of discourses and texts should not be concerned with the intentions and ideas of authors.

Deconstruction The method of reading texts by an examination of their internal characteristics, their inconsistencies, the multiple and varying meanings of their constituent parts. Pioneered by Jacques Derrida, deconstruction became one of the principal elements of **poststructuralism**.

Deduction Reasoning that starts with general premises and goes on to the particular. Often speculative in character. The Aristotelian thinking of medieval Europe would be one example.

Diachrony The emphasis on the change in history.

Dialectic The characteristic method of Marx and Hegel. Dialectics has a long intellectual history stretching back to the ancient Greeks. This method encompasses the **unity of opposites**, **totality**, **negation of the negation**.

Dialectic of nature The idea associated with Engels that not only was human history dialectical, but so too was nature itself. This was the subject of a debate within Marxism and relates to the question of science.

Determinism (1) The idea that phenomena can be attributed to particular causes. (2) All phenomena are the inevitable result of sufficient causes.

Dialectical materialism A term for Marxism stressing its dialectical and philosophical character. See **dialectic**.

Discourse analysis The analysis of the patterns of language associated with Michel Foucault and poststructuralism.

Dualism or **dichotomisation** or **binary oppositions** The separation into opposites, such as mind and body, black and white, rich and poor. These are then considered separately. The dialectic suggests that these opposites are not separate but united in the same totality.

Economic reductionism An approach that reduces different social phenomena to economic causes. An accusation often levelled at Marxism.

Empiricism The view that experience is the only source of knowledge. Facts speak for themselves. Knowledge is the accumulation of facts by observation and experiment.

Enlightenment The seventeenth- and eighteenth-century intellectual movement which believed that science could bring human progress through the increasing knowledge of our world.

Enthusiasm of 1968 The radicalisation of a generation connected to civil rights and anti-war movements and revolts of students and workers across the globe.

Epistemology The philosophy or theory of knowledge, truth or science.

Essentialism The view that (social and historical) categories correspond to fundamental, real or essential characteristics.

Exploitation The appropriation of a **surplus** from production by a non-producing often dominant class. An intrinsic feature of all class societies.

Fall of communism (1989–91) The collapse of the 'communist' regimes of Eastern Europe, which ended the Cold War. This led to transition to market economies and liberal democratic political structures. Some interpreted this as the death of Marxism. Others objected that these regimes had little in common with Marx's vision of socialism.

Falsification (1) The notion (especially developed by Karl Popper) that science and knowledge advance through the falsification of erroneous views; (2) the conscious distortion of history (for example, that practised by Stalin).

Forces of production (or productive forces) This concept combines the means of production and labour power. Development of the forces of production includes the development of tools and machinery, changes in the labour process (new skills, techniques), opening or discovery of new raw materials, sources of energy, lands, education, growth of population.

Formalism Analysis concerned with the outward, conventional or formal characteristics.

Frankfurt school A group of Marxist intellectuals originally based in the 1920s at the Frankfurt Institute for Social Research. It included such thinkers as Adorno, Reich, Benjamin, Horkheimer and Marcuse. Most fled to the USA with the onset of Nazism and war. They increasingly revised key elements of Marxism, such as the approval of science and the centrality of the working class. Very influential in aesthetics and cultural studies.

Hegemony   Intellectual or moral leadership, particularly by one class or part of a class over others. A term particularly associated with Antonio Gramsci.

Hermeneutics   The art or theory of interpreting texts.

Historical materialism   The Marxist view of history. Sees 'ultimate cause and the great moving power of all important historical events in the economic development of society, in the changes in the modes of production and exchange, and in the struggle of these classes on against another' (Engels, *Socialism: Scientific and Utopian*).

Historical sociology   In the 1960s a number of scholars sought to fuse history and sociology. Key sociological thinkers, most importantly Max Weber, Norbert Elias and Émile Durkheim were deployed to write a new kind of history that exhibited a greater sociological awareness.

Historicism   This term is used in a number of contradictory ways. In this text it has been taken to mean the radical division of the past and the present and the idea that each historical individual, event and phenomenon is unique and that therefore there is no overall shape or pattern to history. The view might be summed up by the phrase ' the past is a foreign country' or, as Ranke put it, 'equally close to God'. However, Karl Popper and others have taken historicism to mean the very opposite: the view that history is governed by a law-like logic.

History from below   This idea rejects the view that history is the preserve of 'great men'. History from below or history from the bottom up asserts the importance of the common people to the historical process.

History of mentalities (or **mentalités**)   The notion of a particular outlook or belief system specific to a given time and place. History of mentalities posits the existence of collective belief systems or mentalities or mental structures shaped in part by the environment and everyday life. Associated with the French **Annales** school and anthropological approaches to history.

Humanism   The view that human beings make history and that human activity should be at the centre of history. The history from below of the British Marxist historians is sometimes described as socialist humanism. Opposed by **structuralism**.

Idealism   This is the idea that the primary or sole motor of historical change is ideas or consciousness.

Identity Characteristics that allow recognition of individuals or groups, one's (and others') perception or definition of those individuals or groups. Identities often combine family, national, class, gender and ethnic (self-) perceptions.

Ideology (1) The ideas of the ruling class in any given society. (2) A particular system or body of (often political) ideas. (3) The realm of ideas.

Induction Reasoning that starts from the particular and goes onto the general: for example, the experimental science of the empiricists of the seventeenth century.

Intentionalism The view that history or society can be understood by the analysis of the actions of individuals pursuing their own intentions. Contrasts with structuralist approaches.

Linguistic turn Richard Rorty's term associated with **postmodernism** and **poststructuralism**, indicating the greater emphasis on language and discourse.

Lumpenproletariat The idea of a social rabble or the dregs of society not part of the proletariat and liable to become, in Marx's phrase, 'the bribed tool of reactionary intrigue'.

Materialism All reality is essentially material. Denial of independent existence of ideas.

Mediation According to the **dialectic** changes in quantity bring about changes in quality, so a single process will be transformed into qualitatively different stages. Thus different stages in a process may be mediated by a number of intervening stages. Mediation is therefore the characteristic of intermediary stages.

Mentalités See **history of mentalities**.

Mode of production A particular stage of history characterised by the most common form of production, e.g., primitive communism, **Asiatic mode of production**, ancient mode of production, feudalism, **capitalism**, socialism, communism. Marxist historians often make the useful distinction between mode of production as a general concept and social formation that concerns specific societies which may combine different modes of production.

Modernism A cultural term to denote the dynamic new literary, artistic, musical and architectural forms of the nineteenth and twentieth centuries.

Modes of emplotment Hayden White's term for the forms of narrative plot: tragedy, romance, comedy, irony.

Moral economy E.P. Thompson developed this concept to describe the way in which the crowd in eighteenth-century England had very strong notions of fair prices and just economic practices, and this shared morality and sense of justice shaped collective attitudes and actions (such as bread riots).

Narrativism The method of analysis and writing which elevates the narrative or story-telling qualities of writing.

Negation of the negation According to the dialectic, one thing (e.g., an acorn) becomes another thing (an oak). The oak negates the acorn. But the oak itself becomes another thing (rotting matter, furniture, etc.) and so is in turn negated itself. Therefore the negation has been negated, or we have the negation of the negation. The negation of the negation is a description of the continuous process of change.

New history The term given to the new directions that became prominent in history especially in the 1960s and 1970s. This would include the **history of mentalities**, **history from below**, cultural history, oral history, women's history, black history, the history of sexuality, and the **linguistic turn**, etc. This label was a convenient way of distinguishing 'new history' from 'old' or 'traditional history' in which the political, diplomatic, biographical, the history of great men history and the narrative of great events were to the fore.

Nietzsche, Friedrich (1844–1900) German philosopher who reacted against the **Enlightenment** (therefore science, progress, reason, modernism) and Christian ethics (he stated that God was dead). He proposed that human relationships were based on the **will to power** and that conventional notions of morality (good and evil) were an inauthentic distortion of our nature. Modern society drowned the talents of the natural elite in a growing mediocrity and a new elite of supermen should attempt to transcend this situation. Nietzsche was a key influence on the development of **postmodernism** and **poststructuralism**. For example, Michel Foucault once described himself as a Nietzschean Marxist.

Nominalism The view that categories are nominal, arbitrary and in the mind.

Organic intellectuals The development of an intellectual minority growing alongside or within a class that is able to exert intellectual and moral leadership or hegemony.

Patrician A noble person, originally in Ancient Rome. Often used in conjunction with the plebs (plebians). Often has the connotation of a philanthropic or paternalistic aspect to the relation to the poor.

Permanent revolution Trotsky's theory that socialism was possible in Russia despite its lack of industrial capitalist development. This was because of the existence of small pockets of highly developed capitalist industry in Russia, a small but militant working class and the international character of the revolution.

Plebeian Of the plebs or the common people, originally in Ancient Rome but often used in the case of the urban and rural propertyless poor before the Industrial Revolution.

Polyphony A postmodernist technique which uses many contemporary voices to narrate a particular historical event thereby supposedly displacing the historian as the narrator.

Positivism The notion of a science of society pioneered by Auguste Comte (1798–1857). Factual study and the establishment of scientific laws of society allow the prediction of human behaviour and social improvement through social engineering.

Postcolonial studies A recent branch of social studies, interdisciplinary in character, and concerned with the study of the former European colonies before and after independence often incorporating **poststructuralist** methods.

Postmarxism Denotes historians and thinkers who have either broken with Marxism or who seek to retain some elements of Marxism as a plural and eclectic body of thought incorporating elements of **poststructuralism**.

Postmodernism Literally the phase of history, the arts, etc., beyond **modernism**. In place of the bold innovative character of **modernism**, postmodernism is ironic, sceptical, detached and often nostalgic. In the study of society, postmodernism is sceptical towards universal theories or 'grand narratives'.

Poststructuralism A body of thought that went beyond **structuralism** which suggested rigid determinism. Instead knowledge was less certain. Poststructuralism is particularly concerned with the openness of language to many meanings. **Deconstruction, textualism** and **discourse analysis** are all aspects of poststructuralism. Poststructuralism is seen as one part of postmodernism.

Praxis   The synthesis or unity of theory and practice. A term used by both Gramsci and Lukács to denote the importance of the dialectical unity of these opposites. Sometimes Gramsci employed philosophy of praxis as a synonym for Marxism.

Reductionism   This means explaining a process according to one of its constituent elements. Marxism is often accused of economic reductionism because it supposedly explains all in terms of economics.

Reification   Transformation into matter. A term used by Lukács to express the transformation of **social relations of production** into things to be bought and sold through commodification.

Relativism   The denial that knowledge or ethics can be absolute or certain or universal but is instead relative. It can mean that there can be no (objective) criteria to judge the superiority of one view over another.

Revolution   A rapid far-reaching historical process distinct from the normal pace of historical change. A social revolution draws the masses into rebellion against the old order and may lead to the passage from one mode of production to another.

Saussurrian (or sometimes **Saussurrean**)   Following Saussure's linguistics.

Scepticism   The doubting of the truth or authenticity of aspects of history and society, sometimes taken to the extreme position of doubting the possibility of all knowledge.

Semiotics   The theory of signs. Associated with anthropology and used in new history.

Signifier – signified – sign   This denotes the fact that language is constituted by the vocal sound or written symbol (signifier), the concept (signified) and information-carrying entities (signs – which can be symbols, icons, etc.).

Social relations of production   Specific human relations within society and between humans and the natural world that are created as a consequence of production. Sociologists are more likely to employ the terms social structure and class structure which are roughly equivalent.

Socialist humanism   See **humanism**.

Stalinism   A term that can denote (1) Stalin's personal rule; (2) a doctrine associated with Stalin; (3) a particular socio-economic system that was established under Stalin's rule and spread to the rest of Eastern Europe and China, the interpretations of which vary from the view that this was 'actually existing socialism', totalitarianism, bureaucratic collectivism, a degenerated workers' state or state capitalism.

Standard of living debate   Historical controversy over the impact of the Industrial Revolution on the welfare and standard of living of the British working population.

Structuralism   The view that society is reproduced according to patterns of behaviour, attitudes and rules. The focus on structures of society can obscure or even deny human **agency**.

Surplus   This occurs when production exceeds the basic needs of society.

Synchrony   The emphasis on continuity and inertia in history.

Textualism   The method of privileging the text over the context or authorial intent in analysis and of considering all phenomena as if they were texts. This method is particularly associated with the French poststructuralist, Jacques Derrida, who stressed the multiple meanings of texts.

Thing-in-itself   A philosophical term to express the problem of knowing the reality of external objects. Kant believed that we could not know the thing-in-itself as our knowledge of the world was organised by concepts created within our minds.

Thirty Years' War (1618–48)   A war that involved several European powers covering much of central Europe, noted for its brutality and devastating effects on population. Diplomatic, dynastic and religious rivalry mixed together. The war ended with the Treaty of Westphalia which signalled the frustration of the Habsburgs' attempt to secure control over Protestant parts of central Europe, in particular the Dutch Republic.

Totality   The whole. A term used by Hegel and Marx to denote the conviction that processes cannot be understood by the understanding of particular constituent parts but only by the totality of those processes (i.e., the whole is greater than the sum of the parts). This led Marx and Hegel to view human history as a totality. Others, such as the **Annales** school, also attempted to develop a total history. Critics assert that such universal views are inherently totalitarian.

Transition   A term often used to describe the replacement of one **mode of production** by another (e.g., the long and complex process whereby **capitalism** developed out of the crisis of European feudalism).

Unity of opposites   According to the **dialectic**, opposites mutually define and are interconnected with one another in a total changing process. Light could not be understood without darkness and the relationship between the two is in a permanent state of flux. Important examples of the unity of opposites include: the exploiting and exploited classes, mind and matter, structure and agency, **base and superstructure** and theory and practice.

Utterance   A linguistic term denoting a speech act.

Villeinage   The servile status of a serf in medieval Europe.

Vulgar Marxism   Crude interpretations of Marx, such as economic **reductionist** accounts.

War of movement   The phase of war which is characterised by rapid advances or retreats. For Gramsci this might denote a phase of revolution and counter-revolution.

War of position   The attritional phase of war. Used by Gramsci to denote a phase in the **class struggle** which is slow moving and therefore requires long-term strategy (this is particularly the case in stable capitalist democracies).

Weberianism   A school of sociological thought derived from the writings of the German sociologist, Max Weber (1864–1920). His work is often compared to Marx because of its historical and sociological character. His accounts pay greater attention to such features as individuals, status, charisma, modern bureaucratic rationalism and authority. His most famous work, *The Protestant Work Ethic and the Rise of Capitalism* underlined the importance of Protestantism to the rise of **capitalism**. Sometimes historical sociologists are called neo-Weberians.

Will to power   Nietzsche's notion that human beings are naturally driven by the urge to attain power and dominate others.

Notes

(The place of publication is London unless otherwise specified.)

▶ Introduction

1 K. Marx and F. Engels, *Selected Works in One Volume* (1991), p. 412.
2 http://bbc.com/news, BBC News online (1 October 1999).
3 M. Kettle, 'When fame is an open book', *The Guardian*, 14 September 1999.
4 G. Iggers, *Historiography in the Twentieth Century: From Scientific Objectivity to Postmodern Challenge* (1997), pp. 78–9.
5 E. Hobsbawm, *On History* (1997), p. 223.

▶ 1 The Wide Panorama of Marxist History

1 W. Benjamin, *Illuminations: Essays and Reflections* (1973), p. 248.
2 I. Deutscher, *Prophet Armed: Trotsky, 1879–1921* (1954), *Prophet Unarmed: Trotsky, 1921–1929* (1959), *Prophet Outcast: Trotsky, 1929–1940* (1963); I. Deutscher, *Stalin: A Political Biography* (1967; 1st edn 1949).
3 I. Deutscher, *The Prophet Outcast: Trotsky, 1929–40* (1963), pp. vii–viii.
4 T. Mason, quoting Marx in J. Caplan (ed.), *Nazism, Fascism and the Working Class: Essays by Tim Mason* (Cambridge, 1995), p. 226.
5 J.S. Cohen, 'The Marxist contribution to economic history', *Journal of Economic History*, 38 (1978).
6 J. Saville, *1848: The British State and the Chartist Movement* (Cambridge, 1987), p. 202.
7 W.E.B. Du Bois, *Black Reconstruction in America, 1860–1880* (Cleveland, 1969; 1st edn 1935); see also his historical work before he became a Marxist: W.E.B. Du Bois, *The Suppression of the African Slave-Trade to the United States of America* (New York, 1969; 1st edn 1896).
8 R. Fraser, *The Blood of Spain* (1979); L. Passerini, *Fascism and Memory* (Cambridge, 1987). They collaborated together on R. Fraser (ed.), *1968: A Student Generation in Revolt* (1988), another fine example of oral history.

9 For the earlier generation of Marxist historians see P. Buhle, 'American Marxist historiography, 1900–40', *Radical America*, November 1970.

10 H. Zinn, *A People's History of the United States* (1980), pp. 570–4.

11 V. Kiernan, *Eight Tragedies of Shakespeare: A Marxist Study* (1996); P. Siegel, *The Gathering Storm: Shakespeare's English and Roman History Plays, a Marxist Analysis* (1992); P. Siegel, *Shakespearean Tragedy and Elizabethan Compromise* (Washington, DC, 1983); P. Siegel, *Shakespeare in His Time and Ours* (Notre Dame, 1968); V. Kiernan, *Shakespeare, Poet and Citizen* (1993).

12 R. Hilton, 'The origins of Robin Hood', *Past and Present*, 14 (1958), reprinted in the collection of essays: S. Knight (ed.), *Robin Hood: An Anthology of Scholarship and Criticism* (Cambridge, 1999), p. 192.

13 G. Bois, 'Marxisme et nouvelle histoire', in J. Le Goff (ed.), *La Nouvelle Histoire* (Paris, 1988), p. 271.

14 G. De Ste Croix, *Class Struggles in the Ancient Greek World* (1981).

15 G. Bois, *The Transformation of the Year One Thousand: The Village of Lournand from Antiquity to Feudalism* (trans. J. Birrell) (Manchester, 1992; 1st French edn 1982); P. Anderson, *Passages from Antiquity to Feudalism* (1974).

16 C. Wickham, 'The other transition', *Past and Present*, 103 (1984); C. Wickham, 'The uniqueness of the East', *Journal of Peasant Studies*, 12 (2 and 3) (1985). Wickham argued that Marx's notion of the Asiatic mode of production was fundamentally flawed because these civilisations usually combined tributary (i.e., a highly centralised state taxing the peasantry) and feudal modes of production. They were neither static nor immune to class struggle.

17 For Wickham's view of Michael Mann see C. Wickham, 'Historical materialism, historical sociology', *New Left Review*, 171 (1988); of W.G. Runciman, see C. Wickham, 'Systactic structures: social theory for historians', *Past and Present*, 132 (1991).

18 Bois, *The Crisis of Feudalism*; Anderson, *Passages from Antiquity*.

19 J. Day and G. Bois, 'Crise du féodalisme: et conjuncture des prix: un débat', *Annales*, 34 (2) (1979).

20 P. Anderson, *Lineages of the Absolutist State* (1974). Anderson also criticises the notion of an Asiatic mode of production.

21 R. Hilton (ed.), *Transition from Feudalism to Capitalism* (1978).

22 T. Ashton and C. Philpin (eds), *The Brenner Debate* (Cambridge, 1987).

23 R. Brenner, *Merchants and Revolution: Commercial Change, Political Conflict, and London's Overseas Traders, 1550–1653* (Princeton, NJ, 1993).

24 C. Harman, *The Lost Revolution: Germany 1918–23* (1982); P. Broué, *Révolution en Allemagne* (Paris, 1971).

25 J. Stewart's preface to G. Lefebvre, *The French Revolution*, 2 vols, (1964), p. ix.

26 E. Burke, *Reflections on the Revolution in France* (Harmondsworth, 1968; 1st edn, 1790).

27 G. Rudé, *The Crowd in the French Revolution* (Oxford, 1959); G. Rudé, *Wilkes and Liberty: A Social Study, 1763 to 1774* (Oxford, 1962). John Wilkes was MP for Aylesbury and then Middlesex and Lord Mayor of London. He was the focus of agitation in the 1760s and 1770s when crowds cried for 'Wilkes and liberty'.

28 M. Vovelle, *Religion et Révolution: la Déchristianisation de l'An II* (Paris, 1976); M. Vovelle, *La Révolution contre L'Église: de la Raison à l'Être Suprême* (Paris, 1988).

29 *Sunday Times*, book supplement, 21 May 1989.

30 B. Anderson, *Imagined Communities* (1983); H. Kaye (ed.), *History, Classes and Nation-States: Selected Writings of Victor Kiernan* (Oxford, 1988); E. Hobsbawm and T. Ranger (eds), *Invention of Tradition* (Cambridge, 1983).

31 R.S. Neale, *Writing Marxist History: British Society, Economy and Culture since 1700* (1985); 'History' in Kaye, *History, Classes and Nation-States*.

32 E. Hobsbawm, *On History* (1997), p. 221.

33 G. De Ste Croix, 'Class in Marx's conception of history, ancient and modern', *New Left Review*, 146 (1984), p. 110.

34 S. Rigby, *Marxism and History: A Critical Introduction* (1987); L. Althusser and E. Balibar, *Reading Capital* (1970), N. Levine, *The Tragic Deception: Marx contra Engels* (1976).

35 G. Elton, *The Practice of History* (Glasgow, 1982; 1st edn 1967), p. 53.

36 G. Himmelfarb, *The New History and the Old* (Cambridge, MA, 1987).

37 G. Enteen, *The Soviet Scholar-Bureaucrat: M.N. Pokrovskii and the Society of Marxist Historians* (University Park, 1978), p. 62; see also N. Troitski, 'The first period of soviet historiography', *Russian Studies in History*, 32 (1) (1993); J. Barber, *Soviet Historians in Crisis, 1928–32* (1981).

38 Enteen, *The Soviet Scholar-Bureaucrat*, pp. 151–2.

39 A. Dorpalen, *German History in Marxist Perspective: The East German Approach* (1985).

40 D. Martin, *The Making of a Sino-Marxist World View: Perspectives and Interpretations in the People's Republic of China* (Armonk, NY, 1990).

41 E.P. Thompson, *The Poverty of Theory and Other Essays* (1978), pp. 270–6 and 324–34; S. Ashman, 'Communist Party Historians' Group', in J. Rees (ed.), *Essays on Historical Materialism* (1998), pp. 154–7.

42 G. Lukács, *History and Class Consciousness* (1971), p. 1.

43 R.J. Evans, *In Defence of History*, (London, 1997) p. 4.

44 H. Abelove *et al.* (eds), *Visions of History* (Manchester, 1983), p. 11.

45 Abelove *et al.*, *Visions of History*, p. 170.

46 Later editions renamed and revised: T. Cliff, *State Capitalism in Russia* (1974).

47 R. Bahro and D. Fernbach, *Alternative in Eastern Europe* (1978); M. Djilas, *New Class: An Analysis of the Communist System* (1957); M. Djilas, *Unperfect Society: Beyond the New Class* (1969).

▶ 2 Marx and Engels's Conception of History

1 E. Gibbon, *The History of the Decline and Fall of the Roman Empire*, 2 vols (1994; 1st edn 1776); G. Vico, The *New Science of Giambattista Vico: Unabridged Translation of the Third Edition* (1984; 1st edn 1744).

2 G. Tagliacazzo (ed.), *Vico and Marx: Affinities and Contrasts* (New Jersey, 1983); L. Simon, 'Vico and Marx: perspectives of historical development', *Journal of the History of Ideas*, 42 (1981), pp. 317–31.

3 A. Smith, *An Inquiry into the Nature and Causes of the Wealth of Nations* (Oxford, 1976; 1st edn 1776), pp. 689–723.

4 F. Engels, *Ludwig Feuerbach and the End of Classical German Philosophy*, in K. Marx and F. Engels, *Selected Works in One Volume* (1991), p. 614; D. McLellan, *Karl Marx: His Life and Thought* (St Albans, 1976), p. 95; M. Löwy, 'The poetry of the past: Marx and the French revolution', *New Left Review*, 177 (1989).

5 F. Lyotard, *The Postmodern Condition* (Minnesota, 1984), p. xxiv.

6 J. Rees, *Algebra of Revolution: the Dialectic and the Classical Marxist Tradition* (1998), pp. 75–8.

7 F. Engels, The *Condition of the Working Class in England* (Oxford, 1993).

8 F. Engels, *Letters on Historical Materialism 1890–4* (Moscow, 1980), pp. 7–8.

9 F. Engels, *Socialism: Scientific and Utopian*, in Marx and Engels, *Selected Works*, p. 367.

10 R. Levins and R.C. Lewontin, *The Dialectical Biologist* (Cambridge, MA, 1985); S.J. Gould, *An Urchin in the Storm* (1990), pp. 153–4; R.C. Lewontin, S. Rose and L.J. Kamin, *Not in our Genes: Biology, Ideology and Human Nature* (New York, 1984).

11 F. Engels, *The Part Played by Labour in the Transition from Ape to Man*, in Marx and Engels, *Selected Works*, p. 342.

12 G. Childe, *What Happened in History?* (Harmondsworth, 1946), pp. 7–13.

13 There is a debate over the role of the productive forces. Rigby sees Marx as possibly a 'productive force determinist': S. Rigby, *Marxism and History: A Critical Introduction* (1987), pp. 27–55; A. Callinicos, *Making History: Agency, Structure and Change in Social Theory* (1987), pp. 42–64; G. Cohen, *Karl Marx's Theory of History: A Defence* (1979); H. Kaye, *The British Marxist Historians* (London, 1995), pp. 232–41.

14 K. Marx and F. Engels, *The Communist Manifesto*, in Marx and Engels, *Selected Works*, p. 36.

15 T.R. Malthus, *An Essay on the Principle of Population* (1996; 1st edn 1798).

16 K. Marx, *Preface to A Contribution to the Critique of Political Economy*, in Marx and Engels, *Selected Works*, pp. 173–4.

17 Marx, *The Communist Manifesto*, p. 36.

18 Marx and F. Engels, *The German Ideology* (student's edn, 1991), p. 45.

19 Marx, preface to *A Contribution to the Critique of Political Economy*, p. 173.

20 J. Diamond, *Guns, Germs and Steel: The Fate of Human Societies* (1997), p. 149.

21 P. Fryer, *Black People in the British Empire* (1989), pp. 61–5.

22 F. Engels, *The Origin of the Family, Private Property and the State*, in Marx and Engels, *Selected Works*, pp. 577–8.

23 Marx and Engels, *The German Ideology*, p. 64.

24 Engels, *The Origin of the Family*, p. 578.

25 P. Siegel, *The Meek and the Militant: Power and Religion across the World* (1985), for a general Marxist history of religion.

26 F. Engels, *Ludwig Feuerbach and the End of Classical German Philosophy*, in Marx and Engels, *Selected Works*, p. 614.

27 K. Marx, *Critique of Hegel's Philosophy of Right*, in D. McLellan (ed.), *Karl Marx: Early Texts* (Oxford, 1971), pp. 122–3.

28 Marx and Engels, *The German Ideology*, p. 57.

29 K. Marx, *Introduction to A Critique of Political Economy*, in Marx and Engels, *The German Ideology*, p. 124.

30 K. Marx, *Theses on Feuerbach*, in Marx and Engels, *Selected Works*, p. 29.

31 Marx and Engels, *The German Ideology*, p. 59.

32 K. Marx and F. Engels, *Holy Family,or the Critique of Critical Criticism*, in K. Marx and F. Engels, *Collected Works, vol. 4: 1844–45* (1975), p. 93.

33 Engels, *Ludwig Feuerbach*, p. 612.

34 H. Beynon, 'Class and historical explanation', in M. Bush (ed.), *Social Orders and Social Classes in Europe since 1500: Studies in Social Stratification* (1992), p. 232.

35 J. Kochanowicz, 'Between submission and violence: peasant resistance in the Polish manorial economy of the Eighteenth Century', in F. Colburn (ed.), *Everyday Forms of Peasant Resistance* (1989), pp. 34–63.

36 G. Brown, *Sabotage: A Study in Industrial Conflict* (Nottingham, 1972).

▶ 3 The Historical Writings of Marx and Engels

1 H. Abelove *et al.*, *Visions of History* (Manchester, 1983), p. 271.

2 Consider, for example, Engels's *Peasant War in Germany*, *The Origins of the Family, Private Property and the State*, Marx's *Eighteenth Brumaire of Louis Bonaparte*, *Class Struggles in France*, *Civil War in France*.

3 K. Marx, *The Eighteenth Brumaire of Louis Bonaparte*, in K. Marx and F. Engels, *Selected Works* (1991), p. 93.

4 H.C.G. Matthew, *Gladstone 1809–1874* (Oxford, 1986), p. 1.

5 Marx, *The Eighteenth Brumaire*, p. 93.

6 Marx, *The Eighteenth Brumaire*, p. 93.

7 Marx, *The Eighteenth Brumaire*, p. 94.

8 Marx, *The Eighteenth Brumaire*, p. 95.
9 Marx, *The Eighteenth Brumaire*, p. 160. The June Days pitted the Parisian workers against the National Guard over the closure of the national workshops which had been set up after the February revolution to alleviate unemployment.
10 Marx, *The Eighteenth Brumaire*, p. 160.
11 D. Renton, *Fascism: Theory and Practice* (1999); D. Beetham, *Marxists in the Face of Fascism: Writings from the Inter-War Period* (Manchester, 1983).
12 Marx, *The Eighteenth Brumaire*, p. 162.
13 Marx, *The Eighteenth Brumaire*, p. 161.
14 D. LaCapra, *Rethinking Intellectual History: Texts, Contexts, Language* (Ithaca, NY, 1983), pp. 268–90; H. White, *Metahistory: The Historical Imagination in Nineteenth-century Europe* (Baltimore, MD, 1973), pp. 320–7; *Tropics of Discourse: Essays in Cultural Criticism* (Baltimore, MD, 1985), pp. 15 and 67–8; *The Content of the Form: Narrative Discourse and Historical Representation* (Baltimore, MD, 1990), pp. 46–7 and 101. The error is to overlook the fact that Marx's condemnation stemmed from the lumpenproletariat's reactionary role in the struggles of 1848–51. Marx's alternative would have been to romanticise the poor in a condescending manner out of keeping with his partisanship for working-class struggle.
15 Marx, *The Eighteenth Brumaire*, p. 164.
16 Marx, *The Eighteenth Brumaire*, p. 169.
17 Marx, *The Eighteenth Brumaire*, p. 168.
18 F. Engels, *The Peasant War in Germany* (Moscow, 1977), p. 27. It was first published as a series in the *Neue Rheinische Zeitung* in 1850 and reprinted as a book with a new preface in 1870 and 1875. It first appeared in English in 1926.
19 P. Blicke, *The Revolution of 1525: The German Peasants' War from a New Perspective* (Baltimore, MD, 1981), p. xii in translators' (T. Brady and H. Midelfort) preface.
20 J. Bak (ed.), *The German Peasant War of 1525* (1976), p. 89. This was a special edition of the *Journal of Peasant Studies* to celebrate the 125th anniversary of Engels's work and the 450th anniversary of the war itself. Debate of Engels's piece constituted a significant section of this work with a number of discussants. See also E. Wolf, 'Peasant War in Germany: Engels as social historian', *Science and Society*, 51 (1) (1987).
21 Engels, *The Peasant War*, p. 8.
22 Engels, *The Peasant War*, pp. 7–8.
23 Engels, *The Peasant War*, p. 41.
24 A. Dorpalen, *German History in Marxist Perspective: The East German Approach* (1985).
25 Engels, *The Peasant War*, pp. 39–40.
26 Engels, *The Peasant War*, p. 41.

27 D. McLellan, *Karl Marx: His Life and Thought* (St Albans, 1976), p. 347.

28 W. Morris, 'How I became a socialist', in G.D.H. Cole (ed.), *William Morris: Selected Writings* (1946), p. 565.

29 K. Marx, *Capital*, 3 vols; I (1954), pp. 686–93 (this edition used unless otherwise stated).

30 Marx, *Capital*, p. 686.

31 Marx, *Capital*, p. 685.

32 K. Marx, *Capital*, I (Harmondsworth, 1976), pp. 606–7.

33 Marx, *Capital*, p. 252.

34 Marx, *Capital*, p. 712.

35 Marx, *Capital*, p. 703.

36 F. Engels to C. Schmidt, 5 August 1890 in K. Marx and F. Engels, *Selected Letters* (Peking, 1977), pp. 72–3.

37 F. Engels to J. Bloch, 21–22 September 1890, in F. Engels, *Letters on Historical Materialism 1890–4* (Moscow, 1980), p. 10.

38 Engels to Bloch, in Engels, *Letters on Historical Materialism 1890–4*, p. 11.

39 Engels to Bloch, in Engels, *Letters on Historical Materialism 1890–4*, p. 11.

40 Engels to Bloch, in Engels, *Letters on Historical Materialism 1890–4*, p. 11.

41 Engels to Bloch, in Engels, *Letters on Historical Materialism 1890–4*, p. 10.

42 F. Engels to W. Borgius, 25 January 1894 in Engels, *Letters on Historical Materialism 1890–4*, p. 26.

▶ **4 The Second Generation and the Philosophy and Writing of History**

1 A. Gramsci, *Letters From Prison* (New York, 1973), p. 273.

2 I. Deutscher, *The Prophet Outcast: Trotsky, 1929–40*, (1963) p. 218.

3 A.L. Rowse, *End of an Epoch*, pp. 282–3 quoted in Deutscher, *The Prophet Outcast*, p. 220.

4 L. Trotsky, *History of the Russian Revolution*, 3 vols (New York, 1980; 1st edn 1932); I, p. xvii.

5 Trotsky, *History of the Russian Revolution*, I, p. xxi.

6 Trotsky, *History of the Russian Revolution*, II, p. vi.

7 Trotsky, *History of the Russian Revolution*, I, pp. 5–6.

8 Trotsky, *History of the Russian Revolution*, II, p. xviii.

9 Trotsky, *History of the Russian Revolution*, II, p. vii.

10 Trotsky, *History of the Russian Revolution*, I, p. 118.

11 Trotsky, *History of the Russian Revolution*, III, p. 198.

12 Trotsky, *History of the Russian Revolution*, II, p. vii.

13 Trotsky, *History of the Russian Revolution*, II, p. vi.

14 Trotsky, *History of the Russian Revolution*, III, p. 291.

15 Trotsky, *History of the Russian Revolution*, I, p. 330.

16 L. Trotsky, *The Lessons of October* (1987; 1st edn 1924).

17 Trotsky, *History of the Russian Revolution*, I, p. 435.

18 Trotsky, *History of the Russian Revolution*, I, pp. 435–6.

19 Deutscher, *The Prophet Outcast*, p. 221.

20 A. Gramsci, *Selections from Prison Notebooks* (1971), p. 238.

21 For example, V. Kiernan, 'Antonio Gramsci and the other continents', in V. Kiernan and H. Kaye (eds), *Imperialism and its Contradictions* (1995); V. Kiernan, 'Antonio Gramsci and Marxism', in H. Kaye, *History, Classes and Nation-States*.

22 Gramsci, *Selections from Prison Notebooks*, p. 324.

23 Gramsci, *Selections from Prison Notebooks*, p. 324.

24 Gramsci, *Selections from Prison Notebooks*, p. 323.

25 Gramsci, *Selections from Prison Notebooks*, p. 325.

26 Gramsci, *Selections from Prison Notebooks*, p. 333.

27 Gramsci, *Selections from Prison Notebooks*, p. 340.

28 Gramsci, *Selections from Prison Notebooks*, p. 341.

29 A. Gramsci, *Selections from Cultural Writings: Language, Linguistics and Folklore* (1985), p. 320.

30 H. Kaye, 'Political theory and history: Antonio Gramsci and the British Marxist historians', *Italian Quarterly*, 25 (97–8) (1984). This article detailed the acknowledgements of Thompson, Hill, Hilton, Hobsbawm and Rudé to Gramsci. The article also stressed the value of Gramsci's notion of class consciousness compared to Lukácsian or Leninist views, thereby stressing what distinguished them and underplaying the common ground between these views.

31 *Tailism and the Dialectic*, written in 1925 or 1926 as part of the polemics that ensued Lukács's *History and Class Consciousness*. It was rediscovered in Moscow archives and published for the first time in 1996. It is published in English translation in G. Lukács, *A Defence of History and Class Consciousness: Tailism and the Dialectic* (2000).

32 G.S. Jones, 'The Marxism of early Lukács', in New Left Review (eds), *Western Marxism: A Critical Reader* (1977).

33 G. Lukács, *History and Class Consciousness* (1971), pp. 10–11.

34 Lukács, *History and Class Consciousness*, p. 48.

35 Lukács, *History and Class Consciousness*, p. 154.

36 Lukács, *History and Class Consciousness*, pp. 154–5.

37 Lukács, *History and Class Consciousness*, p. 98.

38 Lukács, *History and Class Consciousness*, p. 102.

39 Lukács, *History and Class Consciousness*, p. 181.

40 Lukács, *History and Class Consciousness*, p. 184.

41 Lukács, *History and Class Consciousness*, p. 1.

42 Lukács, *History and Class Consciousness*, pp. 12–13.

43 Lukács, *History and Class Consciousness*, p. 204.

44 Lukács, *History and Class Consciousness*, p. 74.

45 Lukács, *History and Class Consciousness*, p. 69.

▶ 5 'Rescuing the Poor Stockinger': History from Below

1 C.L.R. James, *The Black Jacobins* (1980; 1st edn 1938) p. ix.

2 W. Morris, 'The Lord Mayor's Show', first appearing in *Justice*, 1 (44) (15 November 1884); reprinted in *William Morris, Political Writings: Contributions to Justice and Commonweal* (Bristol, 1994), p. 66.

3 E. Hobsbawm, 'Communist Party Historians' Group 1946–56', in M. Cornforth (ed.), *Rebels and Their Causes: Essays in Honour of A.L. Morton* (1978), p. 26.

4 Hobsbawm, 'Communist Party Historians' Group 1946–56', pp. 25–6.

5 H. Butterfield, *The Whig Interpretation of History* (1931); L. Namier, *The Structure of Politics at the Accession of George III* (1929).

6 A school of economic history named after Sir J.H. Clapham, the British economic historian (1873–1946). See J. Clapham, *A Concise Economic History of Britain from the Earliest Times to 1760* (Cambridge, 1949); J. Clapham, *An Economic History of Modern Britain* (Cambridge, 1930).

7 E. Hobsbawm, 'Progress in history', *Marxism Today*, February 1962, p. 46.

8 *Past and Present*'s subtitle was changed in 1958, signalling the loss in confidence in the scientific character of history as a number of Marxist historians parted company from Stalinism.

9 Hobsbawm, 'Communist Party Historians' Group 1946–56', p. 32.

10 Hobsbawm, 'Communist Party Historians' Group 1946–56', p. 30.

11 P. Fryer, *Hungarian Tragedy*, (1956); P. Fryer, *Staying Power: Black People in Britain since 1504* (New Jersey, 1984); P. Fryer, *Black People and the British Empire* (1988).

12 J. Morrill, *The Nature of the English Revolution* (1993), p. 273.

13 C. Hill, *The Collected Essays of Christopher Hill. Volume 3: People and Ideas in 17th-Century England* (Brighton, 1986) p. 97.

14 C. Hill, *England's Turning Point: Essays on Seventeenth-Century English History* (1998), pp. 294–5.

15 C. Hill, *The World Turned Upside Down: Radical Ideas during the English Revolution* (1972), pp. 292–3.

16 Hill, *The World Turned Upside Down*, p. 12.

17 C. Hill, *The Intellectual Origins of the Revolution* (Oxford, 1965). This proved to be a controversial work which prompted a debate over the relationship

between Puritanism and science. See C. Webster (ed.), *The Intellectual Revolution of the Seventeenth Century* (1974).

18 M. Kishlansky, 'Desert island radicals', *Times Higher Education Supplement*, 7 September 1984.

19 C. Hill, *The Intellectual Consequences of the English Revolution* (Wisconsin, 1980), p. 60.

20 Hill, *The World Turned Upside Down*, p. 312.

21 C. Hill, *The English Revolution 1640* (1979; 1st edn 1940), p. 62.

22 J.H. Hexter, *On Historians* (1979), pp. 227–54.

23 C. Hill, *The Collected Essays of Christopher Hill. Volume 2: Religion and Politics in Seventeenth-Century England* (Amherst, MA, 1986), p. 51; *England's Turning Point*, p. 294.

24 E.P. Thompson, *The Making of the English Working Class* (Harmondsworth, 1968; 1st edn 1963), p. 13.

25 H. Kaye, *Why Do Ruling Classes Fear History? And Other Questions* (London, 1997; 1st edn 1995), p. 205.

26 Thompson, *The Making of the English Working Class*, p. 9.

27 Thompson, *The Making of the English Working Class*, p. 10.

28 Thompson, *The Making of the English Working Class*, p. 217.

29 Though he would object to much of the poststructuralist content of J.W. Scott, 'Women and the Making of the English Working Class', in J.W. Scott (ed.), *Gender and the Politics of History* (New York, 1988), for a critique of Scott's views see B.D. Palmer, *Descent into Discourse: The Reification of Language and the Writing of Social History* (Philadelphia, PA, 1990), pp. 78–86 and 172–86.

30 E.P. Thompson, *Whigs and Hunters: The Origin of the Black Act* (1990; 1st edn 1975), p. 262. Thompson (and Linebaugh) underscored the importance of capital punishment through the term 'thanatocracy', meaning a government that relies heavily for its power on the use of the death penalty.

31 Thompson, *Whigs and Hunters*, p. 267.

32 E.P. Thompson, *Customs in Common* (1993; 1st edn 1991), p. 7.

33 P. Linebaugh, *The London Hanged: Crime and Civil Society in the Eighteenth Century* (1985), p. xvii.

34 Linebaugh, *The London Hanged*, p. xxi.

35 H. Gutman, *The Black Family in Slavery and Freedom 1750–1925* (Oxford, 1976), pp. 3–4.

36 E. Genovese, *Roll, Jordan, Roll: The World the Slaves Made* (New York, 1975), pp. 25–6.

37 Genovese, *Roll, Jordan, Roll*, p. 26.

38 Genovese, *Roll, Jordan, Roll*, p. 148.

39 D. Chakrabarty, *Rethinking Working Class History: Bengal 1890–1940* (Princeton, NJ, 1989), p. 69.

40 E. Said, *Orientalism* (1985); S. Sarkar, 'Orientalism revisited: Saidian frameworks and the writing of modern Indian history', *Oxford Literary Review*, 16 (1–2) (1994).

41 Though others have also taken the Thompsonian route to postmodernism as well see M. Steinberg, 'Culturally speaking: finding a commons between post-structuralism and the Thompsonian perspective', *Social History*, 21 (2) (1996).

42 R. Chandavarkar, ' "Making of the Working Class": E.P. Thompson and Indian history', *History Workshop Journal*, 43 (1997), p. 191.

▶ 6 Marxism, Structuralism and Humanism

1 B. Hindess and P. Hirst, *Pre-Capitalist Modes of Production* (1975), p. 312.

2 Hindess and Hirst, *Pre-Capitalist Modes of Production*, p. 309.

3 Hindess and Hirst, *Pre-Capitalist Modes of Production*, p. 311.

4 G. Eley and D. Blackbourn, *The Peculiarities of German History* (Oxford, 1984). In part this was written as a critique, using the German example, of the French model of bourgeois revolution used by Tom Nairn and Perry Anderson.

5 E.P. Thompson, *The Poverty of Theory and Other Essays* (1978), p. 225.

6 Thompson, *The Poverty of Theory*, p. 359.

7 Thompson, *The Poverty of Theory*, pp. 205–6.

8 Thompson, *The Poverty of Theory*, p. 300.

9 R. Johnson, 'Edward Thompson, Eugene Genovese, and Socialist-Humanist History', *History Workshop Journal*, 6 (1978), p. 85.

10 Johnson, 'Edward Thompson, Eugene Genovese, and Socialist-Humanist History', pp. 87–8.

11 E.P. Thompson, 'The politics of theory', R. Samuel (ed.), *People's History and Socialist Theory* (1981), p. 398.

12 C. Hill, *England's Turning Point: Essays on Seventeenth-Century English History* (1998) p. 294.

13 E.P. Thompson, *Customs in Common* (1993), p. 73 quoting K. Marx, *Grundrisse* (Harmondsworth, 1973), pp. 106–7.

14 R.S. Neale, *Writing Marxist History: British Society, Economy and Culture since 1700* (1985); K. Marx and F. Engels, *The German Ideology* (student's edn, 1991), pp. 48–50. Roughly speaking the 'four moments' are: (1) the need to produce in order to live; (2) the consequent development of the forces of production; (3) the social relations that this implies; (4) the historical development that these relations go through. These moments are the premises of human history and consciousness. G. Hening, 'R.S. Neale 1927–85', *Australian Economic History Review*, 26 (2) (1986).

15 Thompson, *The Poverty of Theory*, p. 288.

16 A. Prinz, 'Background and ulterior motive of Marx's "Preface" of 1859', *Journal of History of Ideas*, 30 (3) (1969).

17 E. Hobsbawm, *On History* (1997), p. 201.

18 V. Kiernan, 'Problems of Marxist history', *New Left Review*, 161 (1987), p. 107.

19 D. Blackbourn, *Populists and Patricians: Essays on Modern German History* (1997), p. 72.

20 P. Anderson, *Arguments within English Marxism* (1980), p. 33.

21 T. Adorno and M. Horkheimer, *The Dialectic of the Enlightenment* (1979; 1st edn 1944), pp. 3–4.

22 C. Hill, 'Marxism and history', *Modern Quarterly*, 3 (2) (1948), p. 57.

23 C.L.R. James, *Black Jacobins: Toussaint L'Ouverture and the San Domingo Revolution* (1980; 1st edn 1938), p. xi.

24 Anderson, *Arguments within English Marxism*, p. 12.

25 Thompson, *The Poverty of Theory*, p. 298.

26 P. Linebaugh, 'Commonists of the world unite!', *Radical History Review*, 56 (1993).

27 G. De Ste Croix, *The Class Struggle in the Ancient Greek World* (1981), p. 43

28 B. Palmer, *E.P. Thompson: Objections and Oppositions* (1994), pp. 85 and 107.

29 Thompson, *Customs in Common*, p. 7.

▶ 7 Marxism and Postmodernism in History

1 K. Marx and F. Engels, *The German Ideology* (student's edn, 1991), p. 46.

2 Including *Past and Present*, *Social History*, *International Review of Social History* (1993 for special supplement on 'The end of labour history?'), *Journal of Modern History*, *Central European History* (special issue: vol. 22, 1989), *American Historical Review*, *Labour History Review*.

3 A. Marwick, 'Two approaches to historical study: the metaphysical (including postmodernism) and the historical', *Journal of Contemporary History*, 30 (1) (1995) and H. White, 'A response to Arthur Marwick', *Journal of Contemporary History*, 30 (2) (1995).

4 P. Joyce, 'The end of social history?', *Social History*, 20 (1995), p. 73; only for the journal's editors to rebut the claim: G. Eley and K. Nield, 'Starting over: the present, postmodern and the moment of social history', *Social History*, 20 (1995), p. 355. This was part of a long-running debate: D. Mayfield, 'Language and social history', *Social History*, 16 (1991); D. Mayfield and S. Thorne, 'Social history and its discontents: Gareth Stedman Jones and the politics of language', *Social History*, 17 (1992); J. Lawrence and M. Taylor, 'The poverty of protest: Gareth Stedman Jones and the politics of language: a reply', *Social History*, 18 (1993); D. Mayfield and S. Thorne, 'Reply to "The poverty of protest" and

"imaginary discontents" ', *Social History*, 18 (1993); N. Kirk, 'History, language, ideas and postmodernism: a materialist view', *Social History*, 19 (1994); J. Vernon, 'Who's afraid of the "linguistic turn"? Politics of social history and its discontents', *Social History*, 19 (1994).

5 J.-F. Lyotard, *The Postmodern Condition* (Minnesota, 1984), p. xxiv.
6 P. Anderson, *The Origins of Postmodernity* (1998).
7 Vernon, 'Who's afraid of the "linguistic turn"?', pp. 96–7.
8 S. Sim (ed.), *Postmarxism: A Reader* (Edinburgh, 1998), p. 2.
9 J. Derrida, *Specters of Marx: The State of the Debt, the Work of Mourning, and the New International* (New York, 1994); P. Curry, 'Towards a postmarxist social history: Thompson, Clark and beyond', in A. Wilson (ed.), *Rethinking Social History: English Society 1570–1920 and its Interpretation* (Manchester, 1993); P. Joyce, 'The return of history: postmodernism and the politics of academic history in Britain', *Past and Present*, 158 (1998); E. Laclau and C. Mouffe, *Hegemony and Socialist Strategy: Towards a Radical Democratic Politics* (1985).
10 A. Koestler, I. Silone, R. Wright, A. Gide, L. Fischer and S. Spender, *The God That Failed: Six Studies in Communism* (1950).
11 Eley and Nield, 'Starting over', p. 357.
12 C. Issawi (ed.), *An Arab Philosophy of History: Selections of the Prolegomena of Ibn Khaldun of Tunis (1332–1406)* (1950); G. Vico, The *New Science of Giambattista Vico: Unabridged Translation of the Third Edition* (1984; 1st edn 1744).
13 With the French revolution, for example, revisionist historians have scrutinised festivals, Marianne (the mythical revolutionary heroine), public representations of the body, the declaration of the rights of man, the use of the Phrygian cap (first given to emancipated slaves in ancient Rome) and the liberty tree to reinterpret the great events. See M. Agulhon, *Marianne into Battle: Republican Images and Symbolism in France, 1789–1880* (Cambridge, 1981); J. Harden, 'Liberty caps and liberty trees', *Past and Present*, 146 (1995); L. Hunt, *Politics, Culture and Class in the French Revolution* (1984); E. Gombrich, 'The dream of reason: symbolism of the French revolution', *British Journal of Eighteenth Century Studies*, 2 (1979); M. Ozouf, *Festivals and the French Revolution* (1988); D. Outram, *The Body and the French Revolution: Sex, Class and Political Culture* (New Haven, CT, 1989); C. Blum, *Rousseau and the Republic of Virtue: The Language of Politics in the French Revolution* (New York, 1986).
14 R. Samuel, 'Reading the signs I', *History Workshop Journal*, 32 (1991).
15 G.S. Jones, *Languages of Class: Studies in English Working Class History* (Cambridge, 1983), p. 1.
16 Jones, *Languages of Class*, pp. 7–8.
17 Jones, *Languages of Class*, p. 8.
18 P. Joyce, *Visions of the People: Industrial England and the Question of Class* (Cambridge, 1991), p. 23.

19 J. Vernon, *Politics and the People: a Study in English Political Culture c. 1815–67* (Cambridge, 1993), p. 333.

20 O. Figes and B. Kolonitskii, *Interpreting the Russian Revolution: The Language and Symbolism of 1917* (1999), p. 125.

21 T. Childers, 'The social language of politics in Germany', *American Historical Review*, 95 (1990).

22 A. Lüdtke, 'The honour of labour. Industrial workers and the power of symbols under National Socialism' in D. Crew (ed.), *Nazism and German Society* (1994), p. 6; P. Baldwin, 'Social interpretations of Nazism: reviewing a tradition', *Journal of Contemporary History*, 25 (1990) p. 6.

23 A. Briggs, 'The language of class in early nineteenth century England' in J. Saville and A. Briggs (eds), *Essays in Labour History* (1960), p. 44.

24 M. Foucault, *The History of Sexuality*, I (Harmondsworth, 1978; 1st edn 1976), p. 11.

25 Quoted in A. Callinicos, *Social Theory* (Cambridge, 1999), p. 280.

26 J.W. Scott, 'Women in the Making of the English Working Class', in Scott, *Gender and the Politics of History* (1988).

27 Scott, *Gender and the Politics of History*; C. Steedman, 'Bimbos from Hell', *Social History*, 19 (1) (1994).

28 Joyce, 'The end of social history?', p. 74.

29 K. Jenkins, *Rethinking History* (1991), p. 32.

30 B. Southgate, *History: What and Why? Ancient, Modern and Postmodern Perspectives* (1996); B. Southgate, *Why Bother with History?* (2000).

31 H. White, *Metahistory: Historical Imagination in Nineteenth-Century Europe* (Baltimore, MD, 1973), p. ix.

32 A. Callinicos, *Theories and Narratives: Reflections on the Philosophy of History* (Cambridge, 1995), p. 51.

33 S. Schama, *Citizens: A Chronicle of the French Revolution* (Harmondsworth, 1989); O. Figes, *People's Tragedy: The Russian Revolution 1891–1921* (1996); L. Stone, 'The revival of the narrative', *Past and Present*, 85 (1989).

34 Marx and Engels, *The German Ideology*, p. 47.

35 K. Marx, *Poverty of Philosophy* (1847), chapter 2 at http://csf.colorado.edu/mirrors/marxists.org/archive/marx/works/1840/pov-phil/ch02.htm.

36 M. Holoborow, *The Politics of English: A Marxist View of Language* (1999).

37 V.N. Volosinov, *Marxism and the Philosophy of Language* (Cambridge, MA, 1996; 1st edn 1973), p. xv.

38 V.N. Volosinov, *Marxism and the Philosophy of Language*, p. 2.

39 C.L.R. James, *Beyond a Boundary* (1963). James was echoing Rudyard Kipling in this phrase.

40 Volosinov, *Marxism and the Philosophy of Language*, p. xv.

41 D. McNally, 'Language, history and class struggle', in E.M. Wood and J.B. Foster (eds), *In Defense of History: Marxism and the Postmodern Agenda* (New York, 1997), p. 32.

42 K. Marx, *Theses on Feuerbach* (1845) in K. Marx and F. Engels, *Selected Works in One Volume* (1991), p. 28.

43 D. McLellan, *Karl Marx: Early Texts* (Oxford, 1971), p. 122.

44 McLellan, *Early Texts*, p. 116.

45 Marx and Engels, *The German Ideology*, p. 48.

46 A. Woods and T. Grant, *Reason in Revolt* (1995). Consider for example Heisenberg's uncertainty principle which posits that at the sub-atomic level the mass and velocity of neutrons and electrons depends upon the observer. Einstein's theory of relativity also sparked long-running controversies over relativism.

47 That is, *de omnibus dubitandum*, quoted in D. McLellan, *Karl Marx: His Life and His Thought* (Frogmore, 1976), p. 457.

48 S. Gould, *Leonardo's Mountain of Clams and the Diet of Worms* (1998).

49 E. Hobsbawm, *On History* (1998).

50 Kirk, 'History, language, ideas and postmodernism'.

51 J. Cronin, 'Language, politics and the critique of social history', *Journal of Social History*, 20 (1) (1986).

52 Kirk, 'History, language, ideas and postmodernism', p. 235.

53 Kirk, 'History, language, ideas and postmodernism', p. 237.

54 Joyce, 'The end of social history?', p. 80; Evans, *In Defence of History*, p. 293.

55 Palmer, *Descent into Discourse*, p. 189.

56 Palmer, *Descent into Discourse*, p. 215.

57 A. Callinicos, *Against Postmodernism: A Marxist Critique* (Cambridge, 1989), p. 168.

58 See also A. Callinicos, 'Postmodernism, poststructuralism, postmarxism?', *Theory, Culture and Society*, 2 (3) (1985). Callinicos argued that the three major strands of social theory that inform views of modernity and consequently history are derived from Nietzsche, Saint-Simon and Marx. He maintained that Marxism through Volosinov and Bakhtin provides a sophisticated alternative to poststructuralism.

59 Wood and Foster, *In Defense of History*, p. 5.

60 Callinicos, *Theories and Narratives*, p. 66.

61 H. White, 'Historical emplotment and the problem of truth', in S. Friedlander (ed.), *Probing the Limits of Representation: Nazism to the Final Solution* (Cambridge, MA, 1992), p. 37.

62 C.S. Maier, *The Unmasterable Past: History, Holocaust, and German National Identity* (Cambridge, MA, 1988). The *Historikerstreit*, or 'historians' dispute', took place in the mid-1980s when a number of German nationalist historians

tried to deny the uniqueness of the Holocaust. This resulted in a sharp set of exchanges in journals, books and the press.

63 J. Derrida, 'Like the sound of the sea deep within a shell: Paul de Man's war', *Critical Inquiry*, Spring 1988. Dominck LaCapra also addressed the *Historikerstreit*, Heidegger and Paul de Man from a poststructuralist perspective (with a psychoanalytical twist of Freud and Lacan) in D. LaCapra, *Representing the Holocaust: History, Theory, Trauma* (Ithaca, NY, 1994).

64 J.-F. Lyotard, *The Differend: Phrases in Dispute* (Minneapolis, 1988), pp. 56–7.

65 T. Mason, *Nazism, Fascism and the Working Class* (Cambridge, 1995), p. 230.

66 G. Elton, *The Practice of History* (1967); G. Elton, *Return to Essentials* (Cambridge, 1991); for similar views from a conservative American historian see G. Himmelfarb, 'Postmodernist history and the flight from the facts', *Times Literary Supplement*, 16 October 1992.

67 Callinicos, *Theories and Narratives*, p. 209.

68 Joyce, 'The end of social history?', p. 90.

69 R. Samuel, 'Reading the signs I', p. 107; see also the second part in *History Workshop Journal*, 33 (1992).

70 S. Gould, *The Mismeasure of Man* (1996), p. 27.

71 Eley and Nield, 'Starting over', p. 359.

72 J. Saville, 'The crisis of labour history: a further comment', *Labour History Review*, 61 (3) (1996), p. 323.

▶ Conclusion

1 G.S. Jones, 'The determinist fix: some obstacles to the further development of the linguistic approach to history in the 1990s', *History Workshop Journal*, 42 (1996), p. 18.

2 G. Himmelfarb, *The New History and the Old* (Cambridge, MA, 1987), p. 93. The French ex-Marxists she refers to include, amongst others, François Furet, the revisionist historian of the French Revolution and author of a number of anti-communist works. See F. Furet, *The Passing of an Illusion: the Idea of Communism in The Twentieth Century* (Chicago, IL, 1999). In other words, Furet is the kind of former Marxist an American conservative can admire.

3 P. Linebaugh and M. Rediker, *The Many-Headed Hydra: The Hidden History of the Revolutionary Atlantic* (2000), p. 353.

4 A. Sokal, 'Transgressing the boundaries: toward a transformative hermeneutics of quantum gravity', *Social Text*, 14 (1 and 2) (spring–summer 1996).

5 Interview by P.J. Walker with Dorothy Thompson, *Radical History Review*, Spring 2000, pp. 17–8.

6 See, for example A. Jones, 'Words and deeds: why a post-post structuralism is needed and how it might look', *Historical Journal*, 43 (2) (2000); Alex Callinicos also makes this point in his final chapter of *Social Theory: A Historical Introduction* (Cambridge, 1999).

Further Reading

(The place of publication is London unless otherwise specified.)

▶ Chapters 2 and 3

Marx spelt out his general views on history with varying degrees of accessibility in the *Communist Manifesto* (chapter 1) and *The German Ideology* (part 1). In the preface to *A Contribution to the Critique of Political Economy*, he concentrated on the broadest sweeps of history and famously outlined his views on modes of production, productive forces and relations and base and superstructure. In contrast, in *The Eighteenth Brumaire of Louis Bonaparte* (1852), he was concerned with applying his general theory to a particular case study and, as a result, gives much greater insights into the role of the individual and the peculiarities of the French political and social structure of that time. Engels's *Socialism: Utopian and Scientific* (1880) provides an accessible introduction to Marxist thought written for the European workers' movement. Engels also discusses the character of history in a series of letters collected as *Letters on Historical Materialism* (1890–4) and in *Ludwig Feuerbach and the End of Classical German Philosophy* (1886: part 4). The entire works of Marx and Engels can found on the internet at http://csf.colorado.edu/psn/marx. There is a mass of writing on Marx's ideas. For some of the best introductions to his ideas see, for example, A. Callinicos, *The Revolutionary Ideas of Karl Marx* (1983), and his more detailed account of Marx's philosophy of history, *Making History* (1987). S. Rigby's *Marxism and History: A Critical Introduction* (1987) is also valuable but is less forgiving in that it accentuates the inconsistencies of Marx's work. For those requiring a biographical framework for Marx's life's work, see David McLellan's *Karl Marx: His Life and Thought* (1976). J. Mahon, 'Marx as a social historian', *History of European Ideas*, 12 (6) (1990) examined Marx's views on suicide, crime, women, money and health.

▶ Chapter 4

Both Tony Cliff and Isaac Deutscher have written multi-volume biographies of Trotsky. Apart from his *History of the Russian Revolution*, Trotsky wrote prolifically on a range of issues relevant to the historian such as Nazism, the Spanish Civil War and France in the 1930s. Pathfinder Press has published collections of his writings on these subjects. His *Revolution Betrayed* (1937) was at the time a path-breaking analysis of Stalin's Russia. Cultural historians have neglected Trotsky's writings but two collections of his writings, *The Problems of Everyday Life: and other Writings on Culture and Science* (1973) and *Literature and Revolution* (1991), are a good starting point.

Read J. Joll, *Gramsci* (1977) or C. Boggs, *Gramsci's Marxism* (1976) for good short introductions to the life and thought of Antonio Gramsci. For a biography, see G. Fiori, *Antonio Gramsci: Life of a Revolutionary* (1975). For an essay on Gramsci's newspaper articles on fascism as a form of contemporary history, see W. Fillanpoa, 'Gramsci on fascism: journalism as history', *Italian Quarterly*, 24 (93) (1983). There are several collections of Gramsci's writings in English: *Prison Notebooks* (1996); Quentin Hoare (ed.), *Selections from Political Writings 1910–20* (1977); Quentin Hoare (ed.), *Selections from Political Writings 1921–1926* (1978); David Forgacs (ed.), *A Gramsci Reader: Selected Writings 1916–1935* (1988); David Forgacs (ed.), *Selections from Cultural Writings* (1985), *Letters from Prison* (1973). For the relationship between the British Marxists and Gramsci, see H. Kaye, 'Political theory and history: Antonio Gramsci and the British Marxist historians', *Italian Quarterly*, 25 (97–8) (1984). For the links between Gramsci and postmodernism and subaltern studies, see R. Holub, *Antonio Gramsci: Beyond Marxism and Postmodernism* (1992); A. Patnaik, *Gramsci's Concept of Commonsense: Towards a Theory of Subaltern Consciousness in Hegemony Processes* (Calcutta, 1987); and C. Mouffe (ed.), *Gramsci and Marxist Theory* (1979).

Lukács's key writings for Marxist history are: G. Lukács, *History and Class Consciousness* (1971), *Lenin: A Study in the Unity of his Thought* (1997); G. Lukács, *A Defence of History and Class Consciousness: Tailism and the Dialectic* (2000). For useful biographical accounts of Lukács, see G. Lichtheim, *Lukács* (1970) or M. Löwy, *Georg Lukács: From Romanticism to Bolshevism* (1979). For an influential but flawed essay on Lukács's view of history, see G.S. Jones, 'The Marxism of early Lukács', in *New Left Review* (eds), *Western Marxism: A Critical Reader* (1977).

▶ Chapter 5

There is no substitute for reading the works of the authors discussed in this chapter. Christopher Hill's long intellectual career has produced a very substantial *œuvre*. His essays have been reprinted in various collections that are well worth pursuing. Perhaps Christopher Hill's most celebrated work is *The World Turned Upside Down* (1972) which charts religious radicalism in the revolutionary interlude. He linked the revolution to the longer-run evolution of secular thought in his *Intellectual*

Origins of the English Revolution (1965) and *Some Intellectual Consequences of the English Revolution* (1980). Examining the importance of religious thought to the process of revolution are *Antichrist in Seventeenth-Century England* (1971) and *The English Bible and the Seventeenth-Century Revolution* (1993). Affirming his continued intellectual vitality, *Liberty against the Law* (1996) examines the relationship between popular liberties and the growth of the rule of law, and it includes the seminal essay on the Norman yoke (the idea that tyranny had alien origins with the invasion of the Normans). E.P. Thompson's first major work was a biography of the English revolutionary socialist, *William Morris* (1955), with whom Thompson identified on a number of different levels, not least of which was his moral vision of Marxism. His *The Making of the English Working Class* (1963) is essential reading for an understanding of the development of social history and Marxist history, especially history from below. For a collection of his writings on the eighteenth century see E.P. Thompson, *Customs in Common* (Harmondsworth, 1993) and also *Whigs and Hunters: The Origin of the Black Act* (1975). To understand Thompson's affinity with Blake's romantic anti-capitalism, read his *Witness against the Beast: William Blake and the Moral Law* (1993). Other notable 'British Marxist' historians' works are Rodney Hilton's *Bond Men Made Free* (1973), E. Hobsbawm's *Age of Revolution* (1962), *Age of Capital* (1975), *Age of Empire* (1987) and *Age of Extremes* (1994), and V. Kiernan's *The Lords of Humankind* (1969), to name but a few.

In addition there are a number of texts that might act as a useful supplement. On the forerunners to British Marxist historians, see R. Samuel, 'British Marxist historians 1880–1980 part I', *New Left Review*, 120 (1980). For a first-hand account of the Communist Party Historians' Group, consult Hobsbawm's article in M. Cornforth (ed.), *Rebels and Causes: Essays in Honour of A.L. Morton* (1978). Try also D. Parker, 'Communist Party Historians' Group', *Socialist History*, 12 (1997), and J. Saville in *Socialist Register* (1976) for his and Thompson's break from the party in 1956. For an introduction to the group and the subsequent careers of its members see H. Kaye's *British Marxist Historians* (1984). H. Abelove *et al.*, *Visions of History* (1978) collects interviews with several Marxist historians. B. Palmer has written two major studies of Thompson: *The Making of E.P. Thompson: Marxism, Humanism and History* (1981) and *E.P. Thompson: Objections and Oppositions* (1994). H. Kaye and K. McClelland edited *E.P. Thompson: Critical Perspectives* (1990).

▶ Chapter 6

The landmarks in the debate over humanism and structuralism took place on the pages of the *History Workshop Journal* and are summarised in R. Samuel (ed.), *People's History and Socialist Theory* (1981). R. Johnson's 'Edward Thompson, Eugene Genovese, and Socialist-Humanist History', *History Workshop Journal*, no. 6

(December 1978) started the controversy and the debate continued in the next two issues. B. Hindess and P. Hirst, *Pre-Capitalist Modes of Production* (1975), was a key example of the structuralist method as applied to theory in different historical epochs. E.P. Thompson, *The Poverty of Theory, and Other Essays* (1978), was a major attempt to undermine the influence of the structuralists. For one direction of structuralist Marxism see the 'regulation school' of political economy in M. Aglietta, *A Theory of Capitalist Regulation: The US Experience* (1979); R. Boyer, *Accumulation, Inflation, Crises* (Paris, 1983); A. Lipietz, *Mirages and Miracles: The Crisis of Global Fordism* (1987). For a Marxist humanist critique of the regulation school, see R. Brenner and M. Glick, 'The regulation approach: theory and history', *New Left Review*, 188 (1991) and R. Brenner, 'Uneven development and the long downturn: the advanced capitalist economies from boom to stagnation 1950–1998', *New Left Review*, 229 (1998). For a structuralist Marxist contribution to the proto-industrialisation debate, see P. Kriedte, H. Medick and J. Schlumbohm, *Industrialisation before Industrialisation: Rural industry in the Genesis of Capitalism* (1981).

▶ Chapter 7

For a collection of Marxist essays on the postmodern challenge to history, see E. M. Wood and J. B. Foster (eds), *In Defense of History* (1997). For an excellent introduction to the broader movements of social history within which poststructuralism is one aspect see R. Samuel, 'Reading the signs I', *History Workshop Journal*, 32 (1991). A range of Marxist accounts of postmodernism and history exist that are worth reading: A. Callinicos, *Against Postmodernism: A Marxist Critique* (1989); N. Kirk, 'History, language, ideas and postmodernism: a materialist view', *Social History*, 19 (2) (1994); A. Callinicos, *Theories and Narratives: Reflections on the Philosophy of History* (1995); B.D. Palmer, *Descent into Discourse: The Reification of Language and the Writing of Social History* (1990); G. Eley and K. Nield, 'Starting over: the present, the postmodern and the moment of social history', *Social History*, 20 (3) (1995). For a well-received non-Marxist critique of postmodernism see R.J. Evans, *In Defence of History* (1997). For an introductory reader on the question of postmodernism in history, see K. Jenkins, *Postmodern History Reader* (1996). For an introduction to the relationship between poststructuralism and feminist history, see Joan Wallach Scott, *Gender and the Politics of History* (1988).

Index